Indian Women Writers

edited by

R.K. DHAWAN

PRESTIGE

Kamala Markandaya

Nayantara Sahgal

Stemming the Rot: The Rising Woman with Promising Vistas Ahead

K.K. SINHA

Generations have trod, have trod, have trod;
And all is seared with trade;
And wears man's smudge and shares man's smell: the soil
Is bare now, nor can foot feel, being shod.

G.M. Hopkins, "God's Grandeur"

A few months ago, while going through *Women in Indo-Anglian Fiction*,[1] I came across an article by Shashi Deshpande[2] wherein she has enumerated various influences that helped in shaping her into her present form. A few poignant lines from the article occasion this presentation of mine:

> Gender is undoubtedly one of the most important factors in our lives. The first question asked when a child is born, is 'boy or girl?' Our lives are, to a great extent, shaped by our gender. . . . I also realised that in a world dominated by male values, while the class and the class-struggle are taken seriously, the gender struggle is not.

Let us ponder over the question of gender bias in this era of war and peace between God's two favourite creations: Man and Woman (Man decidedly getting more than equal share, going by the popular notions held, the mythological, Biblical, religious records available).

Woman is the partner of man in the advancement of civilisation. But the sad fact remains that down the ages, there has been utter discrimination against women; so much so that one half of humanity has been reduced to a microscopic minority in the matter of rights: the abject treatment given to women may be sufficient to embarrass even the Devil himself. A casual look at the daily newspaper at the breakfast table or the late night recap of the main stories of the day repeat the same story in different permutations and combinations. Infants are raped maliciously and women are molested. Adolescents are deprived of the bliss of childhood and life. From the womb to the tomb, a woman's life seems to be a series of ordeals systematically arranged. As a child she plays in the lap of a servant or a scheming 'uncle' who happens to drop in occasionally especially so when the parents are away at work. She passes through acts, the meanings of which she doesn't even understand and all the while it is she who is 'to blame' partially, if not wholly.

It is a generally experienced fact that a boy's birth is supposed to bring happiness, a girl's birth, a bane. The woman in India is referred to as the Goddess of the house (Grihalakshmi) and the girl-child born is said to be the arrival of Lakshmi (Goddess of wealth)—but that is the preaching part of the gospel; in practice, she is supposed to be an all-in-one servant round-the-clock. The middle class girl has hardly any choice. She learns to live on the physical (or even emotional) left-overs of her elder or younger brothers. Parents would gladly spend a fortune to ensure coveted education or anything for their sons, the girl is supposed to make-do with the limited resources. Even if the girl is lucky enough to be born in a liberal family, she has to move out to face the gender-bias of a prejudiced (and often predatory) host of humanity that seems to have grown invisible claws in the eyes, hands, tongue.

Female foeticide is on the rise—abortion clinics have mushroomed all over—ultrasound and other facilities have been criminally misused just to ensure the coming of the new incumbent with a pendant between its thighs. The war against women is perpetrated not only by men but also by women. Women are involved in abetting crime against women—overtly or covertly. Sometimes even the woman's mentality seems to have undergone a change in her role as mother—in spite of the sufferings she herself might have been subjected to. There are certain compelling factors no doubt, but isn't it high time we stopped to see the slush and mud we are wallowing in? Materialism has blinded us and our souls have become insensitive, numb, so to say. Being habituated to our own ways of muck and might, we can't see the course we are taking. Our feet have become insensitive being shod in the shoes of selfish materialism; guided by rules and regulations being framed since long by man—the maker and breaker of such laws that have degraded the woman: the mother of humanity.

It would, perhaps, not be in the fitness of things to aver that the woman was supposed to be a slave or a menial from the very beginning. Most of our practices and customs have their origins in *Manu-Smriti* or Manu's Code. Though against freedom of any kind to women, Manu rules at many places that the woman ought to be respected and given due rights:

> Jamayo Yani Gehani Shapantaya Pratipoojita
> Tani Kritya hataneeva vinashyanti samantatah
> (Doomed to be destroyed is that house whose woman, for not getting proper regard, curses it to be destroyed.)
> Shochanti Jamayo Yatra
> Vinashyaotyashu tat kulam—
> (Annihilated will be that family or clan where women are in misery—the clan or family of a happy woman is bound to prosper.)
> Yatra narayastu poojyante ramante tatra devatah
> Yatra taastu na poojyante, sarvast trafalah kriyah
> (Gods themselves abide in places where women are worshipped or kept happy. Labours never bear fruit where women are not respected.)
> Santushto bharyaya bharta, bharta bharya tathaivcha
> Yasminnaiv kule nityam kalyanam tatra vai dhruvam
> (Blessed is that home in which the husband is perfectly

happy with his wife and the wife is in perfect happiness with her husband.)

The roots are all right no doubt, then, why did the stem and branches go astray? There are many reasons—some feel that with successive inroads of fighting races into India, the woman was relegated to the background; others attribute it to the growing complexity of human life. But, to me, the most plausible reason seems to be the unbridled power in the hands of man who believes in conquering and subjugating. His crusades outside have not satiated his ego—he wants to subdue at home, too. His defeats abroad invariably have their chain reactions in his family who have to bear the brunt of his frustrations. He does not win over by love—it has more of violence and autocracy. He thinks (and is made to think from the very beginning) that he is monarch of all he surveys in his home and his wife (given assorted names—Bhagyavan, Ardhangani, Grihalakshmi, Malkin, better-half and what not?) is nothing but a robot of flesh and blood supposed to be ever at his service because he provides for her, he gives security and shelter.

In modern times, even she works but that hasn't shifted her responsibilities—she has become the joint bread-winner for the family but her lord has not come forward to share her responsibilities (it is taken for granted that a woman's duty is to run a good home—man is for taking rest and making others slog for him at home) she's supposed to do everything at home in order to maintain harmony in the family. Things are changing though not at desirable pace. A stray woman asserts herself here and there, but the moment she decides 'to be,' her male counterparts, preferring it the other way round, gang up to cry 'Foul! foul!'

Look at a woman working in an office. There is gender bias and even her subordinate male staff have an inbred feeling of superiority—they never seem to feel normal: they can hardly digest the fact that they (they! who do all the bossing around their women at home,) should be bossed over by a woman at the office! Simply preposterous (or is it?). It takes some time and sometimes a few unpalatable assertive and authoritative steps from the female boss to show people their respective places at work.

Optimistically enough, a phase of transition has set in, promising to bring about a greater role to be played by the future woman of India. Politically, the woman is on the verge of getting one-third reservation of seats in Parliament (and subsequently expected at other places, too). She is fast becoming a force to reckon with. Not that she can't make it without being given preferential treatment—but more so because she does not want to lag behind. If others have availed themselves of the facility; if the competent warders of the nation have considered government jobs as spoils of the War of Independence with the booty being shared proportionately according to political clout and voting ability, why should she lag behind? She, too, has pressure groups and has learnt to pull the strings at the opportune moments. Though at the receiving end in society, she is learning fast how to protect herself, her individuality. There have been quite a few cases of Babbitisation which have served to disillusion unscrupulous elements to some extent. The change is visible and it is to the peril of male chauvinists (basking in their self-concocted glory) if they do not notice it. Laws have been enacted umpteen number of times. But strict implementation of the laws seldom sees the light of the day, gagged as it often is, by quizzing lawyers whose main concern seems to be tc save their clients even if it be done at the cost of human values. It is now or never (more than ever) for the New Woman. She has come to stay: to assert herself—not as a beneficiary, but as an equal participant in the advancement of civilisation.

The era of change is round the corner—more so in metropolitan India. There is more confidence in the New Woman's manner of walking, talking, acting and almost everything. She is discovering (or re-discovering?) herself: her needs, her identity. In classrooms and in fields, she has made a name. She has shown that she can walk shoulder to shoulder with man—even ahead of him, given the opportunity.

The problems of women have been raised in the works of many Indians writing in English. R.K. Narayan, Bhabani Bhattacharya, Kamala Das, Nayantara Sahgal, Anita Desai, Shashi Deshpande, Namita Gokhale, Shobha De and Arundhati Roy are a few of the prominent names in this field. Kamala Das may perhaps be said to be the first voice of the woman, for the woman, by a woman. A variety of shades of a woman's mind and plight is reflected through Indian writings in English. Rosie (R.K. Narayan's *The Guide*) has one crucial reason for parting ways from her husband: "I'd have preferred any kind of mother-in-law if it had meant one real, live husband."[3]

Savitri is a passive sufferer in *The Dark Room* who breaks away temporarily to revolt against her philandering husband. And then there is Daisy in *The Painter of Signs* who defies all traditions to live in her own way. How cabin'd, cribbed and confined a woman's lot is, can be seen in Bhabani Bhattacharya's *Music for Mohini* (1952) and Anita Desai's *Voices in the City* (1965).

Another way of revolt against unbearable oppression is divorce: a supposedly good riddance to bad rubbish. Nayantara Sahgal deals with the theme in three of her novels—*This Time of Morning* (1966), *Storm in Chandigarh* (1969) and *The Day in Shadow* (1971). Sahgal has reasons valid enough to bring the prevalent Hindu traditions under scrutiny.

Along with Nayantara Sahgal and Shashi Deshpande (*The Dark Holds No Terrors*), Shobha De and Namita Gokhale take us not only into the bedroom of their characters and their behavioural patterns, but also focus on the factors that account for unconventional actions presented in the course of their novels. To some observers, Shobha De seems to be shockingly audacious in her descriptions—unmentionable earlier. But literature is supposed to be the mirror of life and now, to the New Woman of India, the quest of her identity is the main concern. The prevailing norms of purity and chastity for the woman and promiscuity for the man, are giving way to more considerate points of view—the urges and the raw calls of the body and sublime demands of the soul. Extra-marital sex (though pricking at times) has come to be regarded with greater understanding or flexibility, depending on the circumstances: If men have reasons for a particular line of action, women may have theirs, too!

The De phenomenon has come to stay. She presents the confident, enterprising, ambitious, and individualistic New Woman who demands attention, equality and peace; not on compromising terms but on terms at par with man—even asserting herself for her rights, should the exigencies of the situation so demand.

Men will no longer be wolves, should the woman decide not to play the lamb any more: both belong to the same species: both have to play ball to keep the tournament of life running.

NOTES

1. *Women in Indo-Anglian Fiction*, ed. N.K. Jain (New Delhi: Manohar, 1998).
2. Shashi Deshpande, "Of Concerns, Of Anxieties," p. 33.
3. R.K. Narayan, *The Guide* (Mysore: Indian Thought Publications, 1983), p. 76.

Women's Liberation Movement and Indian Women Novelists

SHUBHA TIWARI

In our country almost no one minds the text books of children showing a woman as cooking, churning butter water or washing clothes and a man riding, writing or playing or doing just anything. When the world at large is aflame with ideas of unbiased role models for men and women, our magazines, textbooks, advertisements, television serials and movies are encouraging the ageold traditional role models for men and women.

What this movement stands for and from what women are demanding "liberation"? "Women's liberation refers to liberation from the traditional female role, which effectively serves to limit the things women can do and the ways she can behave."[1] When Mary Wollstonecraft came out with *A Vindication of the Rights of Women*, she created the beginning of the history of feminism. The American women were among the first to get voting right in 1920 with the nineteenth amendment to their constitution. During 1960s, the movement resurged with a growing number of women realizing the onesidedness of the social arrangement. Women felt that housekeeping was a thankless job. People never paid attention and importance to what women were doing and always expected ideal demi-goddess behaviour from a woman. As a writer puts it. "Have to go on a business trip? She will pack your suitcase with clean clothes which she washed and ironed or sent to the cleaners (after picking them up off the floor where you dropped them). Want to talk? She will listen eagerly. Woman. She will look like a goddess at the crack of dawn and stand in the door as you leave for work and be standing there waiting for you when you come home."[2]

Perhaps the most important event in the history of women's liberation movement was the publication of *The Feminine Mystique* by Betty Friedan in 1963. In this book Friedan explains the psychological urges of a woman. A woman wants to be more than an ideal wife, sister and mother. A woman wants to establish her identity. She has a right to develop her inner potential to the maximum. Above all, women aware of the concept of liberation are fighting patterns of Machismo. Machismo can be described as behaviour of a man full of dominance, rashness, virility, bravery and total absence of emotions and feelings. Some experts have also interpreted "machismo" as destructive behaviour by a man to overcome his weaknesses and inability.[3] The macho treats women only as objects. Many myths, social practices, fairy tales, religious concepts boost this macho image of man. Women activists are fighting against it.

Last, but not the least, women are to be liberated from their own mental chains. Women's liberation is not liberation from men; it is a liberation of women from their own psychological fears and enslavement. Women automatically and unnecessarily confine themselves to a very limited and suffocating social stereotype and rigid behavorial patterns.[4]

The Women's liberation movement is not a movement against men; it should not be viewed in that light. The aims, objectives and strategies of the movement are clear and well defined. They include first of all, equal pay for equal work. No one feels odd when magazines report that an actor gets seven lakhs for doing a movie and an actress gets two. In the private sector and in the case of manual labour, women are still getting lesser amount for equal work as men. Jobs should not be given on the basis of sex. There should be adequate child care programmes especially for the children of working women. A woman should have an equal say in controlling and planning the family. Exploitation of women in any form under any circumstances is to be fought down. Above all, a woman must have the freedom to choose her lifestyle, her profession, her general behavorial pattern. Being a woman, she need not look less competent than men. Being a woman, she need not look very attractive all the time and smile unnecessarily or lisp instead of talking or swing instead of walking. A woman is an ordinary and normal human being with all strong as well as weak human characteristics. The activities of the movement have been wide and varied. Women assemble and talk openly about their urges. Different organisations give an opportunity to women to come closer and develop companionship. The role of these organisations becomes crucial in providing support to women who are trying new role models. Women are kept well informed about their rights. They are counselled. They are given legal and medical aid. On a higher plane, these groups should try to explain to people at large that self-sacrifice, forbearance, lack of ambition, general passivity and extreme sentimentality are hypocritical concepts thrust on women by society for ages for mere convenience.

When this movement started, it was believed to be just another fashion fad and craze. Instead, the women's liberation concept has come a long way. The first fighters were rebuked by the society and were termed as "unfeminine," "masculine" etc. Today, people have started realizing its worth and seriousness. Media covers women's liberation issues seriously and constantly. "Far from evaporating into thin air like the latest fad or having been consumed in the intensity of its own fire, the Movement has had an immense effect on every area of life."[5] The role of women in education, medical profession and in employment scene in general has increased remarkably during past two, three decades. Many conscious and educated people now use words such as "person," "human being," "one" rather than "he" or "man" in referring to humanity in general.

Any discussion of the topic would be incomplete without mentioning the hurdles on the way. In the govt. system, official network as well as private channels, people try to delay a woman's progress as much as possible. It is very difficult for society to digest (so to say) a rising and competent woman. Talking in the field of abstract ideas requires no effort and therefore people easily do it. But when it comes to obeying a female boss, dealing with a female colleague, people fail to leave behind the traditional role of a male patronizing and a female humbly being patronized. It is these outdated sick minded people that are working as parasites on society. They do not know that they are harming their own daughters.

One of the most deep-rooted obstacles in achieving the goals of women's liberation is the ideologies in the form of religion. Major religions all over the world preach the superiority of men over women. Whether it is Koran dictating dominance of men over women[6] or The New Testament which goes on to say—"It is a shame for women to speak in the church."[7] A male Jew thanks Almighty Lord in his prayers that "I was not born a woman."

In contrast, Hindu religion in its fundamental form, gives women a place of deep respect in society. In fact, power, the ultimate and final source of energy is embodied in the feminine form of SHAKTI. Invasions from abroad and the influence of various alien cultures on Hindu society have cast a negative impact in this connection. Great writers all over the world have written with the assumption that behind every successful man is a woman. Shakespeare's heroines are known to be the moving force of his plays. Ruskin goes on to say: "Shakespeare has only heroines; no heroes." George Bernard Shaw believed and propagated the theory that women are the pivot and central driving force of this world.

Advertisements, propaganda and films have just one motto and that is to make maximum profits. Anything is okay there as long as it sells. So we have a woman advertising spices and a man advertising an insurance company. There should be some law that prohibits traditional portrayal of role models for men and women. In most of the films and T.V. serials, a female enters either to sing or to shed tears. They are not treated as normal females of the human species.

II

Indian women novelists can be said to be highly conscious of the women's liberation movement. By and large they have portrayed women and their stories with consciousness of the injustice being meted out to women by society. These novels have a feminist undercurrent. Usually these novels have a woman as the central character. If we look at these fictional female characters, a large number of them rebel against the existing social set up. They discard the idea of being submissive, suffering and sacrificing. Rebellion is no easy process. It demands determination and a will to stand by the cause of rebellion at any cost. These heroines in the novels of Indian women novelists have often come up to paying the prize of their rebellion rather than submitting and dying through suffocation.

Awareness on the writers' part of the individual needs of women like self-fulfilment and identity formation have resulted in these novels in patterns of alienation, communication gap, broken relationships and identity crises. Women in the novels of Nayantara Sahgal are liberal and unconventional. Saroj in *Storm in Chandigarh* refuses to succumb to socially acceptable norms of feminine behaviour. She craves to establish herself as an individual whereas for her husband Inder, she is a mere wife. A woman's longing for love and understanding is beautifully depicted in the novel. Similarly, in Sahgal's *The Day in Shadow*, it is the heroine, Simrit's yearning "for a free communication of ideas with her husband"[8] that proves disastrous. An egoist that Som is, he fails in listening and sharing his wife's ideals and values. "Sahgal's women seek to establish a new order with changed standards where women can be their true selves, where there is no need for hypocrisy and where character is judged by the purity of heart."[9]

Ruth Jhabvala as a major woman novelist is less concerned with the personality development of her women; she is attracted by the double standards of Indian women in general. She can be said to have dealt with distortion of modernity and women's liberation. Her women do not go against traditions out of any firm conviction; they do so in order to pose modern.

Shashi Deshpande is one novelist who is rising like a star feminist among women novelists of India. Her women are educated, self-conscious and sensitive. Their revolt against the rigid social and family set up comes out of necessity. Saru in *The Dark Holds No Terror* pays the price in terms of being brutally insulted by her husband simply because she is superior to him mentally as well as socially. She goes through traumatic experiences simply because she is a woman and is highly skilled, intelligent and competent. She lectures the school girls sarcastically about the one-sided social system which is totally partial in favour of men: "Listen, girls, . . . you won't be happy . . . until you get married and have children. A wife must always be a few feet behind her husband. If he's an M.A., you should be a B.A. If he's 5′4″ tall, you shouldn't be more than 5′3″ tall. If he's earning five hundred rupees, you should never earn more than four hundred and ninety-nine rupees. That's the only rule to follow if you want a happy marriage. Don't ever try to reverse the doctor-nurse, executive-secretary, principal-teacher role. It can be traumatic, disastrous. Women's magazines will tell you that a marriage should be an equal partnership. That's nonsense. Rubbish. . . . You can nag, complain, henpeck, whine, moan, but you can never be strong. That's a wrong which will never be forgiven. They will tell you about economic independence and an independent identity. Forget the words."[10]

In her novels like *That Long Silence* and *A Matter of Time*, Deshpande has subtly and accurately described the silence which has been thrust on Indian women for centuries. Deshpande's first novel *Roots and Shadows* has two strong female characters Akka and Indu.

Kamala Markandaya's women present a mixed spectrum. Even when her heroine conforms to the social set-up, she does not lose her identity and strength of mind. Rukmani, the narrator heroine of *Nectar in a Sieve* is a woman living according to the set social norms. Different factors like economic upheaval, husband's infidelity and children's disobedience tear her world apart. But she remains intact. She does not break any relationship. She does not escape or withdraw. She faces life and faces it with remarkable strength.

Mira in Markandaya's *Some Inner Fury* is a liberated woman who chooses to live in her country rather than go after her love,

Richard. Markandaya has not shown her women to be as radical as shown by Sahgal and Deshpande but has bestowed them with tremendous inner strength.

Raji Narasimhan is a minor Indian woman novelist but her novels nevertheless present "protagonists in search of self-fulfilment, in search of something that eludes the grasp."[11]

Anita Desai's importance in Indian fiction in English is indeed great. She has touched the nuances and subtleties of fiction hitherto unknown in Indian fiction in English. A feminist reading of her novels reveals that almost all her women are not only liberated but go much beyond to the region of psychological and philosophical depths. For example, Nanda Kaul in *Fire on the Mountain* is fully and painfully conscious of her need to live for herself. All her life she has lived in mock pleasure and pseudo status. She is enjoying the bliss of silence and an existence entirely for herself. But the point is that her story does not stop here. It goes far beyond into intellectual regions. So it is with almost all women portrayed by Desai. Her concern does not lie with radical feminism and women's liberation. She lives and paints a scene where women can be presumed to be liberated. The narration starts after the independent identity is established. Whether it is Maya in *Cry, the Peacock* or Monisha in *Voices in the City*, the women of Anita Desai are mentally advanced in the real sense of the word.

All these novelists seem aware of the negative aspects of illogical feminism. Loss of moral values is not women's liberation. Breaking and destroying social harmony and institutions is not the purpose of this movement. Women's liberation is a state of mind.

An analysis of the novels by Indian women novelists with a feminist view reveals that these novelists have written with immense concern and understanding for their female characters. The hidden and suppressed world of Indian women comes to full light in these novels. Indian feminine sensibility can be fully felt by reading these novels. It will not be wrong to call these novelists the most powerful forerunners of Women's liberation movement in India.

NOTES

1. McNeil and Rubin, *The Psychology of Being Human*, 1974, p. 414.
2. Lester, 1970, p. 31.
3. Aramoni, *The Mind of a Machismo*, 1972, p. 73.
4. Phyllis Chester, 1971.
5. Edmiston, *Out from Under! A Major Report on Women Today*, 1975, p. 160.
6. "Men are superior to women on account of the qualities in which God has given them pre-eminence." The Koran, the sacred book of Islam.
7. "Let your women keep silence in the churches; for it is not permitted unto them to speak, but they are commanded to be under obedience, as also saith the law." *The New Testament* (1 Cor. 11:14).
8. Meera Bai, *Women's Voices* (New Delhi: Prestige), p. 623.
9. A.V. Krishna Rao, *Nayantara Sahgal*, p. 58.
10. Shashi Deshpande, *The Dark Holds No Terror* (Penguin), p. 137.
11. Atma Ram "Raji Narasimhan" *The Indian English Novelists*, ed. Madhusudan Prasad (New Delhi: Sterling, 1982), p. 184.

The Predicament of Women as Reflected in the Works of Contemporary Indian Women Writers

SANGEETA DAS

Women are held in a great esteem in India. They are termed as 'Devi' by men. In Hindu custom, men pay obeisance to young girls deifying them as incarnation of deities. All this sounds very impressive and mind-boggling too. A feminist writer would certainly be shocked to read these lines. Yes, certainly, because all is not so well as it appears to be. This is a picture when seen through rose tinted glasses and is definitely not the sole truth. There is another side to the picture, rather bizarre and dark.

Age long suppression and torture both mental, physical and emotional has forced her to lift the cudgels and stand up to fight the male chauvinistic society. Previously, women were deprived of the privilege to education whereas men were given all the facilities and prerogatives in this field. Women's role was to accompany men in their beds, provide them with emotional and egoistic satiation so that they were re-affirmed of their supremacy from time to time. This aspect has been affirmed by Kamala Das who also feels that it is only on sexual grounds that the women have to supplicate before man. Therefore in *My Story*, her autobiography, she says that though she had mental and emotional compatibility with her husband and loved her children, she denied any physical access to her husband. This was her way of self-assertiveness against the male-domination.

But because of her dubious approach towards male-influence on the life of women, she has been denied place among the feminist writers. The point of contention in her approach was compatibility with her husband and at the same time her cause to uplift the women folk from male domination.

It was in the later part of the twentieth century that women writers like Anita Desai, Kamala Markandaya, Nayantara Sahgal, Ruth Prawer Jhabvala and Shashi Deshpande have achieved recognition.

Anita Desai has given quite a diversive image of woman emancipation in *Bye-Bye, Blackbird*, *Voices in the City*, *Cry, the Peacock*, *Where Shall We Go This Summer?*, *Fire on the Mountain*. In *Bye-Bye Blackbird*, the protagonist is educated and a foreign based Indian. He selects a foreigner as his wife, and in his selection he is guided by the typical Indian male instinct i.e. a docile woman who could comply to the whims of male chauvinism. The following lines would highlight this aspect: "English wives are quite manageable really, you know. Not as fierce as they look—very quiet and hard-working as long as you treat them right and roar at them regularly once or twice a week." (29) Sarah tries her best to satisfy Adit, her husband, and in her futile attempt transforms herself so much that she loses her self. A stage comes in her life when she is finally compelled to live a stranger's life and she happily accepts the change in order to satisfy the ego of her husband. This is the predicament of practically all Indian women. Either she gives in or she lives a life of disgrace where she is ostracized by the whole society. If she can live with the stigma she stays alive, if not she is sexually assaulted and her self-respect is destroyed and consequently her life. Rape implies the highest injury and insult to the women's pride and dignity. This Anita Desai tried to explore in *Fire on the Mountain*, in which Ila is raped by Preet Singh because she had interfered in the matter of his seven-year-old daughter's marriage to an old man. He did this to humiliate Ila for the injury she had caused to his male ego. This depicts the helplessness of the women in the world. In some cases, women are raped repeatedly, i.e. when they are forced into mis-matched alliances. In Anita Desai's *Where Shall We Go This Summer?*, Sita is compelled by circumstances to stay married to Raman as she is mother of four children and pregnant with a fifth but she does not wish to give birth to the child nor does she want to abort it. She is psychologically broken and tired by temperamental incompatibility between her husband and her self. She also feels insecure because her four children are more close to their father. Distraught totally, she wants to run away to her childhood home in the island of Manori. Actually, in the Indian society, woman is always placed second to a man, no matter whatever height she may score. She is directly under the guardianship of man since birth to her death. First, she is under the control of her father, then husband and at the final stage, her son. Without male-shelter, woman is vulnerable to the criticisms of society. In Desai's novels, the protagonists either reconcile with their circumstances—Sita and Sarah give up their dreams of emancipation, they get wise and mellowed with time and realize the futility of their freedom—or they end their lives—like Maya and Nanda Kaul.

Mamta Kalia and Imtiaz Dharker represent two major religious faiths. Mamta hits at the root by pinioning her father, somewhat following Virginia Woolf's well-known phrase "Killing the Angel in the house." Mamta Kalia likes to stick to her own philosophy of life and refuses to subjugate to the patriarchal standards prevalent in the society. In her novel, the protagonist is repelled by the very idea of marriage but she is forced to accept it. Unlike Anita Desai's protagonists, Mamta Kalia's protagonist dominates over her husband threatening him with leaving the house if he did not meet her requirements properly. The tables are turned on the antagonist himself in her novels. In the novels of Kamala Das and Anita Desai, the protagonists are victimized and humiliated to the extent of either committing suicide or giving in to the imperative patriarchal society. Anita Desai and Kamala Das state the various ways in which the women are tortured physically, mentally and emotionally and instigate them to rebel against the atrocities but do not suggest or indicate any substantial alternative which take their protagonist to a vacuum where they find themselves helpless and thwarted. No wonder, they either come back and reconcile as Sita did or commit suicide and end their lives as Nanda Kaul did in *Fire on the Mountain*.

Imtiaz Dharker's emphatic nature is posited by her taking the whole Muslim community to task. The atrocities meted out to Muslim women and the high-handedness of the patriarchy receives proper laceration at her hands. Though born and brought up in an Islamic family where conventional rigidity is prevalent, she acquired a cosmopolitan outlook by her exposure to western ethos in Britain. She lashes out fiercely against purdah system which she feels curbs the personality of the woman.

The second issue which she attacks, taking it to be an insult to a married lady, is the mehar which a woman is promised by her husband when divorced. It makes her a marketable commodity and jeopardizes the very infrastructure of the marriage which is based on faith.

Again, a muslim girl is expected to marry within her religion. The moment she marries a lad of another religion, she is declared dead by her own family as is evident in the following lines.

> The table is laden at Mohurram
> and you are remembered
> among the dead
> No going-back,
> The prayer's said.

Besides all these instances of humiliations, she is subjected to another which questions her biologically and becomes a disqualification with regard to her participation in religious ceremonies and prayers. Her periods become an Achilles's heel for her to enter the mosque. How embarrassing that man who takes its origin from it has the audacity to defile it. It is extremely inhuman on the part of man to question its own source of life. How can he be so brutal and abuse its own existence when 'God the compassionate, the merciful, created man from clots of blood.' Religion never teaches segregation, it always teaches inclusion but whichever prayer excludes women can only be an outcome of malice and hatred. God never prevails in such an environment.

Imtiaz Dharker has been brave enough to take such a daring stance with regard to her religion. Her poems are suggestive, thought-provoking and argumentative.

In Indian society, the identity of a woman is attributed to her husband. She is a decorative appendage who is expected to accompany her husband everywhere and meet the people her husband approves. She can never expect to have her own associations and definitely not of the opposite sex or else she is relegated as infidel. This is the scene in Markandya's *A Silence of Desire*. Sarojini, in her quest for solitude, abstains herself from her home and her husband. This makes her husband subtly interrogate her and doubt her fidelity. How atrocious? In a society where woman cannot question her male counterpart about his whereabouts, she has to give account of her activities to her husband or rather the master who had her destiny in his hand. Why? She is expected to attend to the family requirements directly related to her husband and children. Her existence is restricted to this alone. The moment she desists from this, the family faces discomfort and regards her a failure and her very identity is at stake. It was not just Sarojini's absence from home but her growing inefficiency in kitchen matters, sexual abstinence and evasive responses to Dandekar's subtle interrogations which was enough to trigger his doubts regarding her fidelity. This questions the very existence of women in Indian society. Thus her identity encircles her husband alone and she is victimized under the male chauvinistic wave which awash the entire society. Has she taken birth only to give comfort to the men? Does she have no time for herself? In Desai's *Clear Light of Day*, Bim remains a spinster to keep herself free from the shackles of family life. But she cannot enjoy this freedom for long. Death of her mother shifts the responsibility of her handicapped brother Baba to her shoulder; her elder brother Raja does not take up the responsibility. Thus she is enmeshed in the trap from which she had tried to escape. In the end, she finds solace in the wondrous song of Mulk's aged guru. There arises a feeling of detachment and renunciation in her and she gives up the idea of independence of women. There is no satisfaction in Desai's novel for a woman who vehemently opposes male-supermacy and wishes to fulfil her desire of equality.

Nayantara Sahgal tries much to fill the vacuum created in my mind after reading Anita Desai. In her novel *The Day in Shadow*, the protagonist, Simrit, is an educated woman, a professional writer who is fully exploited by Som, her husband, whose sole concern is to earn wealth and secure himself monetarily. In his quest to earn money, he forgets about the existence of his wife, who had herself chosen Som as her husband and allowed him to use her till it became unbearable. She was forced to take a divorce and consequently turned toward Raj, not for sexual satisfaction but for mental and emotional support. Though she had married Raj who was not much different from Som, remarriage was Raj's idea whereas Simrit herself was disinterested. After marrying Raj, she was also given the opportunity to allow the writer in her to flourish. Raj took interest in her work and was besotted by her. Simrit hero-worshipped Raj and he in turn admired Simrit's integrity and grit despite his feministic convictions. The differences between the two men are particularly apparent in the way they respond to Simrit's basic need of tenderness.

Raj is more or less the type of husband an Indian woman can think of, who would recognise a woman's integrity and conside her a human being with feelings and not a doormat to be used as and when wished and then forsaken. In *The Day in Shadow*, at least one woman clearly repudiated her role of victim and believed that she had achieved autonomy. The authenticity of that autonomy lies not with the woman alone but also with the man who is the counterpart of woman and both are equally important for each other.

Like Virginia Woolf and Anita Desai, Shashi Deshpande is also a prose rhapsodist of sentiments, feelings and emotions passing through human consciousness. In her novels, the protagonist is in a pursuit of self-knowledge. Jaya, her protagonist, believed that love came before sex but her marriage with Mohan revealed that it could be the other way round. She gave up writing for the joy of getting married and having children but the secondary position meted out to her by her husband greatly disappointed her. Her fierce giggle at Mohan when he needed consolation for his nervous irritations owing to his suspension, humiliates him so much that he leaves the house. But if the cause of her unexpected attitude is probed into, it would show that continuous piling of frustrations, bitterness and disgust with the role of a docile secondary status of a wife was behind the sudden upheaval. An Indian male concept of women as less than themselves in mental capacity and reason and often discouraging them from developing any interest in their work was acceptable to the ancient Indian women but today woman has developed much and is working in such fields where tremendous balance of mind and brain is required.

Times have changed and women have come out of their shells and spread their wings to fly into the sky of achievements. They distinguished themselves in those fields which were strictly men's privilege and were never expected to be attained by women. They have thrown away the shackles of stereotyped Indian women and have taken up careers besides being wives. They have yet not been able to free themselves from the grip of the spirit of Indian women who need men to stand beside them like a sheltering tree. She feels incomplete without the company of man. Her thirst for family life compels her to come to terms with man. She comes to terms with her conditions. In Shashi Deshpande's novel, Jaya revolts to the dual role that is thrust on her by her husband viz. of a housewife serving her husband and son and the second role to befriend her husband's C.E. for his protection and this leads to her rebellion. She wanted equality in treatment from her husband which is the basic need of not only Jaya but each Indian woman. It is lack of recognition of her entity by the male counterparts which has forced the women to raise their heads in rebellion against them. It is due to the persistent male chauvinism in spite of the change in female standards which has triggered off a mammoth growth in feminist writers flaunting their pens as swords to slice at male ego and carve out a niche for woman in society where she is treated equal to men.

Where Shall We Go Hence? The Question of the Indian Woman's Voice and Choice in the New Millennium

K.K. SINHA

> Turning and turning in the widening gyre
> The falcon cannot hear the falconer;
> Things fall apart; the centre cannot hold . . .
>
> W.B. Yeats, "The Second Coming"

Yes, the second coming is at hand; Indian society, reflected in the literature of the age, is passing through a phase of transition; nothing seems to hold on for long; things are falling apart and tradition fails to hold individuality in check. What will the prospects and possibilities of Indian English literature be in the New Millennium is a question that has haunted us time and again.

Within the limited scope of this paper I propose to bring out certain prevailing trends with special reference to some of the novelists writing in the later part of the last century. The focus is on the condition of the woman as portrayed through their novels tracing her sense and sensibilities, responses and reactions in the Indian social milieu and arrive at the possible trends of the coming era.

Since time immemorial the woman has felt that she deserves a better deal at the hands of man. The development of the woman's mind asserting equality has been described by Elaine Showalter.[1] Showalter states that there are three phases in women's fictional writing. The first phase of male superiority was when everything revolved round men. Women, too subscribed to this view taking on male pseudonyms. They "imitated the dominant male modes and internalised their aesthetic and social values."[2]

The second phase or the phase of protest (the Feminist Phase) seeks to look at life from the woman's point of view. The third phase (also called the Displacement Phase) shows the search for core identity: the quest for freedom is turned inward and aimed at the goal of self-discovery. Men no more matter to women as they once used to.

Change is the law of life and a state of changelessness is said to be stagnation. The woman in India has long been worshipped using the choicest terms of address. But the woman of independent India is not ready to enter another abysmal era of blind hero-worship. With cumulative wisdom being passed down to her through the ages, she has learnt to recognize herself. She has learnt to put awkward but pertinent questions. The picture of society had always been depicted through the literary works of the relevant periods whether it be Gunter Graas (*The Tin Drum*) or Salman Rushdie (*Midnight's Children, The Satanic Verses, Shame*). The image of a cabined, cribbed and confined woman has been delineated through the works of many Indian novelists: R.K. Narayan, Anita Desai, Kamala Das, Kamala Markandaya, Shashi Deshpande, Nayantara Sahgal, Namita Gokhale, Githa Hariharan, Shobha De et. al. One notices two main tendencies in the Indian social framework today—one may be called the centripetal while the other has come to be termed as centrifugal, or, running away from the centre or the family. Neither of the two trends can be said to be completely in vogue. Often, they overlap, and the nature of a particular character is the sum total of all the actions and experiences in the course of the work of art. The spirit of revolt arising out of mechanical life, mismatched marriage or wayward ways of the husband have forced the woman to come out in the open to register her dissent. But the revolt does not take her out of her home. The home still remains for her the only refuge. There may be temporary withdrawals but on the whole, a centripetal spirit of compromise can be seen on the part of the woman.

Savitri in R.K. Narayan's *The Dark Room* (1938) revolts against her husband's philanderous ways and leaves her home in sheer disgust:

> I'm a human being. . . . You men will never grant that. For you we are playthings when you feel like hugging and slaves at other times. Don't think you can fondle us when you like and kick us when you choose.[3]

Her helpless condition is a result of psychic compromise with tyranny: "We are responsible for our position; we accept food and shelter." (113)

Savitri moves out of the house to be on her own, but all in vain. A woman in the Indian social context is a non-entity without a man. Savitri returns on the fourth day, not to her husband but to her children, making the spirit of compromise evident: "A part of me is dead," (208) she reflected.

Other works also throw ample light on the predicament of women. Monisha in Anita Desai's *Voices in the City* (1965), Jaya in Rama Mehta's *Inside the Haveli* (1977) or the incarcerated woman in the so-called Big Houses in Bhabani Bhattacharya's *Music for Mohini* (1952) are some cases in point. Kamala Markandaya's *Nectar in a Sieve* and *A Handful of Rice* present the woman in a traditional role asserting that above all, she is a living being. In almost all her works, Markandaya has an end in view: "autonomy for the self, nurturance for the family and fellow feeling for the community of men and women."[4]

Though Anita Desai does not proclaim herself to be a feminist writer, the fact remains that she attempts to discover life as it is. Until *Clear Light of Day*, Desai's women are sensitive and emotional misfits trying to maintain their individuality: "either withdrawing into a subjective world, often acting in ways society considers neurotic or mad; or they cultivate coldness or indifference, refusing to give in."[5]

A change in attitude comes with *Clear Light of Day* and she "nurtures her feminine self through acceptance and accommodation rather than withdrawal and rejection."[6]

The issue of incest, considered unmentionable earlier has received Desai's attention in the novel: "She felt an immense almost irresistible yearning to lie down beside him on the bed stretched out limb to limb, silent and immobile together."[7]

The God of Small Things describes Estha-Rahel fixation and R.K. Jha's *The Blue Bedspread* also deals with the theme of incest: the roots may be traced back to Vedic literature in the delineation of Yama and Yami relationship.

In Desai's subsequent novels, too, the malaise in human relationship is rooted in a mismatched sense and sensibilities of the male and female characters.[8]

In spite of the tendency to revolt within the social framework, these had simultaneously a centrifugal urge in the fettered woman to break free finally. R.K. Narayan's Daisy[9] and Rosie[10] recognize their own selves and walk out of unbearable circumstances that threaten to fossilize their very existence. Rosie is even more assertive as Nalini and prefers her affirmity for dancing to Raju her lover.

The transition in the woman's consciousness has continued. The Indian woman is well on her way to move from the feminine or feminist phase to the phase of displacement and self-discovery. Self-assertion seems to have become the keynote of the expressions of the evolving woman. To escape the deadlock perpetrated by the unilateral dictates of a perniciously effective patriarchal form of society, the New Woman comes out in more prominent contours in succeeding works. War is the last resort—and the New Woman of India has recourse to divorce as the only means of salvaging her lost self. This centrifugal revolt takes definite shape in Nayantara Sahgal's novels. Divorce has been depicted as an alternative way of life to escape the drudgery perpetrated through discriminatory laws promulgated by lawmakers like Manu and enthusiastically supported and implemented by the succeeding generations of men deeply steeped in their complacence to toe the line. Three of her novels, *This Time of Morning* (1966), *Storm in Chandigarh* (1969) and *The Day in Shadow* (1971) need special mention in this regard. Sahgal describes the plight of Simrit, a divorced woman in *The Day in Shadow* through the following lines:

> . . . a passive creature to whom things happen. She is culture *the typical Indian woman: marginalized and ductilized into conformity* tradition, *of sub-ordination* a patient enduring passivity *sterilized, etherized into a state of perennial numbness by the customs of a sclerotic society.* (My italics)

Sahgal is an iconoclast in her own right as she succeeds in demolishing the hitherto held myths and images of the Indian woman: the 'pati-parmeshwar'[11] image: the husband is God.

Co-existing with the trend of moving out of a marriage ruined by the vicious atmosphere is the tendency to remain within the, framework of society and register protests and individuality from the centre itself. This trend may be said to be the continuation of characters like Savitri (*The Dark Room*) and many characters of Anita Desai. Divorce is still regarded as a stigma by most Indian women, who do not jump into marriage or out of it on an impulse. This concern of the woman to save her marriage often forces her to become the willing victim. Shashi Deshpande's novels throw much light on this aspect of the woman's mind. Deshpande's women are professionals—one is a doctor while two are writers. Jaya in *That Long Silence* feels that a woman's domestic life is a failure and, on introspection, finds that it is she who is to blame. Like Savitri in *The Dark Room*, she says:

> With whom shall I be angry?
> With myself, of course.[12]

Jaya decides to speak up and erase that long silence between her and her husband. She does not want to be taken for granted. She rejects the role model of Sita going into exile with her husband or Savitri winning back her husband from the jaws of Death. Her predilection is for Maitreyi, Yagnavalkya's wife who rejected his offer of half his property asking: "Will this property give me immortality?"[13]

It is clear that at the turn of the century in India, the types of Sita and Savitri seem to be on the receding whereas the bold and assertive Maitreyis are ever on the increase. The details of personal/private life may differ but the message is clear: self-respect and self-recognition by the Indian woman. Though Deshpande denies being a woman writer, her works have given us an in-depth view of "The vulnerability of women. The power of women. The deviousness of women. The helplessness of women. The courage of women."[14]

Jaya's recall of Lord Krishna's words to Arjuna towards the end of the novel is symbolic. Deshpande herself seems to exhort womankind of posterity to rise and stop not till the goal is reached: "I have given you knowledge. Now you make the choice. The choice is yours. Do, as you desire." (192)

This is a message to the awakening woman—the woman who has attained knowledge of her individuality: the epicentre of power-distribution on the earth. The message?—a woman's destiny is ultimately in her own hands. The old barriers are crumbling. A daughter can talk to her father about domestic violence. *The Dark Holds No Terrors* throws ample light on progress in social/interpersonal relationships. Saru's confessions of marital violence and domestic rape are worth citing:

Saru: I know you're my father and I'm your daughter . . . but still you're a man and I'm a woman. Can we talk such things?

Father: Go on. . . . Tell me everything.

Saru: He's cruel to me . . . in bed.

Many works in the recent past have shown that the definitions of virtuous woman have been modified considerably. Premarital sex (Manju Kapur's *Difficult Daughters*) and extramarital sex (Shobha De's *Socialite Evenings* and *Second Thoughts*, for example) have received sympathetic treatment. Sex is no more a taboo. Modern society seems to be awakening to the fact that sex does act as a rejuvenating force in a relationship that has become eclipsed by the mechanical and dreary routine of the hectic life.

Adultery is viewed with more leniency and the emphasis today is on giving a first hand account of the inner sanctum of family life. No inhibitions, no holding back. Even octogenarian Khushwant Singh has finally taken a plunge in this deep pool of unholy waters with much pomp and show (though not necessarily matched by a proportionate virility): "Occasional adultery, Mohan was convinced, did not destroy a marriage; quite often it proved to be a cementing factor as in cases where the husband could not give his wife as much sex as she needed, or, where the wife was frigid. It was silly to condemn adultery as sinful; it often saved marriages from collapsing."[15]

Namita Gokhale and Shobha De present the world of the rich and affluent people. In this race of materialism, the middle-class refuses to be tethered to morality—the only ethics of success and survival. Women assert themselves: they have their own priorities. Bodily needs are not neglected. Premarital or extra-marital affairs hold no terror to her. The language is bold, brushing aside past inhibitions. Women characters have the full appetite for life and the capacity to take in the odd swigs or swags that fall to her lot in the course of her winning spree. Namita Gokhale's *Paro* shows a reckless disposition to live life as fully as she can—she seems to have a sexual appetite so ravenous as to prove a potential incinerator on contact.

Shobha De is even bolder and through her characters, she has hit hard against the prevailing norms. Men and women live liberated lives without hassles (happily or not, is another question to be taken up, perhaps, in another paper). Financial considerations often force the woman to live within the family—but she responds to the call of the body even clandestinely without any bites of conscience. Karuna in *Socialite Evenings* shows the development of a middle class girl who enters the fast life of Bombay but is disillusioned: "My marriage went sour because I'd married the wrong man for the wrong reasons at the wrong time."[16]

Most of the women characters in De talk of lack of emotional involvement, stuck up in a situation because there is nothing better for survival. The same sense of ennui prevails in *Sec-*

ond Thoughts where Maya is locked up with Ranjan in a relationship that didn't satisfy either of them: "Other than the odd mole-hunt, my body remained uncharted territory."[17] Maya's aspirations remained unfulfilled physically, socially and emotionally: "The love-making that followed was always a let-down. Initially, I had blamed myself for it. And then I discovered something. . . . I'd married a virgin." Such circumstances propel people towards the centrifugal attitude—if not permanently, then as a means of temporary escape from exacting surroundings.

The trend continues. So, at the end of the century we do see a trend emerging—a trend which had been present as an exception to the existing traditional mores: but with the passing of time, the callous/uncaring and wilfully negligent attitude of men has forced women to look beyond vistas immediately available. The name of the father is no more mandatory with parents having practically no time for each other, not to mention adequate time and understanding for the emotional demands of their children the stray cases of incestuous relationship may get a wider coverage in the coming age of transparency. Lesbian couples have been known to achieve legal recognition and extremes may drive women to seek sustenance and solace from other women. Genetic engineering has reached the stage of successful cloning and in vitro fertilizations have been made possible by anonymous donations from semen banks; gene mapping and graphing may make the 'child-of-choice' dream come true. All these factors together threaten the traditionally held positions of vantage by man: he may be reduced to the position of just a 'donor' if he chooses to be still reckless to the fervent calls of the human soul. Anxiety is bound to be one of the recurring themes to register their presence in the new millennium. There are chances that most of the books would be written according to formats prescribed by computers. But on the whole, there would still be 'the super-computer' human being at the root of every creative work. The concept of inequality would disappear and there are chances that if the backlash or 'male-bashing' continues at the same pace (De, for example) the 'hunter' (man) may soon become the 'hunted.' The New Millennium could very well see the rise of the New Man fighting hard against the atrocities of emotion and intrigue perpetrated upon him by the 'fair' sex that had become 'unfair' with the passage of time.

Hopefully, there may come about a realisation among men and women that the basic motive behind existence on earth is procreation and enjoyment of the bounties of nature. This may result in the shedding of ego-clashes. Society would then be more understanding and harmonious and life certainly more meaningful and enjoyable. Figuratively speaking, the scenario presented through the works of the age could once again show an elderly couple lovingly snuggled together on a bench in a roadside park, happily munching, by turns, nuts with the help of a single set of dentures between them! After all, means would fail to curb the expression of mutual love as it is the mind that thinks but finally the heart that feels.

NOTES

1. Elaine Showalter, *A Literature of Their Own: British Women Novelists from Bronte to Lessing* (Princeton, N.J.: Princeton University Press, 1977).
2. Savita Goel, *The Coming Age of Shakespeare's Sister: Women Writing: Text and Context*, ed. Jasbir Jain (Jaipur: Rawat, 1996), p. 99.
3. R.K. Narayan, *The Dark Room* (Mysore: Indian Thought Publications, 1988), p. 110.
4. Shanta Krishnaswami, *The Woman in Indian Fiction in English* (Ashish Publishing House: New Delhi, 1984), p. 163.
5. Sharad Shrivastava, *The New Woman in Indian English Fiction* (New Delhi: Creative, 1996), p. 51.
6. Renu Juneja, "Identity and Feminity in Anita Desai's Fiction," *Journal of South Asian Literature*, 22.1 Summer, Fall, 1987: 66.
7. Anita Desai, *Clear Light of Day* (London: Penguin, 1980), p. 166.
8. Maya and Gautama in *Cry, The Peacock*, Sita and Raman in *Where Shall We Go This Summer?*, Nanda Kaul and her Vice-Chancellor husband in *Fire on the Mountain*. The solitary Bimla

with her cramped stuttering suitor Dr. Biswas in *Clear Light of Day* show this incongruity in detail.

9. R.K. Narayan, *The Painter of Signs* (1977; Mysore: Indian Thought Publications, 1991).
10. R.K. Narayan, *The Guide* (Mysore: Indian Thought Publications, 1983).
11. 'Pati-parmeshwar' image: the husband is God as prescribed by the Laws of Manu, 5.154, p. 115, which rules that 'A virtuous wife should constantly serve her husband like a god, even if he behaves badly, freely indulges his lust and is devoid of any good qualities.'
12. Shashi Deshpande, *That Long Silence* (New Delhi: Penguin, 1989), p. 192.
13. The reference originally pertains to *Brihadaranyaka Upanishad* (IV.V.4). Source: *Women in Indo-Anglian Fiction*, ed. Naresh K. Jain (New Delhi: Manohar, 1998), p. 15.
14. Shashi Deshpande, "On the Writing of a Novel," *Indian Women Novelists*, ed. R.K. Dhawan (New Delhi: Prestige, 1991), vol. 5, p. 34.
15. *The Company of Women*, Khushwant Singh (King Press, 1999), p. 8.
16. Shobha De, *Socialite Evenings* (New Delhi: Penguin, 1989), p. 65.
17. Shobha De, *Second Thoughts* (New Delhi: Penguin).

Ranjana Harish in conversation with Lakshmi Kannan

Transcribed by Neeta Khurana

RH: Lakshmi, it is really wonderful to have you on the campus of Indian Institute of Advanced Study, Shimla. Before we begin the interview, let me congratulate you for the work you have been doing. You have travelled a lot and published a lot both in English and in your mother tongue Tamil.

LK: Thank you, Ranjana.

RH: Lakshmi it is interesting to note that you write under your name while writing in English but you use pen name 'Kaveri' while writing in Tamil. Why so?

LK: You see, when I began to write in Tamil, I became naturally, very very aware of this regional audience/ readership, maybe that brought about a change in me and in my sensibility for that moment when I was writing in Tamil, and although we are all cosmopolitan, still that 'Tamil identity' became a big shock and I realised that I am slightly qualitatively different when I write in Tamil. Because I felt different, I wanted a name, so, I went back to the river that I am very fond of 'Kaveri.' I grew up with it as a child when I was in Mysore, there my grandfather, a civil engineer, and an outdoor man used to take me out for picnics and I was an outdoor sports minded girl. Very often I used to go out on picnics and excursions with him and the memory of 'Kaveri' is something like a great surging river, that I remember holding his forefinger. I am so emotional about this. It is like a memory of my grandfather.

RH: I see, so it was in the memory of your grandfather and the great times you had with him.

LK: Yes, I still remember, how firmly he used to hold me by the hand lest I run closer to the water. I have wonderful memories.

RH: So it is something personal. It does not have to do anything with religion.

LK: No. Over a period of time, as I grew, I just took 'Kaveri' to be a perennial river, a river that never dries, the river that I am fond of, a river that looked so wonderful. All through my childhood, it kept me busy and I associated it with my grandfather, but over a period of time, I have also grown to the 'cultural load' that it has. It has great religious significance in the South, people there bathe in 'Kaveri' on particular days, it is almost like a Goddess for them. Later, I married a man from Tamil Nadu, where 'Kaveri' flows and my husband said that it is an 'apt metaphor for you as it flows into my city.'

RH: You had all this background in your mind, but you never had the slightest association with the religious aspect of the name 'Kaveri' When you took it, was it just personal?

LK: Yes, when I took it, it was just spontaneous.

RH: And when you grew as a writer, you realised how right it was?

LK: As I grew, my unity with the South made me feel that it was right. Moreover, the richness of an encounter with a serious man or woman from Tamil Nadu made me realise its importance. The minute they came to know that my name is 'Kaveri,' they had two or three wonderful lines on 'Kaveri.' They have the rich repository of knowledge and reaction to the sacred river, so by and by I got educated in what 'Kaveri' meant to them. Even now, whenever I go to Chennai or Madurai, my name evokes a similar response, and the elders have something wonderful to say about Kaveri. I feel enriched.

RH: You wouldn't like to have any pen name when you write in English. Why?

LK: No. I have always written in my name in English.

RH: As a woman, do you think that deep down in your psyche, you were apprehensive of the society, of the audience, for which you were going to write? Hence the pen name? Carolyn Heilbrun says in *Writing a Woman's Life* that she had a pen name because she wanted to write something which would not be expected from a University faculty.

LK: There also is George Eliot who wrote under a pen name. In a way Heilbrun's observation is very right.

RH: Yes, but George Eliot is a different case, she did not write something which was below dignity, but with Heilbrun it was different. She was a University faculty writing thrillers. She did not have any space in her house, so psychologically, by writing thrillers, she created a space for herself, under a pen name.

LK: This is very interesting. Perhaps, we can come to the conclusion that when there are two different things happening to a writer at the same time, then s/he would take up a pen name.

RH: Coming to the audience do you think that the Tamil audience or any other 'bhasha' audience in India would be closer to the writer compared to the English reading audience. You have written in both the languages very successfully. What are your views on this?

LK: You see, in early eighties, when I started writing in Tamil, I had already published a bit of poetry and a lot of criticism and 1 was known as 'Lakshmi Kannan' in English. I was not readily accepted in Tamil. My Tamil was suspected. 1 was looked upon as somebody from the English faculty and people questioned as to what she is going to offer and so on. Fortunately, I found very disarming critics, quite unspoiled and I was very pleased with this unspoilt area in the Tamil literary field which is smaller, intense and quite uncorrupted by the populous stereotype.

They are very discerning, so somewhere along the line, I felt being a stereotype brings lack of knowledge. We have notions about the reader that they will not accept this or that, but then I got accepted and a whole lot of books followed and they were translated and, now I have a Tamil readership as well as an English readership. Now, you know, it surprises me to say this, but it is the truth and I am so glad that you gave me this opportunity by asking me such a searching question, it is because you yourself have a bilingual sensibility coming from Gujarat.

RH: Thanks.

LK: Now, for a long time, 'she's different, she's interesting' that epithet got stuck to me, now I have a niche for myself, which I lacked. They know that this is what they expect from her.

RH: Once Shashi Despande told me that she envied the 'bhasha' writers as compared to English readership; the bhasha readership is more concerned and immediate. Do you also think so?

LK: Yes, I do. I am very happy with them. For instance, the heroine of *Going Home*, Gayatri, accepts Damodaran on a platonic level, and she says that it is wonderful to have such a relationship. Gayatri is a married woman. The English readers who read this book had some snide remarks to make but with the Tamil readers, it went down very well. They were sensitive.

RH: How surprising!

LK: Yes, a Tamil critic has just written a review saying that Gayatri may have had failures in her life, but she has had a gift of friends. So you see, it is the Tamil audience who have taken it well. I recall another instance. A story about a lesbian woman.

RH: You mean Maria?

LK: Yes, the same. I wrote this much later, even after I was accepted as a Tamil writer. I had written it but I had misgivings about it as I felt that if I write about lesbian relationships, the Tamil audience would not take it well. But

I am proved wrong. I am glad for this. I am beginning to feel that the Tamil audience/readers and the critics have some kind of natural sophistication. When this novel was published, the critics went as far as to say. "Why should she hide Damodaran? When he is just a nice man who takes an interest in a lady on an intellectual level? Why does not she come out in the open? and then I wrote about Maria the lesbian woman. I wrote it in Tamil, because it came to me in Tamil, I reacted to her in Tamil. After writing it I was unsure about sending it, thinking no one would want to publish it, but then when I did, my publisher was so happy that I had explored this area, he said that there is such a human level to Maria, she has gone through such a horrible life, maybe that has led to aberrations and still you have reacted to her as why should it happen to her? For the cover of the book he found a Greek statue, which is half male and half female and made it the key. About six months ago, I had misgivings about Tamil writing, but when it was translated into English it was very well received.

RH: While reading 'Maria' I was feeling that the narrator has the right attitude towards Maria. She is so sympathetic. When men are celebrating homosexuality, poor Maria is being labeled and ostracised, only because she is a lesbian.

LK: And that too on just a mere suspicion she got branded, here the men are openly reading about homosexuality and nobody bothers. In Tamil the response I got was very good. They questioned as to "why is it discriminatory," but in English, the response was lukewarm and they gave some value judgements, so I am beginning to wonder and I am not able to locate this English reader, I think, he's diffused and uneven. As for myself, as a writer and as a woman, I sympathise with Maria who is a writer and a woman, how she is totally, severely alone and so is sympathetic to the woman who gives her vegetarian food and comes to her and cares for her.

RH: Well, this is the quality which I have noticed in all your writings. I have read all your books and in them I find that there is a very special sympathy towards women, say for example Gayatri and Rama, the relationship and friendship that they have is very rare.

LK: Yes, it is very rare. Another review quoted from Virginia Woolf's *A Room of One's Own* saying that "it is rare to have an enduring woman to woman relationship" this was said years ago, I think.

RH: Yes, that was in 1929 in *A Room of One's Own*.

LK: It is unfortunate that such relations are not easy to find. You know, why it doesn't blossom/flourish as much as a man to man relationship? Incidentally some of my best friends, my wonderful friends are women and what wouldn't I do to make them happy, to solve their problems if I can. Very early in life, I made it very clear to my husband that I value my women friends, and that I am not going to be a friend to a man that is there and this is my avenue, when I see sensitive, intellectual women full of emotional depth, then these are the people I want to be friends with.

RH: That is your personal experience as an individual human being, but coming to literature, when you transform that experience, that conviction that you have into literature, it so happens, that you are supporting the latest Gynocentric agenda i.e. instead of asking men to help you, to support you, or instead of wasting your energy on criticising how unfair the man has been, the best thing that a senior woman could do is to see that the younger generation women are supported.

LK: That's what "India Gate" depicts. When "India Gate" was published in Tamil and after some time it was translated into English and later into Hindi in "Hans" and Marathi, it had a tremendous response. Loveless relationship is impossible. Even for the sake of children one cannot go on with such a relationship. Just to keep up one's image as a 'good wife' one cannot sacrifice life. Such models of femininity are outdated, I guess.

RH: You have made the same point in one of your man centered stories. I appreciated that, I like the way you have handled the story, in which a man, a widower is going up the hill, to pray to Ganesha, and he has been thinking of the model of masculinity, that a man is not supposed to cry, he is love-less, heart-broken and then finally in front of the God, when the Pundit blesses him, he cries.

LK: Very true, the kind of situation faced by another man called Sheshadri in a story called "Pain," a terminal cancer patient, who faces a situation where nobody is sensitive to his feelings. While speaking of his wife people keep on saying, "She's going to die Sumangali, she is so lucky," nobody is consoling the poor man who is going to die. He is alone in the story.

RH: You have brought in so many regional and cultural things in your stories which make them very Indian. Is it deliberate, so that one can understand them.

LK: That is your own experience. When you are writing, things, ideas and words come to you and you can be yourself.

RH: In your book there is the concept of "Sumangali," or certain myths as for example "Ganesha" or that woman who aspires to go out and is not allowed and finally she is making Rangoli and invoking the Goddess to come and help.

LK: Yes, she is a thwarted mathematician, very brilliant.

RH: There are dancers, writers, mathematicians, scientists, aspiring medicos and not being allowed by men to take up jobs.

LK: Some of them.

RH: Career for women is looked upon by men as something very minor.

LK: At one point they were like that.

RH: Why did you turn to novel form in *Going Home*. Is it more fulfilling?

LK: This was obviously a novel stuff. For a long time I had been wanting to write it. I had written three or four novellas, so that was a discipline that taught me how to extend a theme. The Tamil novella has had its own kind of influence from European novella, it dramatises, sometimes you can adopt that, but format appeals to me and this format is not extended, it is more dramatic to put into the Beginning, the Middle and the End. The Beginning will give you a sense of foreboding that something is going to happen. The Middle will develop it and the End will explode in quite an unexpected manner. This appeals to me and I wanted to explore it, so I wrote.

RH: The introduction that you have written for the novel *Preface* shows that you have been a student of literature and you have been a very serious critic.

LK: *Preface* is a recent novel. Yes, I have taught literature for about seventeen years and it greatly helps and exposes you to the Western literature, and of course to the masters of literature. Doesn't it?

RH: Yes, I guess so. Being exposed to Western currents and bringing them into your own literature is great. You feel a sense of happiness as you are doing a service to your own people. While I was thinking about why you could have probably taken to novel form, I thought perhaps you are interested in experimenting with different genres.

LK: Short stories give me great scope for the epithenic in life and as someone who is very fond of reading and writing poetry, the epithenic element in life—which comes to all of us who are receptive—it is very appealing, so short stories gives me the maximum scope, it can be accommodated in a novel, but then Novella was a very good discipline, particularly that mode I adopted in the three novellas I wrote. One of them has not been translated into English, although it has been into Hindi, it is a woman-oriented novella. It's about three female academics.

RH: What is the title?

LK: In Tamil it is "Purudurra Vanna" i.e. how you change the colours. It deals with the changing attitude of the male boss towards the three women from three different age groups, it is done with an undercurrent of humour. It has a surprising end as all the three women realize the truth about their boss and gang up against him and have a good time at his expense.

RH: It is wonderful to know that you have also tried your hand at the comic. Often women are dismissed off as incapable. They lack sense of humour—people believe.

LK: I think it is offensive.

RH: Coming back to the novel writing and short story writing. Once you come to novella writing, do you think you would be going back to short stories or are you doing both the things parallel?

LK: I have just finished a short story. It depends whether you get the idea.

RH: That's right. Once I was talking to one of the very important creative writers in India and she began as a short story writer and she was very good at it and then she started writing novels and now she is writing novels only. I asked her as to why she doesn't write short stories and she told me that now she can't. She's not capable and I asked why?

LK: This is very curious, because even in Tamil, there are stalwart figures who are failures as short story writers.

RH: Once while interviewing a famous Indian writer who started as a short story writer I was told that novel writing was like a marathon race. The athlete who runs a marathon becomes almost useless for running short distances i.e. after turning to novel one cannot go back to short story.

LK: I am afraid I don't agree with this. I have noticed that some very good writers are failures when they write short stories and short stories is a very different genre in itself. Complete in itself if you ask me. It gives you a glimpse, it has its temporality, it is fascinating, it ends very dense, it makes you think. Sometimes it is very apocalyptic. It has its revelation, so it takes another kind of talent and I don't think every novelist has it in him, I know major writers in Tamil who are failures at short stories. For me, it is a very favourite form. I grew up on short stories. When I went for an International Seminar I was very fascinated by a participant from Brazil called Charles, he is a short story writer. He told us that probably he will remain a short story writer, because in that country you don't have to write a novel to prove yourself, you can make your reputation on short stories and I was envying him the cultural values of his country because on the basis of his short stories alone he has this reputation.

RH: Tell me, how is the reading value of India? What kind of people are we? Do we, as readers, expect our favourite writers to give us novels and only then do we accept him as a full-fledged writer?—

LK: I think there is an undercurrent, a tacit expectation that you have to write a novel to be taken seriously.

RH: Don't you think that is something very wrong?

LK: I think so. In an international perspective or even within India, there are such tremendous short story writers.

RH: As you have been going abroad so often, tell me how does the world think about our literature? Do they care about Indian literature?

LK: You know, the first thing that strikes us is, how we devalue ourselves within the country and in the name of postcolonialism, we tend to be a little apologetic. But if you go in an international setting, you realise that India is greatly respected. It is not respected for its anglicised aspect, rather, it is respected for its Indianness. This is the paradox that hits you and it amuses you when you are there, because when you come back to India there are people bending backwards to show the West that they are as good as they are, they are like them. Whereas, there you are distinct to them only if you are culturally distinct. The artistic lot in the International community are very drawn to the Indianness. The stories that got anthologised abroad are the stories that are very ethnic like "Muniakkam."

RH: I noticed that the Indian words that you have used in your stories, are not translated. Like any African writer, Achebe for example, you have just used them.

LK: Yes very right. This was not necessary at all. English is great as a medium. As soon as you function in English you throw open the windows and the world can relate with you and it is wonderful.

RN: Even technique wise you learn so many things through English. What you are suggesting is that as an Indian writer, writing in English, you have an advantage of being acquainted with the western current, as you have been a student of English literature, a teacher, a critic, a seminarian and then a writer.

LK: And I continue to write poetry also.

RH: Right and poetry also. So on one side you have the English current going on and on the other you have the local 'bhasha' thing going on—and this is my observation—that as an author if I have to define you, I'll define you as an author who stands at the meeting point of East and West, and you are receptive to the form and the technique i.e. you are getting inspiration from the West so far as the technique is concerned, for example, the use of 'stream of consciousness' technique in the novel *Going Home*, or addressing the diary, these are the techniques which you find in the West and you have brought them to our literature.

LK: I have had tremendous inspiration. I am receptive to the techniques of the West, any innovative technique, anybody who is of any nationality, that really appeals to me if it is inventive and if it really works.

RH: So your technique is influenced by the world current.

LK: You are absolutely right. The first reaction to the Tamil original was that "she writes with a strength that comes with her exposure to the West," that was a very perceptive remark made by a woman critic who runs a magazine. I loved the perceptiveness. She says here is a writer who writes, in the guise of 'Gayatri' in the first person narration as Gayatri starts a diary. The critic enjoyed the paradox and appreciated the technique employed in the work. This discussion regarding technique reminds me of my Nigerian friend. We met in a seminar and became great friends. He has written a novel in which I am a protagonist and the main character is America. The technique in this novel is very impressive. His technique was amazing. He became a woman who records for her husband and sends him cassettes. Her husband is in Africa and is lonely and wants to hear her voice. So he wrote the novel like a cassette and that gave him a chance to revise and in print he was trying to be like a cassette.

RH: This is fascinating.

LK: Yes it is. The novel is called *From Iowa with Love.* He has dedicated it jointly to me and to the director Paul Eagle. It was published two years ago.

RH: How wonderful! Do tell me more of such literary experiences.

LK: Thinking of such experiences, an African writer comes to my mind. I had gone to Cambridge to attend a workshop. There was an African, Kenyan, writer. We had a poetry/story reading session. His turn came for story reading and what does he do? Oh! It was a memorable evening. What did he do? He went and got himself a big Beer Mug and said, "this is Calabash." Calabash is root beer that is taken for community sip where it is passed on from person to person. They chat and in between say, "pass the Calabash," his story was called 'Pass the Calabash.' In this story, the people discuss ways of raising funds from the village for a dying woman. It was like a Premchand story. So, men were passing the Calabash, which is a very heady beer and at the same time, as he was reading, we were also saying "Pass the Calabash." So story reading was so alive. By the end of the story, the men were roaring drunk and they forget the woman who finally dies. It's like Premchand's story "The Shroud." It is an oblique commentary on alcoholism. But, what a technique! All that we remembered that night when we parted was "Pass the Calabash."

RH: It almost becomes like an oral narrative, don't you think? How wonderful!

LK: It is. As a modern young writer, I don't like romanticising reality, it won't help. One has to face reality with a touch of fantasy in technique.

RH: Now, about your translations. Lakshmi Kannan as a translator of her own stories and novellas. It is good that you do the translations yourself.

LK: In English, when I translate, I become very aware of the potentialities and limitations of English. Our own languages like Tamil, Gujarati, Hindi, well, some of them have a texture which we cannot translate, for instance, in my literary collection "Rhythms," there is a novella called, "Glass Balls." It is tragic, here a young son of a very attractive mother loses his sanity, he is schizophrenic, the whole family tries to help him. His mother, particularly goes berserk trying to help, and then there is somebody who feels that his attachment is Oedipal. This is a very English concept, yet I questioned as to "what about the mother's point of view?" She does so much, but still the critic maintained that it was Oedipal, because she is drawn to him. I felt, this was because he could not understand and was reading wrong meaning in English, because otherwise in Tamil, the Tamilian could grasp what is called 'Vatsalya.' It is a beautiful word. It is "untranslatable," it is maternal love, it can also be paternal love, it's vatsalya towards the child. It is not translatable very well in English. There are certain words, expressions, I get into problem with in English, but there are certain other things where it opens up.

RH: It is a gateway to the world, I agree. Don't you think bilingualism is a must in today's world?

LK: Of course, yes. It is catching on. There are more and more bilingual people now. You are writing in English and Gujarati, you are already a bilingual critic. These have become special brands of critics in English Departments, ten years ago it never happened.

RH: I think we are getting decolonised.

LK: Yes.

RH: You call yourself a feminist, so please define your shade of feminism?

LK: To me, at this point of time, it has become synonymous with "human rights." It has become as basic as that. Since, I have got used to voice and articulate a woman's point of view with as much clarity as I could muster, I feel that it has become a grounding in my psyche, so I find myself doing it for a man too. When a man is oppressed, it comes into my man centered stories like 'Maze' or when a man is vulnerable—like in one of my stories 'Zeroing in,' it was received very well in Cambridge by most of the men because it shows the terrible situation of man in his workplace. I feel for them. So I find, it is enlarging. "Feminism is human rights."

RH: So, your sympathy is for anybody who suffers.

LK: Now it has become like that, it is widening. It has the same grounding, the same ammunition.

RH: Being a feminist, do you believe that a woman has a right to space, mental as well as physical.

LK: Yes, how can one help it? She must have her own space.

RH: Coming finally to the most forbidden area of feminist assertion in Indian context, do tell me who in your view is the boss of the woman's body? Is it her own estate?

LK: I am very clear about this. She should try to be the boss of her body in every sense and in the Hindu sense particularly. We are lucky we are Hindus, we have a rich religion which teaches you to live within this body.

RH: Excuse me but I recall a metaphor used by you in your novel *Going Home* where the young girl exclaims "0 yes, tenant as we are the tenants in the body."

LK: Yes, so body comes in there, she is there in the woman's body and she has already learnt to suffer all that comes with the package, the biology, some feminists call it "biology's destiny."

RH: Simone de Beavoir rejected it and said that it is all because of gender coding, i.e. acculturation of the body.

LK: It is all very Western or maybe it is a reductive thing, but as a Hindu, as a woman who grows older with books, I have this feeling that it is a temporary dwelling.

RH: Yes, as long as you are in this dwelling it is yours.

LK: It is mine, it should be kept well not only in working order but it should be respected by yourself.

RH: That and by others as well.

LK: If they don't respect it, you will have to teach them how to respect it. I hate physical abuse, I just can't stand it and I don't see how anybody can excuse violence.

RH: Thank you very much Lakshmi for such an inspiring conversation.

East-West Encounter in Kamala Markandaya's Novels

JAYDIPSINH K. DODIYA

Kamala Markandaya is one of the most outstanding Indian novelists writing in English. It is beyond doubt that she occupies a prominent place among Indian English novelists. She won international fame and recognition with the publication of her very first novel, *Nectar in a Sieve*, in 1954. As a novelist she differs from other Indian English novelists in many respects. When she started writing novels, the themes of Hunger and Degradation, East-West Encounter, Rootlessness, Politics and Human Relationships had already been dealt with by a number of Indian English nóvelists. She is not traditional at all from thematic point of view. She provides variety and vividness to these themes. In her novels, the themes include the life in villages, cities, husband-wife relations, social conflicts and lure for modernisation. One of the most remarkable characteristics of her novels is that at no place does she repeat herself.

East-West encounter is the major theme of all Markandaya novels. Having been born and brought up in India, her presentation of the East-West conflict, tension and culture, is characterized by her first-hand experience. This East-West conflict is presented on different levels, namely the political, the social, the human, the technological, the cultural and the artistic. R.M. Verma rightly observes about her novels that they are the bi-cultural world of Kamala Markandaya without any partiality or favour either for the East or for the West. She brings out the various points of weakness and strength of both the cultures. She looks at the West through the eyes of the East and looks at the East through the eyes of the West. The setting may be England or India, city or village. She brings out clearly the barriers of arrogance, colour and cultural differences that keep the East and the West apart. She tries to bring about a reconciliation of the two. C.D. Narasimhaiah rightly remarks: "Generally her novels reflect her strong penchant for Indian values as against the spiritual impoverishment of the English society, but Indians are not spared. Actually her good men and women come from both cultures."

In *Nectar in a Sieve*, Nathan and Rukmani symbolize the East whereas the rapid industrialization and Dr. Kenny represent the West. Both Nathan and Rukmani have to suffer a lot when natural calamities like floods and droughts shatter their whole family. Ultimately their valued possession, their land, is taken away for establishing a tannery. Through the character of Dr. Kenny, Markandya tries to awake the East. Dr. Kenny, an English social worker, loves the Indian people but when he sees their passive acceptance of life, he feels disgusted. He painly tells Rukmani, "I go when I am tired of your follies and stupidity, your external shameful poverty. I can only take you people in small doses." In this world of Dr. Kenny, there is an underlined feeling of sadness and pain over the miseries of poor, innocent people. No doubt, he consoles Rukmani in her sorrows but he also scolds her for passiveness when she feels content with a little rice and hopes that times will be better. He shouts at her, "Times are better, times are better. Times will not be better for many months. Meanwhile you will suffer and die, you meek suffering fools. Why do you keep this ghastly silence? Why don't you demand—cry out for help—do something? There is nothing in this country. Oh God, there is nothing."

Dr. Kenny dislikes the Indian philosophy of fasting for the purification of soul. When Rukmani tells him about the Indian priests fasting and inflicting on themselves severe punishment, he exclaims with disgust: "My God, I do not understand you. I never will. Go, before I too am entangled in your philosophies." Thus the talk between Dr. Kenny and Rukmani reflects the clear perspective of the Eastern and the Western outlook of life.

Kamala Markandaya also points out that the people of the East are passive and submissive whereas the people of the West are active and conscious of their rights. At this stage she also brings out the strong points of the culture of the East. In the East, marriage is a sacrament whereas in the West, marriage is simply a contract. Dr. Kenny tells Rukmani: "My wife has left me. My sons have been taught to forget me."

The East-West Encounter is also reflected in Kamala Markandaya's novel *A Silence of Desire*. In this particular novel, the East-West encounter is in the form of a conflict between the Indian spiritualism and the western modernism. There are no western characters in the novel. The confrontation is depicted through the Western-educated and the Western-oriented individuals like Ghosh on one hand and women like Sarojini and Rajan who are basically Indians in their attitudes to life on the other hand, with Dandekar standing in the middle. C. Paul Verghese rightly remarks: "This conflict between the husband and the wife is treated in the novel as a part of a conflict between Science and Superstition. The novelist in presenting the conflict does not make an outright condemnation of superstition or faith healing swami. She attempts to strike a balance between Science and Superstition."

The novel also has references to the feelings of the East towards the West. In the office, Chari Ghosh and Dandekar discuss the British culture. Chari criticises the British claim of reforming India: "The British have told us many a time of all they have done—they built railways, roads, bridges. Do you think in Russia, China, Japan, where there were no British, there are no roads, railway bridges?"

Possession presents the constant conflict between the Indian spiritualism and the Western materialism, the former winning over the latter. In this novel Caroline Bell makes every possible effort to possess Val anyhow, but the spiritual values of the Indian culture are so deep-rooted in him that he is not easily captivated by her. On the contrary, he succeeds in liberating himself from the clutches. Here the novelist wants to emphasize the fact that the British rulers exploited the Indians and tried to possess them both physically and mentally, but ultimately they failed and had to quit India. Caroline takes Val to England and tries to expolit his talent of painting.

In *A Handful of Rice*, the East-West encounter has been portrayed in the form of difference in the cultural values. Certain traditions and the ways of the East are disliked by the West and vice versa. The novelist's following remark about the shamelessness of the Europeans makes it quite clear: "Ravi had sisters, and so he knew the strict watch that was kept on young unmarried girls in their community, in all communities except shameless ones like the Europeans."

In *The Coffer Dams*, the East-West encounter is on technological as well as human level. On the technological level, the conflict is between the technological power and the forces of nature represented by the turbulent-South Indian river on which the dam is being built and also the heavy rains which try to hinder the task of the construction work. On the human level, the conflict is between the arrogant British officers under their leader, Clinton and the poor hill-tribesmen working as labourers."

In short the theme of East-West encounter is presented in the context of rural India in *Nectar in a Sieve*; in the context of western way of life in *Some Inner Fury*; in a cultural context of traditionalism and modernity in *A Silence of Desire*, *A Handful of Rice*, *Two Virgins* and *Pleasure City*; in the context of Indian spiritual values and western materialism in *Possession*; in the context of racial conflict in *The Nowhere Man* and *The Coffer Dams*; in the context of political movement and freedom struggle in *The Golden Honeycomb*. The theme of East-West encounter can be identified with the idea depicted in E.M. Forster's *A Passage to India* which emphasizes the wide gulf between the Indian and the Eastern life. Markandaya expresses her views on this vital subject through a large variety of situations and characters. It has been rightly said that "she maintains objectivity throughout, and very scrupulously avoids the dichotomy which we find in the works of other novelists."

The Theme of Hunger in Kamala Markandaya's *Nectar in a Sieve*

PRADIPSINH RATHOD

> *In India the countryside too has been polluted but not by the encroachment of industry . . . the pollution comes from within, through starvation.*[1]

Often compared and contrasted with Bhabani Bhattacharya's *So Many Hungers* for the theme of degradation of humanity, with Pearl S. Buck's *The Good Earth* for the treatment of milieu, with Dennis Stoll's *The Dove Found No Rest* for the depiction of social chaos, and with Prem Chand's *Godan* for its realistic approach, Kamala Markandaya's *Nectar in a Sieve* presents a spectrum of themes reflecting the lives of village folk. The fact that the novel portrays the rural Indian life at its best, becomes evident through the realistic picture put forward in all its phases and the minute description of flood, draught, famine, starvation, superstition, struggle for survival and so on. These various aspects need, of course, a stupendous setting to create an everlasting cinematic effect, and the creation of all time Indian village fulfills this necessity. The unbaptized South Indian village of Markandaya symbolises any rural area existing on Indian soil. It stands for the socio-economic/cultural/spiritual and to some extent, socio-psychic upheavals—the insuperable ingredients of India's country people. What is most remarkable is the full-balanced assemblage of these elements; and here lies the actual force of Markandaya's rural realism.

Nectar in a Sieve runs in the first person narration told by the protagonist-narrator Rukmani, a peasant woman suffering almost all the time within the duration of narrative. Her family consists of her husband Nathan, a poor tenant farmer, a daughter, Ira, and six sons. Although poverty-stricken, they are happy and mutually compromise with the conditions they are put into by fate. But the establishment of the tannery initiates miseries for them. Capriciousness of nature accompanied by cruel dealings of their landlord bring their apparent peace to disaster. The unwelcome entry of industrialization not only "invaded our village with clatter and din, had taken from us the maidan where our children played, and made the bazaar prices too high for us,"[2] but also intruded the complete innate atmosphere and the village economy causing devastating social calamity. Rukmani stands in thorough opposition to even a thought of tannery, since according to her, it has been tempting the simple village folk into greed and immoral acts. Her fears come true as not merely the society, but her own family gets dislocated, initially with two of her sons joining the tannery as workers and thus disappointing their father's much awaited desire of farming. However, this separation brings in a thin layer of happiness—perhaps the best period in their lives—to the family and temporarily they get rid of perpetual fear of starvation until both the brothers are dispelled from the tannery and go to Ceylon as labourers, never to return. Apart from the man-made misfortunes, the family suffers at the pitiless hands of nature which was never merciful to them. Drought and flood destroy crops one by one. Rukmani painfully recalls:

> It was as if nothing had ever been but rain. . . . Nathan and I watched with heavy hearts while waters rose and rose, and the tender green of paddy field sank under and was lost . . . there will be little eating done this year. (43-44)

The whim of nature shifts its form again, but the result is same:

> [Drought] continued until we lost count of time. Day after day the pitiless sun blazed down scorching whatever still struggled to grow and baking the earth hard until it split and great irregular fissures gaped in the land. Plants died and grasses rotted, cattle and sheep crept to the river that was no more and perished there for lack of water. (81)

Stability never sets on them after such a series of tragic periods and there can hardly remain any demarcating line between wandering hungry animals in search of food and human beings facing starvation. Hunger observes dictums neither of humanity nor of quality:

> Thereafter we fed on whatever we could find. . . . Early and late my sons roamed the countryside, returning with few bamboo shoots, a stick of sugarcane left in some deserted field, or piece. . . . It was not enough. Sometimes from sheer rebellion we ate grass although it always resulted in stomach cramps and violent retching. (91)

Even the much-sustained human relationships tend to lose their significance if the stomachs are empty:

> Of coconut picked from the gutter . . . other farmers and their families in like plight to ourselves, were also out searching for food; and for every edible plant or root there was a struggle—a desperate competition that made enemies of friends and put an end to humanity. (91)

Still a sigh of solace is possible and practical as well if the disaster is caused by nature only, but tenant farmers like Nathan must not rest as they have to settle the lifelong unsettled accounts with their landlords. The one that Nathan has, is never late in demanding and accumulating his dues, nor troubles his mind to take a note of his tenant farmer's misfortunes and failure of his crops. This exploitation immediately results in perpetual hunger and starvation and their eviction from the tenant land proves the last nail in Nathan's coffin: "To those who live by the land, there must always come times of hardship, of fear and of hunger." (136) Soon the couple, Rukmani and Nathan, is compelled to part with the village and live with one of their sons, Murugan, in the city where they are eventually informed of his deserting the city as well as his family. So they live on charity for sometime before doing some petty jobs till Nathan succumbs to death. Despaired, Rukmani returns to the village, still with the "fear of dark future; fear of sharpness of hunger; fear of the blackness of death." (83)

The delineation of the theme of hunger is obviously one of the remarkable features of *Nectar in a Sieve*, chiefly due to Markandaya's first hand dealing with what she offers. She had been an independent onlooker who witnessed the socio-economic values of village life during her stay in South India. This fact evidently assigns the book to be a vital record of poverty and starvation caused by inhuman exploitation. If the statement is stretched further, some more equally prominent themes such as deterioration and debasement of humanity and devaluation of morality erupt as side-effects of hunger. The same vicious circle entangles beautiful Kunthi in prostitution and compels her to blackmail Rukmani for a handful of rice; provokes Raja, one of Rukmani's sons, to steal from the tannery only to be killed by the authorities; and despairs Ira to sell her body to the tannery people in her desperate efforts to save her youngest brother from starving.

While dealing with such central ideas behind her creative impulse, Markandaya has simultaneously been developing her own world of the proletariate which, according to Cowasjee and Shahane, is "tempered with common sense and sound judgement."[3] And thus, her main theme is her actual concern for the unhappy and poverty-stricken people exploited by the bourgeoisie and misfortunes caused by nature.

NOTES

1. Kai Nicholson, *Social Problems in the Indo-Anglian Novel* (Bombay: Jaico, 1972), p. 116.
2. Kamala Markandaya, *Nectar in a Sieve* (New York: New American Library, 1954), pp. 31-32.
3. S. Cowasjee and V.A. Shahane, "Kamala Markandaya," *Modern Indian Fiction*, p. 104.

The Unconscious Desire and Its Fulfilment in Kamala Markandaya's *A Silence of Desire*

M. RAJESHWAR

Kamala Markandaya's *A Silence of Desire* depicts the unconscious desire of a house-wife, Sarojini, to fight the decay of her self within the marital relationship. She protests unconsciously, but in a manner approved by the society, against her husband, and by extension against the whole society, for giving her a listless and mechanical life which her psyche perceives quite clearly as being responsible for her fast deteriorating self. Her husband, Dandekar, to whom her strange behaviour and defiance come as a big shock, neurotically reacts and goes through a phase of suffering and soul-searching. Since it all happens unconsciously, neither of them has a clear understanding of the real motives for their behaviour. In the light of the knowledge of depth psychology, I would like to integrate into the discussion here such aspects of the novel as Dandekar's jealousy, his rationality and its loss on being subjected to traumatic experiences, the strategies of his psyche to win Sarojini back, Sarojini's preference for a faith-healer over modern medicine and her deep attachment with the Swamy, and argue that the whole effort of Sarojini's psyche has been to voice her desire to protest against the imminent loss of her self and that of Dandekar to get back his peace and domestic harmony and then conclude that both the protagonists emerge wiser than before—she having made her point and he having recognized his 'integral' but non-sexual 'wholeness' with her.

Dandekar bases his life upon some certainties: "Three children, no debts, a steady job, a fair pile of savings that his wife methodically converted into gold-bangles, a necklace, ear-rings and brooches less for ornamentation than the security it represented."[1] As a wife Sarojini is "good with the children, an excellent cook, an efficient manager of his household, a woman who still gave him pleasure after fifteen years of marriage . . . she did most things placidly . . . and from this calm proceeded the routine and regularity that met the neat and orderly needs of his nature." (7) He does not want a change in this routine even in the wildest of his dreams. Even a trivial change like his daughters' buying tiffin provokes him to roundly remonstrate with his wife. This secure world comes off at the seams once its main pivot, his wife, frequently absents herself from the house and lies about it. Dandekar's first feeling is a suspicion of her fidelity. Her lies and his discovery of a stranger's photograph in her trunk strengthen his suspicion. Still, it is strange that after fifteen years of shared living, Dandekar should suspect her fidelity the first thing instead of considering other possibilities. There appears to be an element of abnormally intense jealousy in him which is often the case with people prone to neurotic reaction. His leniency towards his colleagues Joseph and Mahadevan who believe in free love and inherent unfaithfulness of women respectively shows him to be secretly entertaining similar thoughts. But they have undergone a thorough repression. He therefore readily projects his own feelings onto his wife. As Freud puts it, projected jealousy is "derived in both men and women either from their own actual unfaithfulness in real life or from impulses towards it which have succumbed to repression."[2]

The common experience is that marital fidelity is maintained only in the face of great temptations. Persons consciously denying to themselves these temptations, like Dandekar, will find it inevitable to use the unconscious mechanism of projecting their own impulses to unfaithfulness onto the other person to get relief from the pressure exerted by these temptations. Freud continues: "This strong motive can then make use of the perceptual material which betrays unconscious impulses of the same kind in the partner, and the subject can justify himself with the reflection that the other is probably not much better than he is himself." The situation has not varied from the days of Othello and Desdemona. Dandekar's repressed unfaithfulness informs his moral errantry during his neurotic grapple with the difficulties imposed upon him by adverse circumstances.

Dandekar feels so intensely jealous that he makes two attempts to trail Sarojini, risking in the process his reputation and interests at the office. The desire to find out with whom she is carrying on an affair consumes him "like a fire." (68) He succeeds the second time. To his dismay, he finds Sarojini amidst a group of people and in the company of a Swamy to whom she confesses to be going to get cured of a painful growth in her womb by faith and prayer.

It is very interesting to examine Sarojini's reasons for going to the faith-healer and not to a medical doctor. She had a rigid religious tutelage and consequently she has not kept up with the changing times. Upon developing the growth she expects to meet the same fate as her mother and grandmother who suffered from the same disease, underwent an operation but did not survive. She refuses to recognize the tremendous advance made by the medical science. These are the verbalized reasons. However, the important reasons lie in her unconscious. Fifteen years of married life have made it clear to her that the rest of her life is going to be as dull and drab as it has always been. Her life becomes so mechanical and routine that we find her attending to her household chores with a predictable regularity which Dandekar has grown to like so much. She does not betray her emotions at all. Her repressed anger, accumulated over the years, against the person responsible for the meaninglessness of her life assumes a negative identity symbolically put in the novel as the tumour. She knows all too well Dandekar's Western frame of mind and scientific attitude. By going to the Swamy, which she knows will be disapproved of by him, she unconsciously protests against him just as Tara protested against her pedantic husband Brihaspati by physically running away with Soma in the Rigvedic myth. Sarojini does it differently, in a manner that is sanctioned by tradition and achieves the desired effect. In her unconscious the

Swamy plays the lover and the father at the same time as we shall see next.

Once she starts meeting the Swamy regularly, complications develop. It soon becomes impossible to wrench herself free from the magnetic pull of the Swamy. This point calls for a little theoretical enquiry. In offering to heal, all these mystics follow a familiar but complex method discussed at length by Sudhir Kakar in his book *Shamans Mystics and Doctors*. They know that only lonely, neglected and distraught people seek their help. Therefore, the first thing they see to is that an enhancement of the 'individual,' as against the all-embracing community and the isolation of the individualistic society, is assured. Then they annex this newly developed self to themselves which results in a relatively greater childlikeness in the followers. The event becomes a symbolic enactment of a similar experience in childhood. Sudhir Kakar, strongly echoing Freud, put it succinctly:

> The whole transformation process has its roots in, and is a replication of, psychic events in that early period of childhood when the child, in the face of the many narcissistic hurts and disappointments that the ending of infancy brought in its wake, sought to recapture his early feelings of "greatness" through a new route, where he projected his greatness into the idealized image of a parent and then partook of it himself by setting up a configuration in the psyche: "you are great but I am a part of you."[3]

The unconscious substitution of the guru in place of the father requires afresh the mechanisms of idealization and identification. The follower achieves a "psychological symbiosis" with the Master through these processes. Idealization of the analyst and identification with him do happen at certain stages of psychoanalysis too. The difference is that they are tactical and temporary in psychoanalysis whereas in mystical cults they are strategic and are meant to be permanent. The idealization and internalization of the guru is usually sought to be cemented by such strategic methods as meditating upon the guru's face which indeed Sarojini does. The result of all this is that the ailing follower replaces his feelings of dependence, insignificance, inertness, limitation and circumscription with the guru's dependability, omnipotence, energy and all-pervasive presence in the unconscious.[4] It sets in motion the follower's healing transformation similar to what is obtained in psychoanalysis.

The Swamy of *A Silence of Desire* follows a similar method and Sarojini is completely taken in. Markandaya does not go into the healing rituals at the Swamy's place. But enough evidence is offered to strengthen our theoretical perspective:

> She was sitting, cross-legged, on the man's [the Swamy's] right. His hand was on her bowed head, and he was murmuring to her, his voice sometimes falling to a whisper, a soft stream of indistinguishable words. In a rough circle about them sat a small group of men and women, listening—so engrossed that no one turned as he [Dandekar] burst in. No one had even stirred; they were simply unaware of his presence. (79-80)

It is therefore not surprising that Sarojini should feel better every time she goes there. She is aware that the pain is there but it does not touch her in the Swamy's presence. What the Swamy actually ministers to is not the alleviation of the pain her body experiences but the pain her psyche experiences—the pain born of a sense of neglect and worthlessness. Her neurotic need for love and self-importance are amply attended to by him. It produces a temporary euphoria which neutralizes the physical pain for the time being. Before Sarojini knows it, the Swamy's image is internalized and going to him becomes something of an addiction. She lacks the necessary intellectual resources to discriminate between the needs of her body and psyche. She therefore falls into the false belief that "without faith I shall not be healed." (87) As is evident, the Swamy's method works only in the treatment of imaginary illnesses. Rajam, the garrulous cousin of Sarojini, has in fact been cured by the Swamy of her terrible pains which the doctors have diagnosed as imaginary.

While Sarojini is happy in her pain, Dandekar goes through a period of acute mental torture. The certainties of his life appear to be crumbling down. He finds "the pattern of his life being twisted out of shape." (77) The cumulative effect of it is that he grows "withdrawn, questioning, introspective." (98)

His exposure to Western thinking has rendered him particularly unsuitable to uncritically participate in the world of Sarojini. We find him at that point of turning away from religion which Freud thinks "is bound to occur with fatal inevitability of a process of growth."[5] Dandekar is, for example, careful to point out that the tulsi plant which his wife worships with great devotion is merely "a plant; one did not worship plants." (5) His disregard for rituals is symbolic of the reenactment of the overcoming of childhood neurosis which of necessity everybody suffers in the process of taming the unruly instinctual demands. Religion is by extension "the universal obsessional neurosis of humanity: like the obsessional neurosis of children."[6] This much desirable psychic progression of Dandekar is suddenly disrupted by the onslaught of great anxiety caused by his wife the relationship with whom becomes strained and hence the chief source of pain for him. Attempting to work out solutions at the infantile level to problems requiring adult rationality is quite in keeping with the logic of neurosis. He unconsciously believes that his wife, whose love and acquiescence he has taken so much for granted, has deserted him for good and he experiences acute anxiety and pain just like an infant who equates the loss of perception of its mother with the loss of the mother herself and becomes anxious about it.[7] With the passage of a few months Dandekar realizes that his wife can be with him and yet not give him the assurance which she formerly used to give. This, as in the case of an infant, becomes for him "a new and much more enduring danger and determinant of anxiety."[8] His anxiety makes him do things which earlier he would not think of doing even in dreams. Knowing well that he is financially strained he becomes exaggeratedly generous, purposelessly talks aloud, risks his social reputation by visiting houses of ill-fame and commits such blunders in his work that they almost earn him the sack. His rationality deserts him and he sees nothing wrong in worshipping the tulsi himself!

He feels so drained of thought that it requires his kindly colleague Sastri to advise him to initiate some steps to set things right. His genuine efforts to talk some sense into Sarojini's head and his pitiable pleadings with the Swamy to dissuade her from seeing him end up in a fiasco as they are bound to, for reasons we have already considered. In addition, in the Swamy's presence, he feels so detached from himself and attracted to the Swamy that he is moved to donate money to the Swamy's fund. The Swamy seems to touch an atavistic chord in him as he surely does in others including the fierce Deputy District Magistrate, Ghose. Nothing seems to matter in the Swamy's presence.

The realities of life are, however, different. One cannot afford to lose sight of them for long. Dandekar finds it now impossible to reconcile these two worlds. He feels as though he is fighting "something invisible." (170) Questions seize his mind allowing it no respite to find answers.

> "Question, questions, questions," Dandekar's knuckles dug into his forehead. "They crowd into my brain and it's like you [Sastri] said, I don't know the answers. I suppose it's because I've never had to think much about anything until now, but I don't seem able to think straight, do anything. All I know is I can't go on like this." (171)

He is indeed unable to go any further. Nature itself takes care of it. He comes down with severe shingles and is bedridden for fourteen days. The illness serves several purposes simultaneously although Dandekar appears to regard it as mere inconvenience. Firstly, as the doctor rightly diagnoses, it provides a relatively safer outlet for the anxiety that has been brewing in his unconscious for the past few months. Secondly, it becomes a device employed by his unconscious to hold Sarojini down to him. After all no woman, however irresponsible, will leave her husband to suffer and go away for a selfish reason. But here the strategy fails. While not neglecting her duties as a wife, Sarojini nevertheless continues to visit the Swamy. Thirdly, it allows him some breathing space to make some key discoveries about himself and his relation with Sarojini. The "heat and pain and those stabbing, lucid moments" of the two weeks of his illness sensitise him to the suffering of Sarojini and sober him. Her body does not arouse him sexually any more. He now looks at her "from another aspect of love" (191) and sees "the flesh flower pale and beautiful under the thin blue cotton she wore without desire." (191) He wants her back now "not merely because he desired her," but because of "a spiritual ingrowing which made it impossible for him to be whole so long as any part of her was missing." (191) Markandaya subtly conveys the changed perspective of Dandekar through the image of a night storm which is followed by a gentle drizzle in the morning.

Dandekar pins all his hopes on his boss, Chari. Although Chari does not assure him of anything he nevertheless assigns the task of enquiring into the Swamy's activities to his deputy, Ghose, and when that yields only limited results he takes up the matter himself. He does not order the Swamy to quit the place but his efforts do not really go waste. The Swamy is clever enough to see that his position as a spiritual guide and faith-healer has become controversial. He therefore thinks it wise to quietly leave the place. For Sarojini, this proves to be traumatic. She feels so distraught and dazed at the Swamy's disappearance that for a split second Dandekar feels that if it is within his power to bring him back he would do it. Inconsolable as she is with the loss she at the same time realizes, unconsciously again, that she still matters a great deal to her husband. Otherwise why would he suffer so much on account of her? She is therefore restored, body and soul, to Dandekar—to the world of hard facts, her 'honeymoon' with irrationality being over and her 'desire' being fulfilled. Her desire to voice her protest had something revolutionary about it. It was her last ditch effort to save herself from falling into self-preservatory negativism issuing directly from psychological repression unleashed by the social institution of family. She undergoes the required operation and is eventually cured of the ailment.

Dandekar too regains a semblance of happiness by shedding the physical nature of his desire and with the distinct realization that his wife is an essential and indispensable part of his world, that it will not be in his interest to take her for granted and finally that henceforth his relation with her should be on the basis of love and equality.

NOTES

1. Kamala Markandaya, *A Silence of Desire* (London: Putnam, 1960), p. 6.
2. Sigmund Freud, "Some Neurotic Mechanisms in Jealousy, Paranoia and Homosexuality," *On Psychopathology*, trans. James Strachey (1979; Harmondsworth: Penguin, 1983), p. 198.
3. Sudhir Kakar, "The Path of the Saints," in his *Shamans Mystics and Doctors: A Psychological Inquiry into India and its Healing Traditions* (New Delhi: Oxford University Press, 1982), p. 145.
4. *Ibid.*, pp. 146-47.
5. Sigmund Freud, *The Future of an Illusion*, trans. James Strachey (Harmondsworth: Penguin, 1964), p. 227.
6. *Ibid.*, p. 226.
7. Sigmund Freud, "Anxiety, Pain and Mourning," *On Psychopathology*, p. 330.
8. *Ibid.*, p. 331.

East-West Relationship in Kamala Markandaya's *Possession*

MADHU JOSHI

> "Well," said Caroline, "What was India like?"
> "Hot."
> "And London?" queried Anusuya.
> "Cold."[1]

This conversation aptly and succinctly sums up, in less than a dozen words, the very spirit of Kamala Markandaya's fourth novel *Possession* (1963). The clash between the East and the West—between their respective cultures, values, traditions, convictions and, most important of all, between human beings who personify their virtually irreconcilable worlds—remains the focus of attention throughout this novel which many critics consider to be one of Markandaya's less successful works. Even as one cannot help noticing that *Possession* has a number of shortcomings which no discerning reader can overlook, one is forced to admit that one of the greatest achievements of the novel is the manner in which the author dexterously, realistically and impartially handles its major theme—the love-hate relationship between the East and the West, represented by the Swami and Lady Caroline respectively, and the diametrically dissimilar values and convictions which the two embody and personify.

H.M. Williams says of *Possession*: "The novel is one of the most forceful artistic explorations of the distortion of India's national character in the British embrace and of her consequent urge to be free."[2] The central character through whom this 'distortion' is probed, analyzed and discussed is Valmiki, a goatherd blessed with unusual artistic talents who, when Lady Caroline Bell first meets him, is a fourteen-year-old illiterate village simpleton. As soon as Lady Caroline comes in contact with him, she spots his talent and wastes no time in taking possession of him—body, talent, personality, values and soul, as it were. She breezes through the formalities of getting permission from his parents and 'buys' him for five thousand rupees, a fact which aptly exemplifies her possessive and dictatorial instincts. Before the bewildered Anusuya—the narrator through whose eyes the whole drama is seen—can react, she carries Val, as she likes to call him, away to distant London, and then to Switzerland, France, Italy, Greece, America and the Nile delta. Then she begins a continuous process of trimming and chiselling, moulding and conditioning during which Valmiki's own individuality—and this, one must stress, includes the oriental qualities which are an integral part of his make-up and of his soul—seems to be completely subjugated. He assumes the role of a creation of Caroline and she assiduously and singlemindedly fashions and shapes him. Finally, he becomes the living representation of the very image that Caroline had conjured up in her mind, probably as soon as she had first set eyes on him when he was a simple, though prodigiously talented, goatherd "in rags, smelling a little of his goats." (14)

Very soon Valmiki becomes totally Westernized—or so it seems—and acquires Western tastes, values and instincts. All along Caroline ruthlessly and obdurately eliminates all obstacles which she encounters. When "some awful little man [from the Education department]—pestered her with unnecessary questions," (44) she takes Valmiki away to Switzerland because she is convinced that he does not need formal education like other lesser mortals. When Valmiki becomes emotionally and physically involved with Ellie, a pathetic victim of Nazi brutalities, she swiftly and silently gets rid of Ellie, goading the wretched Jewess to commit suicide. Yet once again, when Valmiki deserts her for Annabel she bides her time and strikes only when the moment is ripe. With studied casualness and pretended innocence she reveals before Annabel sordid details about her protege's involvement with desertion of Ellie who was carrying his child. Thus, with one dexterous stroke, she manages to fob off her distant relative for whom Valmiki was ready to forsake her, his ambitions and his artistic career.

However, in spite of all these 'victories' scored by Cardine and despite his own apparent transformation, Valmiki cannot completely sever all his ties with the past, particularly the Oriental values which he had imbibed from his mentor and guide, the Swamy. Therefore, he does not go back to Caroline, even after her triumph over Annabel. After nursing Minou, his pet monkey who eventually dies of double pneumonia, he returns to India and his village cave with Anusuya. He takes up residence with the Swamy and goes back to the business of painting and offering his artistic creations as homage to God. This is the point from which Caroline had arbitrarily and confidently uprooted him. Yet when he returns to his cave he is a wiser, more tempered and chastened man, who has seen and tasted the enticements which the West has to offer, and who has renounced all these Occidental allurements and pleasures so as to find peace of mind and soul in artistic creativity which assumes the form of prayer and thanksgiving.

Thus, by comparing and contrasting Lady Caroline's instinct for possession with the Swamy's spirit of renunciation and detachment, Markandaya once again picks up the theme of East-West relationship which she had first dealt with in *Some Inner Fury*, and to which she was to return in *Coffer Dams* and *The Nowhere Man*. The Swamy and Caroline represent the two antithetical forces which act on Valmiki—the former almost unwittingly exerts spiritual and emotional pressures which Valmiki ultimately succumbs to, while the latter does her best to entice Valmiki with Western glamour, opulence and fame, from the clutches of which Valmiki escapes, at least for the time being, at the end of the novel. From the very beginning, the relationship between Lady Caroline and Valmiki is that of the possessor and the possessed, or the owner and the owned. That would explain why Caroline is ready to go to any extremes in order to make

Valmiki, whom she autocratically treats not merely as a possession but virtually as her own creation, walk along the path she has chalked out for him. Consequently, when, after being uprooted from his native village, Valmiki stops painting altogether—that his only painting from this period is that of something which "looked vaguely like a desert" (48) is highly symbolic—she gets her South-Indian cook to write letters to him. She then pretends before Valmiki, who can neither read nor write, that they come from the Swamy. The letters have the desired effect; Valmiki exclaims enthusiastically, "Now I am happy. . . . I feel good—here—I work again, much work." (62) One must mention at this point that during this arid phase Valmiki's main concern, which he expresses before Anusuya, is, "Then you not tell Swamy." (52) It is clear that, in spite of his initiation into Caroline's world and his obvious attempts at conforming to the rigid codes of her society, it is the Swamy's opinion of him that he values first and foremost.

Again, it is the same proprietorial instinct which prompts Caroline to fight tooth and nail, by fair means and foul, when she finds Valmiki slipping away from her grasp because of his involvements, first with Ellie and then with Annabel. K.R. Srinivas Iyengar aptly sums up Caroline's attitude as "purblindly ruthless and demanding."[3] Valmiki, due to his innate sagacity and shrewdness, realizes from the very beginning that for Caroline he is, to a large extent, a possession. Once, during his early days in London, he is upset when he hears Caroline calling his village and his cave a 'crevice,' and he explodes before Anusuya.

> She does not care for me. She cares only for what I can do, and if I do it well it is like one more diamond she can put on the necklace round her throat for her friends to admire; but when I do nothing I am nothing to her, no more than a small insect in a small crack in the ground. It was not a slip of the tongue, a manner of speaking: [use of the word crevice] it is what she thinks of me when I am as I am now. (56)

That is, certainly, the best way of summing up Caroline's general attitude towards Valmiki.

Yet once again, Valmiki shows that he is aware of being a mere possession—a role which he wholeheartedly resents—when towards the end of the novel he takes Caroline to his cave where she finds all the cheques, that she had sent for him, lying uncashed. It would be best to quote the passage which throws a great deal of light on the Caroline-Valmiki relationship as it stands at the end of the novel:

> "Exhibits," said Caroline, and her eyes narrowed. "Darling, what do they exhibit: my greed? meanness? avarice? cruelty? which of the great iniquities would you lay at my door?"
>
> "My dear—" Valmiki's voice had lost its earlier mocking level. "My dear," he said again, wrung, "None of those things. Only one, that you wanted to own me and it is not an uncommon iniquity." (222)

Indeed, one can safely say that one of the most important reasons for Valmiki's return is the fact that he resents Caroline's possessive attitude towards him since it obviously suffocates not just his artistic talent, but also his personality and his very soul.

Anusuya, too, is aware of Caroline's inclination and intention from the very beginning. Talking about Caroline's relationship with Valmiki in 1955, when the relationship was working out very well, she says, "Caroline was not only possessed, but had also taken possession." (178) She expresses the same sentiment when she warns Annabel, "Caroline thinks Valmiki belongs to her, and in a way she's right. She won't let go. People don't easily give up what they think are their possessions. The English never have." (192) Once again, some time before they sail back for India, Anusuya says: "There's Caroline—always Caroline. She fits into it, she is responsible for some of it. She was born and bred to power, nothing has ever curbed it." Valmiki's answer, "People do not have power unless you allow them to have it," (207) makes it abundantly clear that he harbours no ill-will towards Caroline; he accepts the fact that the desire to possess is not an uncommon one. Furthermore, once he has realized this, he soon reaches the point from where he can break the bond which ties him to Caroline so that he can return to the Swamy.

Valmiki is not the only one who realizes that the instinct to grasp and to retain, human beings as well as other objects, is a universal human failing. At one point Anusuya, too, realizes how difficult it is to let go, even when the possession is an inanimate painting. Thus when she decides to steel the painting that Valmiki had given to her before he had left India, she finds that she wants to keep it. She says:

> Then, I found I could not let it go. Valmiki had given it to me, long ago at the very beginning; it was his very first present to me, I found I did not want to part with it. I tried to think of the issues involved, but all that came was the low wail of a tenacious possessiveness. Possession, I thought appalled: attenuated form of the powerful craving to have, to hold, which was so dominating and menacing a part of Caroline: which left a grey and ugly trail of human misery such as, horribly swollen but not unrecognisable, one saw stumbling in the wake of power-societies and empires.
>
> But for that I would have kept the picture. (210)

When one talks about Anusuya one must also mention that it is partly through her relationship with Caroline that Kamala Markandaya focuses attention on the wide chasm that separates the two cultures—the East and the West. The best way in which one can describe the relationship that Anusuya and Caroline share is to say that they have a love-hate relationship. So different are their two worlds that the Westernized Anusuya, in spite of her unwilling admiration for Caroline, finds that she is often at a complete loss when it comes to understanding her. The following conversation between Anusuya and Caroline amply illustrates this point:

> "I hardly thought you'd mind," I said, "*what* I told you."
>
> "It just shows doesn't it," she said with an ironic edge to her voice, "how little you know me."
>
> "I shall never really understand you," I said, and she nodded at once, looking at me with faint amusement.
>
> "No. It's the classic ailment isn't it?"
>
> "What is?"
>
> "That England and India never did understand one another." (75)

One person whom Lady Caroline herself cannot understand at all is the controversial Swamy. As far as his characterisation is concerned, while K.R. Srinivasa Iyengar merely calls him "modern," (443) Uma Parameswaran minces no words when she insists that, in the Swamy, Markandaya has "created a ludicruous effigy and passed it off as a real spiritualist."[4] Indeed, one cannot help noticing that as a spiritual figure the Swamy is not very convincing, let alone awe-inspiring, in sharp contrast to the Swamy of *A Silence of Desire*. Markandaya does not really succeed in her attempt to portray an ascetic successfully propounding the principles of detachment and renunciation. Indeed, at times, it is difficult to reconcile the picture of this not-too-impressive God-man with the spiritual and emotional hold that he has over Valmiki, as also the ultimate victory that he scores over the strong-willed and impressive in spite of everything Caroline. However, and this one must emphasize, this is obviously just a result of a lack of depth in the characterisation rather than an outcome of any flow in the Swamy's character. Therefore, in order to understand the hold that the Swamy has over Valmiki and even over Caroline, one has to view him as Markandaya obviously intended to paint him, and not as she succeeded in portraying him.

The Swamy, as he comes across in parts of the novel and as Markandaya obviously tried to paint him, is supposed to be an impressive figure—detached yet humane, letting go of Valmiki when Caroline spirits him away to London and being graceful when Valmiki returns to him. Markandaya informs us that "From the very beginning he was the only human being with whom she [Caroline] was ill at ease." (33) When Valmiki is unable to paint in London, she realizes that she has very little influence over Valmiki's creative ability. She becomes aware of the magnitude of the Swamy's hold over Valmiki and she cannot help feeling ineffective in comparison. The passage would lose much of its impact if one were to paraphrase it:

> "It was so. I do not know how, only it was so. He say good, I feel good. He say work for god, I work for god. He say you paint well, I paint well."
>
> "It's not the same, is it," said Caroline, "if I say you paint well. It doesn't work, there's no magic in it."
>
> He was instantly contrite. . . . "Same, yes same. You say good, I feel good. Here, Here." He thumped his heart and head with his fists, shaken by his own sense of guilt, his vehemence.
>
> "But it still doesn't work, does it."
>
> "No. Not work." (53)

One need not add anything to this picture of Valmiki's two worlds and the power that each one has over him. However, one must mention that the delineation of the two worlds and the successful portrayal of the differences and the tensions between them is one of the major achievements of *Possession*.

So strong is the spiritual hold that the Swamy has over Valmiki that the latter feels it even when he is deeply engrossed and apparently lost in Caroline's world. Once he innocently informs Anusuya, "When I want he [Swamy] is always near. . . . He is always near, in the spirit." (61) At the very beginning of his relationship with Caroline, Valmiki instinctively realizes that Caroline, somehow does not fit into the Swamy's world. That would explain why he bars her way when she tries to follow him when he goes to his cave to bid adieu to his gods before leaving his village. An interesting sidelight to this incident is that it is the Swamy who breaks the deadlock between Valmiki and

Caroline as they confront each other angrily, each determined not to give in.

Furthermore, when the Swamy visits England Caroline once again feels his power which she resents. Anusuya recalls,

> She did not go near the Swamy. He subdued her, she was afraid of him, or if not of him of the power he still wielded over the clay she had moulded and caressed to an image she could love. In a way he was something of an obsession, become so partly because she could not bring herself to emasculate it by personal encounter, partly because she was jealously aware of the years that had gone before, before she had had Valmiki. Instead she sought to compensate for the reality by endless questioning, storing away my answers like arms in some secret arsenal to be brought into later use. (139-40)

So upset is Caroline because of what she terms "a seduction . . spiritual if you like" (139) that Anusuya senses that the Swamy and Caroline are virtually locked in a battle for Valmiki's loyalty, indeed for his soul. She reminisces,

> I do not think we recognised it then: but it had come, in a way, to a testing of strengths: between Caroline, who made casualness a religion, applying its supple standards and ingratiating gloss to all aspects of living; and the Swamy, whose principles of morality were both inflexible and majestic, requiring a scrutiny not only of ends but of means, and rejecting as indefensible a plea of lack of knowledge. (144)

It should also be noted that even when Valmiki is most firmly entrenched in Caroline's world and the Western civilization, the Swamy's influence over him does not fade away. Even as he paints a flattering portrait of Caroline, the style of which Anusuya finds "chocolate box, or, cheaper still, worst mid-century paperback," (180) about some of his best works critics comment that he "paints as if unknown to himself he had glimpsed, beyond the horizon, the transcendent powers of Universe, and the refracted light brings a hint of the power and the menace into his own painting." (159) This comment goes to prove that even the superficialities of the West could not totally corrupt Valmiki's art which, at its best, retained the qualities which had been an integral part of it, to begin with.

It is not difficult to say who, of these two combatants, is surer of himself. While the Swamy usually advises Valmiki to listen to his own heart or to "seek the truth," (144) Caroline leaves no stones unturned in order to make Valmiki secure. Not only does she get the cook to write fake letters, and deliberately drives Ellie and Annabel away, she also does her best to break all the ties that Valmiki has with his native land. It should also be noted that for Anusuya, as for Kamala Markandaya, Caroline's attempts to subjugate and transform the very nature of Valmiki is equivalent to, what H.M. Williams calls, "India's historic possession" (and hence distortion of her national psyche) by the British. (87) Viewed in this light, the conclusion of the novel acquires fresher and wider connotations. Caroline's tendency to entice, grasp and possess comes to the fore once again when, after Valmiki's illness and estrangement with her, she uses Minou, his pet monkey, to draw him back.

Indeed, Minou, scarlet jacket, gilt leather collar and silver chain, et al, aptly symbolizes the world to which Caroline introduces Valmiki. He is part of the ensemble—"Muslim Style" (106) clothes, turban with plume and Oriental mannerisms—that Valmiki adopts once he gains a certain amount of fame. When Caroline and Valmiki visit America, the former writes to Anusuya and tells her about Minou "who drew as much attention as a prima donna." (157) Thus, Minou becomes a symbol of the splendour, glamour, attention, prosperity as well as artificiality and superficiality which surround Valmiki during his innings as a successful painter, acknowledged and acclaimed by the West. It is ironic that during his darkest days in the West—soon after the end of his relationship with Annabel—it is Minou, and a sick one at that, that Valmiki turns to for consolation and solace, "clinging to her in this bad patch of his life as he had fitfully done over the years." (204) In India Valmiki always had the Swamy to turn to even when his family had vitually disowned him. However, in London, in spite of his numerous acquaintances, he has no one else besides Minou. This, one must stress, is a very telling comment on the nature of the two cultures, as Markandaya views them.

It is through Minou that Markandaya points out how complete and successful Valmiki's initiation into the materialistic society, where he lives, has been. Valmiki has been nursing Minou and he realizes the folly of the way in which he has used the monkey.:

> "Animals aren't created *for* men are they? . . . "
> "Animals are created in their own right." He spoke gently. "I do not know when I stopped believing that, but I must have, mustn't I, to do what I did? Bought her in a shop, took possession like a god, for ends of my own." (211)

These lines epitomize Valmiki's realization that he has strayed very far and that this straying has not given him any satisfaction or peace of mind. It is very likely that it is at this point that he almost unconsciously decides not to go back to Caroline but to return to India. Furthermore, one cannot understand the full significance of Minou as a symbol unless one notices that it is only after Valmiki has buried Minou—a poignantly evocative symbol of his stay in the West—that he returns to the Swamy, but not before telling Anusuya, "But her grip . . . isn't it marvellous? I can hardly let her go, it's so strong." (214)

However strong the grip of Caroline and the West might have been, once he has made up his mind, Valmiki breaks free from it. When he has freed himself completely, he finds true peace and satisfaction. At this point Markandaya comments on the dissimilar ways in which the West and the East—Caroline and the Swamy, to be precise—respond to art. For Caroline, art is synonymous with money, exhibitions, art galleries, 'art men' such as Leon, and parties. On the other hand, the Swamy thinks of art as a form of worship, or "the work a man does to glorify his god." (223) So dissimilar are their views on the subject of art, as, indeed, on almost all other topics, and the chasm between them is so wide and apparently unbridgeable that Anusuya feels that it succeeds in "carrying them to different continents." (223)

However, it is not as though Kamala Markandaya unrealistically portrays one 'continent' as impressive and majestic at the cost of the other. One cannot help noticing that Caroline instantly responds to Valmiki's talent, in spite of his rags, while he is insulted when he comes to Madras in the same clothes. Even Anusuya admits before Caroline at the beginning of Valmiki's adventure, "You're doing what I wouldn't do . . . but that's only because I know I wouldn't have the nerve or the strength to carry it through." (41) The fact that the author is not taking sides and is merely trying to portray the conflict between the two cultures, as she sees it, is brought out by the impartial ending of the novel.:

> "Now is not for ever," said Caroline. "He has tasted other satisfactions—satisfactions that I have given and which he knows I can give. One day he will crave them again and then—"
>
> "—then he will be free to go," said the Swamy, "but he will never stay until he has an equal freedom to return.". . .
>
> "There is still one thing," she said at length, equably, "to be taken into account: Valmiki is yours now, but he has been mine. One day he will want to be mine again. I shall take care to make him want me again: and on that day I shall come back to claim him."
>
> The Swamy's eyes were troubled, "If that day comes," he said.
>
> Caroline came of a breed that never admitted defeat. "Of course it will come," she said with a faint contempt. (224)

Thus, while the Swamy triumphs in the end, it is Caroline who has the last word—obviously an indication of the author's belief that the conflict has not been resolved and that the tussle continues with newer issues at stake, along with the present one which still hangs in the balance.

Martin Seymour Smith says of Kamala Markandaya that she often fails to include "a context as impressively real . . . as her central characters."[5] In *Possession*, however, while the context and the theme are real enough, the characters are sketchy and not as well worked out as, for example, in *Some Inner Fury* or *A Silence of Desire*. Although Markandaya succeeds in creating, what Meenakshi Mukherjee terms, "particular human beings rooted in their narrow regional identities,"[6] they do not really come alive. While they remain prototypes of the values and concepts that they symbolize, they do not often become living and breathing human beings, except in patches. The final impression is of characters who lack conviction, probably because the author was too busy, in using them as symbols of certain concepts and values, to pay enough attention to making them authentic and convincing human beings.

However, what *Possession* lacks by way of depth of characterisation is made up by the dexterous and convincing handling of its major theme, the East-West relationship; this is achieved in spite of the sketchy and very-often unconvincing characters. The novel is a parable of the subtle tussles as well as the more blatant conflicts that inevitably mar any attempt at rapprochement between the two cultures. In order to achieve this end, Markandaya uses the Swamy to symbolize the essential Oriental, particularly Indian, qualities, while Lady Caroline is made to epitomize the possessiveness, artificiality and superficiality of the West. The skilful and dispassionate handling of the rivalry and the struggle between these two, for 'possession' of Valmiki who is, in a sense, a product of both the East and the West, is what makes *Possession* eminently readable and interesting. Therefore, to be able to understand and appreciate the novel fully, one has to view it, first and foremost, as a "commentary on the Indo-British relationship."[8] (Parameswaran, 99)

NOTES

1. Kamala Markandaya, *Possession* (London: Putnam, 1963), p. 101.
2. H.M. Williams, *Indo-Anglian Literature 1800-1970: A Survey* (Madras: Orient Longman, 1976), p. 87.
3. K.R. Srinivasa Iyenger, *Indian Writing in English* (New Delhi: Sterling, 1985), p. 443.
4. Uma Parameswaran, *A Study of Representative Indo-English Novelists* (New Delhi: Vikas, 1976), p. 97.
5. Martin Seymour Smith, *Macmillan Guide to Modern World Literature* (London: Macmillan, 1985), p. 725.
7. Meenakshi Mukherjee, *The Twice-Born Fiction* (New Delhi, 1971), p. 175.

Nayantara Sahgal's *Plans for Departure*: Towards the "Text"

C.R. VISWESWARA RAO

The novels of Nayantara Sahgal trace the convulsive moments in the growth of modern, secular India towards a democratic and humane society. They further give creative release to feminine sensibility and articulate the birth-pangs of a new socio-political order. Thus an interesting aspect of the modern Indian enlightenment is illuminated in Sahgal's writing which is a response to Western dominance culminating in the great movement of decolonization that happened all across the Third World.

With *Rich Like Us* and *Plans for Departure*, Nayantara Sahgal shows how there is a growing concern in her with the novel as expressing the collective fate of a nation releasing itself from subjugation. She observes in an article in Span that no living literature can claim immunity from the social and political consequences and influences around it:

> Fiction cannot be written as in the past. A story must have some implications for the collective fate, or be meaningless. And as for the question of whether art and other commitment can mix, has this not been answered by the creation of new forms to express new visions in music, paint and words? . . . The success of the mix can ultimately be judged only by the final test of any work of art: its power, and the reverberations this produces long after it is seen, heard, or read, sometimes from generation to generation.[1]

In spite of what her training in "liberal humanist" education has taught her to value in literature, Nayantara Sahgal shows how what has been taught to her as universal and eternal is in fact the creation of a particular historical time and place as well as race, sex, and class. In her tracing of the European ethonography, Sahgal seems to satisfy a postmodernist concern with "local" issues and not with grand reality as it were; with problems to be solved rather than with history itself. Truth in her *Plans for Departure* is replaced by truths, uncapitalized and in the plural.

Plans for Departure takes us back to the colonial past and presents a picture of the sub-continent against the backdrop of the world on the brink of a cataclysmic war and of the Indian Freedom Movement under the guidance of Tilak who, it was feared, could "trigger a native uprising."[2] Anna Hansen, the Danish feminist and student of Indian mythology in search of her true identity, is the protagonist of the novel. She postpones the dedication of her life to an English diplomat, Nicholas, because of her desire for self-realization. She embarks on a travel visiting Copenhagen, London, Madras, Calcutta, and she finally lands in Himapur, a fictive village in the Himalayan ranges. Of the nine important characters in the novel, only two are Indian. Of these two, Nitin is steeped in Western mores and is loyal to the Raj which has knighted him. Nitin, the famous botanist, has fled the crowds to study the neurotic tendencies of celery. Henry Brewster, whose wife has forsaken him, has been exiled for having "suffered from philosophy, and attacks of ruling-class consciousness." (28) He was destined for better things once he had put his flawed reasoning behind him:

> Henry had written cautious screeds recommending policy changes, suggesting everyone was not an assassin and whole populations could not be treated with suspicion. He had implied the heart of the matter was an equal relationship, and it would only come of mixing. (71)

He read the article in *Kesari* for which Tilak was prosecuted and remarked, "Frankly it didn't sound seditious to me." (72) He witnesses Khudiram's execution with an uneasy conscience whereas, in contrast, Stella maintains a poise throughout the proceedings. Henry feels he is the stranger from whom Stella needs protection. The temperamental incompatibility between them is such that Stella finally cuckolds Henry and makes her plans for departure to start a new life with Robert Pryor, another imperialist, anti-India person. The imperialist, anti-Indian adulterers marry by the end of the novel and move into the Governor's house in Bombay, whereas the pro-Indian Henry who still loves his wife, with a "searing constancy" (115) and in whom her memory is "superimposed like a flame across in conscience," (96) dies fighting at Somme. While Henry realizes about Stella that "She didn't even know what I meant by love, and we certainly did not have it in common," (178) Stella, when she hears of Henry's death, comments thus to Pryor: "Poor Henry's dead too. His death made up for everything, didn't it, darling?" (206) This reaffirms how Stella's marriage with Henry couldn't be saved. She comes from a family of military personnel who took pride in their country's military and politcal paramountcy. She represents a female voice that politically and culturally personifies the Raj. She thus believes in the superiority of the imperialists, a view endorsed by Pryor. Here the novel shows how cultural notions of the feminine are inevitably inscribed by and in language. Nayantara Sahgal's concern for temperamental disparity between man and wife dominates this novel where Sahgal is "a weaver of plots and a creator of characters rather than an evangelical political journalist."[3]

There is an increasing political awareness among the women characters in the later novels of Nayantara Sahgal which affects their relationship with men. Shivaji's widowed sister, Devi, in *A Situation in New Delhi* stands committed to the political fortunes of her brother to an extent where she rejects Michael's proposal of marriage. With their conflicting attitudes to communism, Sonali and Ravi Kachru in *Rich Like Us* cannot stand together, especailly when Sonali finds that the flouting of the canons of humanism is intolerable to her. *Plans for Departure* presents a reverse ideology in Stella who deserts Henry because of her anti-imperialist stance.

The marriage of the Crofts too fails for its lack of "the manure of common cause." (192) Lulu does not see the fanatic behind the charismatic leader of the people. Moreover, she does not fit in with the role of an idealist's wife. Even though she is unable to adjust herself to Marlowe's chosen life, Lulu is perceptive enough to realize that Marlowe's church would only be a pipe-dream. Further, as a result of her childhood spent with her dictatorial landlord father and as a result of a growing up based on mistrusting of the locals the way her father had done, she raises "phalanxes of hostility" (119) every time she opens her mouth. A marriage between "two such diametrically opposed" people cannot last and thus Lulu experiences a grim and fearsome predicament when she plans her departure from Himapur: "She had been a fool to imagine she could leave Himapur. She had never made a plan in her life or taken a journey alone. . . . It was like discovering she was a cripple." She realizes that she has closed the doorway to freedom by marrying Croft. "Marlowe had married her but not for love," (146) in his obsessive commitment to the church. But an "inveterate bungler," (163) Lulu can never accomplish her husband-leaving. Her premonition that the rickshaw pullers "will slip on purpose" (32) to land her in the Khud ironically comes true, with our knowledge that her death by "slipping" into a ravine seems credible. This gives scope for motive-hunting. If circumstantial evidence exonerates rickshaw pullers and if the fact that she is universally hated is not sufficient reason for her murder, still Marlowe Croft remains the chief suspect in the eyes of Anna whose mind is invaded by morbid fantasies.

Probing the ravine for clues of this horrifying incident, Anna stumbles on the dead dog, Juliet, which makes her suspect that Henry must have killed his wife. That both these "murders" have taken place on the same side of the ravine leads her to suspect Henry of double murder. With Nitin dissuading her by saying that it is futile for her to pursue justice on behalf of the murdered Stella, Nitin and Anna hasten their plans for departure. The whole incident about the dog's death and Pryor's buying a dog for Jennie (207) is introduced by Nayantara Sahgal to solve a mystery and revoke the suspense in a thriller story as it were. Stella reveals, "She died before the day we left, bitten by a scorpion. Jennie cried so much I thought she'd never get over it." (207) At a late date when Anna is introduced to Stella, now Mrs. Pryor, it is like watching a macabre farce in which the dead are resurrected, as it were. Anna is the protagonist-commentator who comes out of her obsession with an amateurish investigation into Stella's death. Instead of simply watching other's lives, she discovers own life intertwined with this drama. She is forced to accept that, though married to Nicholas, she still loves Henry. He becomes to her a man "who made her think of candles, incense, altars, and the brooding vaults of great cathedrals." (77)

Apart from weaving into the plot a number of plans for departure, Nayantara Sahgal synchronizes a number of bigger events and gives her novel a kaleidoscopic perspective. The 'meta'-sensibility of the postmodern times, this awareness that all our systems of understanding are historically specific human constructs, is in evidence here in Sahgal's writing. It invokes a historical field of reference to show history as a vast theatre in which a drama is unfolding, that of representation. Nicholas writes to Anna thus: "Private matters will soon be at the mercy of bigger outer events, for that, ultimately, is the tragedy of war." (154) Henry writes to Anna that the war has overtaken Europe like retribution. (196) Thus there is a widening of the horizons against which the quest for freedom is examined. The British Jury, Anna finds to her consternation, has struck down Tilak's libel case. Nicholas contemplates thus:

> Bickering little identities had become sovereign nations, monarchies had fallen, three empires had been wiped off the map, because justice had not been done. (202)

Henry felt that if Austria's suppression of the Serbs, Czechs, and Transylvanians bears any significance in relation to the British repression of India, it would be the sacred duty of the Indian people to "shoot their way out of the empire," (38) for it is a "law of moral consequences" (130) which ought to be in operation.

The time in which the novel is set coincides with Tilak's trial, the rumblings of the Indian freedom strugle, and the outbreak of the First World War with its carnage and self-inflicted destruction. This world-wide perspective takes into account the pre-1914 struggles of British Suffragettes, the Mahatma's efforts on behalf of the voteless in South Africa, and the conditions of the oppressed peasants in Central America in the 1950s. The technique is similar to the one employed in *Rich Like Us* where the novel binds together the Sati and the modern sacrificial altar of power and pelf, thereby giving us a perspective on courage and heroism against the background of the powerlessness of law and reason and the domination of custom. Spread on a vast canvas is a vivid tapestry characterizing the convulsing moments of Indian history, including the Moghul period. It is this breadth of vision linking apparently disparate events and historical processes that is the evidence in *Plans for Departure* too where a free thinker in religion and a spirit out of the old Norse Saga endearingly called Tantanna, Anna believes in the tantrics of Hindu religion. Take for example the passage below which relates the struggle for mastery, colonization, and even self-mastery by incorporating in the pattern of the novel a texture of mythic reverberations:

> who wanted a general, an Indra, a Zeus, or a Thor, once wars were over? Indra had his day, but what a day it had been! A change in the wind's direction, a shivering branch, a cloud formation could revive Vedic battles. She [Anna] could see the wild rider recklessly race his three-wheeled chariot across the sky, his hair streaming, his victorious drunken laughter echoing in every gust of wind. The truly discerning traveler might still see the bodies of the slain littering the ground and hear Aryan feasting and roistering that must have sounded as ferocious as battle to the defeated trembling in their hiding places. She could imagine Indra's outrage at being forcibly retired, "I, who cleared

> this land for the Aryan?" But it was easy to see why he had to be replaced. After that ecstasy of conquest the pendulum had swung. Lawless gods were put away. In their place came laws. And to prove that the conquered have the last word, their own awesome Shiva slipped out of remoter antiquity to embody The Law. The age of asceticism had begun. The world and life in it became flimsy outer garments. The struggle for self-mastery was all that was really real. If that was Hinduism in a nutshell, Anna reflected, it was a pity it had not stayed grand and simple, in the nut. (47)

There is a distribution and circulation in the passage cited above of the numerous forces and intensities that saturate a text. This is Anna's mode of putting herself into an "excentric" position with regard to Indian culture. The paradox of this underlining and undermining of cultural "universals" implicitly challenges any notion of centrality in culture. Nayantara Sahgal's complicated politics reflects her multiple locations. Her work reveals the imprint of a complex perspective—a perspective that is shaped by her postcoloniality, gender, and sociopolitical critiques of Indian society. Her use of historical moments which provide the political contexts for the narrative are exploited for contextualizing the theme of freedom of the individual.

This is where *Plans for Departure* shows itself to be a text, though occasionally, and not so much a work. Instead of an organic proccss of maturation or a hermeneutic process of deepening, there is here a movement of dislocations, overlappings, and variations which rely on a metonymic activity of associations and contiguities coinciding with a liberation of symbolic energy. As a text it is thus plural and depends on a stereographic plurality of the signifiers that weave it (etymologically the text is a cloth, textus, from which text derives and means "woven").[4] The text thus relies upon filiation which gives rise, in howsoever a limited fashion, to something of a polysemic utterance. The passage cited above is just that social space occupied by the text which allows no enunciative subject to hold the position of judge or analyst. It stirs up and exposes dormant sediments of meaning settled into its fabric enabling us to glimpse at discontinuities through mythic tracing in the quest for freedom and domination.

NOTES

1. Nayantara Sahgal, "First Person Singular," *Span*, 27:2 (Feb. 1986), p. 11.
2. Nayantara Sahgal, *Plans for Departure* (London: Heinemann, 1986), p. 29.
3. Keki Daruwalla, "On Nayantara Sahgal," *Imprint* (June 1986), p. 89.
4. Roland Barthes, "From Work to Text," in *Textual Strategies: Perspectives in Post-Structuralist Criticism*, ed. & intro. Josue V. Harari (1979; London: Methuen, 1980), pp. 74-76.

The Clue to Who I am is in the Lives before this One: Indeterminacy, Cultural Identity, and Feminist Secular Vision in Nayantara Sahgal's *Mistaken Identity*

JENNIFER KELLY

"I have no politics." This is the apparently simple claim of Bhushan Singh, the narrator of Nayantara Sahgal's *Mistaken Identity* (1988), upon finding himself in jail on charges of conspiracy in India of 1929. "I should never have been arrested," he insists. "I have no politics."[1] The novel, in constructing Bhushan's own re-construction of his life, in weaving together layers of personal and collective histories, ultimately demonstrates, *theorizes*, the falseness, the illusory nature, of any such claim to an apolitical position, to a location separate from familial and national histories, from the complex power relations that shape the political, the national, the past and the future Further, in exploring the multiple determinations and the very *indeterminacies* of personal and collective histories, *Mistaken Identity* dissembles notions of identity as fixed, stable, immutable, "pure"—notions, the work argues, that led to the "mistake" that was Partition.

In his "Cultural Identity and Diaspora," Stuart Hall describes cultural identity as "a matter of 'becoming' as well as of 'being.' It belongs to the future as much as to the past. It is not something which already exists, transcending place, time, history and culture. Cultural identities come from somewhere, have histories. But, like everything which is historical, they undergo constant transformation. Far from being eternally fixed in some essentialised past, they are subject to the continuous 'play' of history, culture and power."[2]

It is, crucially, in its demonstration—and celebration—of the indeterminacy and transformative nature of history and of cultural identities that the power of the feminist vision of a secular India theorized in *Mistaken Identity* lies. The work enacts a transformation of cultural identity through the story of Bhushan. His is an individual story that becomes collective through its telling, simultaneously reaching into India's past and shaping its future. While in prison, Bhushan recalls and re-evaluates his life. Each fragment of his story, of his proclaimed identity as a man who "has no politics," delves further into the past and deeper into Indian politics. In her article "Goodbye to Realism: The 'Ending' of *Mistaken Identity*," Jasbir Jain has described *Mistaken Identity* as "the history of a family, a country and of a dream."[3] Yet the work is more than a history; it comprises a play—a play not only, in Hall's words, of "history, culture and power" but of illusion, reality, and memory, which functions to reconfigure cultural identity anew, to celebrate it as a process of becoming; this is a process, moreover, that can incorporate a feminist politics, that can be grounded in the maternal, for Bhushan's story and vision are his mother's as much as his own. Bhushan's re-vision, crucially, enacts a transformation of identity through his relationship with his mother, through a familial history once silenced yet politicized and revolutionary in its uncovering and re-vision.

The *dream* of Bhushan and his mother is not only that of a lost love found but of a secular India, in which an idealistic Sikh man and a rebellious Muslim woman can unite without fear, in which a ranee can openly declare her love for a Communist worker, in which fate encourages Hindus and Muslims "to roast [their] dogmas in the same bonfire." (129) It is a *dream* of India in which a mother is liberated from the realm of myth and the strictures of traditional roles and can unite with her son in change, in which a woman such as Bhushan's lover Sylla can rewrite *The Scarlet Letter* to rave approval. It is a *vision* in which women can be like Sylla, who is "new every day," (53) and can utilize their transformative energies to make and remake their identities and their circumstances. It is a *vision* in which the political boundaries between Muslim and Hindu are seen as ultimately false because the two groups are united in a timeless past, a past that remains in the present and can shape the future. As Jain writes, *Mistaken Identity* is a commentary "on the role of history, and that of human nature. Man moves towards his destiny to meet it. He is also the maker of his own destiny. It doesn't exist in the abstract." (264) The crucial instance of "mistaken identity" explored in the work is not so much that of Bhushan's arrest but of the long-standing assumption of cultural purity, of difference, between Hindus and Muslims on which Partition was based; *Mistaken Identity* argues, finally, that this massive error is alterable through the transformative energies of revision, of imagination, of dreaming. It is through the demonstration of such creative energies, of the *indeterminacies* between fact and fiction, illusion and reality, past and present, individuality and collectivity, art and history—of, in other words, their potential in political change—that *Mistaken Identity* constructs this revolutionary feminist vision.

Jain recognizes that the reader is compelled to "re-read" the work for missed clues, just as Bhushan re-reads the details of his life, "each time arriving at a different interpretation and point of view." (263) Yet she fails to address how *Mistaken Identity* dissolves boundaries, such as those between Sikh and Muslim, art and politics, dream and history, past and future, illusion and reality, and how this dissolution functions in relation to the work's political vision. Bhushan, for example, persistently enacts this dissolution, as in his comments on his court case (a parody of the British judicial system): "The prosecution would try to invent charges and we would have to counter their tactics with inventions of our own" (108); in another instance he tells the court: "I've dreamed in both languages: My diet, and therefore my digestion, are mostly Muslim, but my blood seems to circulate in Hindu fashion, and my heart beats alternately to each." (156) This is not to deny, however, the implications of the historical setting of the work nor its relation to its political vision. It is set in 1920s India, in a period of India's fight for independence from Britain in which Hindus and Muslims, Gandhians and Communists, momentarily at least, were united politically; it is situated, in other words, in a time when Bhushan's secular dream, momentarily, was realizable.

What I am suggesting, rather, is that *Mistaken Identity* not only offers a re-vision of history but demonstrates the transformative political potential of the very multidimensionality of reality that makes such re-visions, such political dreams, realizable. On one level, for example, Bhushan's tale is exposed as merely that of a hapless and love-crazed Sikh man, the privileged son of a raja, who chases a dream of love with a Muslim woman, makes false assumptions in the process, commits murder based on these assumptions, and eventually lands in jail on charges of conspiracy, apparently the result of a mistake. Thus, in one sense, his arrest as a conspirator appears as absurd as he claims. Yet the reader, like Bhushan, remains unsure as to whether or not Bhushan's mistakes have merely been "a good example of the Potter's brand of frolic. A monstrous trick of fate. . . . And all for nothing." (180) This play among illusion, reality, and memory—of indeterminacy—is sustained productively throughout the work. Bhushan observes at one point that "one doesn't believe everything one sees" (44); he wonders if his co-prisoners's protests are nothing more than "a pearl out of the same illusory necklace we all wear that keeps us from believing what we see, what starkly stares us in the face. . . . Is there no limit to our pearly illusions?" (174) Further, when he discovers that Razia is happily married and well-off, and has remained true to her own sense of self—thus shattering the dreams and illusions on which his actions apparently have been based—Bhushan's words foreground the power of illusion, reality, interpretation, and reinterpretation: "If a message had this stunning, verifiable impact, so forceful that one must obey it, how can it have been wrong? . . . I would never have believed a message so clear could be misinterpreted." (174) Yet it is in such indeterminate movement between illusion and reality, message and interpretation, past and future, that the power of dream and transformation lies.

Mistaken Identity enacts the power of memory to transform both "reality" and "illusion," past and future. The linear paradigm of cause and effect is disrupted constantly in the work, as Bhushan continually is transformed by his interpretation and re-interpretation of his own history. The past is thus shown as embedded in the present and the future, but nothing remains static or unchangeable. Rather, history, like identity, is in a continual process of becoming. And while the reader, this reader, at least, is constantly left in that dynamic space of questioning, it is in this location of indeterminacy that a personal, familial, and collective vision of feminist revolution and secularism is created.

In negotiating through the labyrinth of memory, of silence, of familial and national histories, *Mistaken Identity* demonstrates the immanence of the secular and feminist vision that is its subject and its goal. Viney Kirpal writes that the "techniques and constructive principles of traditional Indian narrative"[4] include episodicity, plotlessness, and the story-within-a-story. Further, she suggests, Indian novels in English of the 1980s "reflect, as never before, the theme of mixed Indian tradition. The controlling temper of the period is synthesis, polymorphism where all religions, all communal groups, including the minorities have an important place." (xxi)[5] In *Mistaken Identity*, the reader is invited to recognize this synthesis, this polymorphism, the very fluidity of Indian cultural traditions and identities. As Bhushan humorously tells the British court when asked if he is concerned with the Bolshevik "threat": "What's the difference? If they're coming, they'll come, won't they? Inevitable. Everyone else has. It's probably their turn next. I glance across at the judge . . . 'Your lot, of course, came the longer way round, by sea.'" (157)

Sahgal, further, has theorized elsewhere on the political potential of this fluidity, a theory aligned with her practice in *Mistaken Identity*.[6] She writes in "Some Thoughts on the Puzzle of Identity" that

> it is through this deepening, expanding, metamorphosing consciousness that identity takes a beating or blossoms, and is perpetually renewed and reshaped. Through this open awareness, historians reinterpret history and people everywhere continually reinvent themselves. We are not what we

> were yesterday nor what we will be tomorrow. But our intelligent recycling of whatever happens to us, the human race—either individually or collectively—can help us transcend even the most brutal and agonizing of these experiences, and transform them into patterns ever more human and humane. (14)[7]

Such is the potential of the play between illusion and reality, and such is the power of dream and of art. Bhushan creates not only a transformed sense of self but a dream for the future, a dream of a poet and, after all, of a revolutionary; a dream described by Bhushan's lawyer: "He is a poet and may be forgiven a poet's vision of a realm where all gods are one. I would go further and say he dreams of a dawn when there will be no dividing characteristics of race, colour, feature, worship left on earth. These are his politics, my lord, this is his vision." (163)

Every incident, every encounter, twist, and turn in the labyrinth of Bhushan's remembered and reconstructed life is drawn, re-interpreted, as connected to other histories, other clues, other stories, all of which are grounded neither in reality or immutable historical "fact," for *Mistaken Identity* suggests that "fact" and dream are equally real and equally illusory. Bhushan's story, rather, is a story of memory, of desire, of the desire to locate dream: "If the key to life's puzzles lay in childhood," he laments, "mine was too wriggling a labyrinth to yield it up. If only I could blast a tunnel through *reality to the dream*." (134: my italics)

In *Mistaken Identity*, Bhushan's story, his dream, inextricably links Hindu, Muslim, and Sikh cultures in the past, the present, and the future; linear time, and narrative chronology become less important than the immanence of the secular dream filtered and transformed by memory. When Bhushan recalls meeting Razia, for example, she is imaged as symbolic of a past unity of India, as embodying a revolutionary transgression of religious stricture in the present, and as a signal of hope for a secular India. Bhushan recalls that in Razia's face he read his dream of revolution:

> I thought of her face. It took me years to decipher its spell and understand why it haunted me. It defied unwritten laws. The Tartar cheekbones of this face should have had slanting eyes above them, but hers were long ovals, the lidded eyes of temple structure. Their width took me unawares when they pounced upon her tonga. It was this manifest racial impurity, a mix belonging to a vision of future communal union, that made it unforgettable, and retreat impossible for me. (60)

Yet even this interpretation is filtered through the transformative power of memory, as Bhushan states, "it took years" for him to draw this conclusion; Razia's face is an image of his creation, a representation of his desire. And yet all his actions are based on his unnamed desire for unity, on a dream and a history that inextricably links Hindu, Muslim, and Sikh cultures. He and Razia make love near a decaying monument, a "small crumbling ruin" (63) marking a battle between their ancestors. In Bhushan's memory, he and Razia "wiped out the grief and carnage with . . [their] bodies on her burka." (65) He consistently asserts the falsity of arguments of difference between Muslim and Hindus: "They don't know, poor sods, we're in each other's blood already." (47) When he kneels to the ground to pray with Razia, he recognizes their shared history and its continuance in the present: "Words I had heard time without number and could have chanted with the muezzin, an untaught inheritance I was surer of that I could be of who had given me birth." (76) His declaration of a shared history between Sikh and Muslim becomes as much fact as dream, as much a vision of the future as a recognition of the past, as much a statement of fact and the expression of a wish. His love poem to Razia, in which he asserts "I am you, there is no other way," (129) is a declaration of this revolutionary desire.

One of the narrative threads of *Mistaken Identity* is thus a re-creation of a shared history on which a secular vision is based, a re-creation that depends on the dissolution of perceptions of cultural purity, of "difference," between Sikh and Muslim. Central to this strategy is the destabilization of Bhushan's personal, familial, and "cultural" history as linear, retrievable, as "pure." Bhushan comes to realize that his own lineage is uncertain, and that this uncertainty lies in both his maternal and paternal inheritances. His re-vision of his past comes to include the possibility that he was fathered not, after all, by the raja but by the cave dweller his mother visited on her famous pilgrimage to conceive Bhushan: "Perhaps that is how it happened, my tireless pilgrim, my mother, or whoever you are, and Father's stray droplets had nothing to do with it." (168) This revelation functions as more than an ironic play on the impotence of Bhushan's apparent father—and, by extension, the crumbling raj system he represents, for it is in the destabilization and unfixing of perceptions of identity, in the recognition of identity as in a constant state of becoming, that the potential for change, for new configurations, new histories and new futures, is located.

This transformation of Bhushan's paternal history, further, is connected to another crucial aspect of *Mistaken Identity*, namely, the transformation, the *theorizing*, the politicization of the maternal. Bhushan's revelation of his uncertain paternity occurs alongside his re-evaluation, via memory and dream, of the maternal—of his mother, his relationship to her, and of her relationship to collective history and change. The revelation that the raja may not have been Bhushan's father, for example, functions also to revise Bhushan's assumptions about the staunch traditionalism of his mother. At one point he claims, "It was useless talking to mother about change. No one could have set out on the journeys she did if she hadn't believed her own world was going to stay securely in place till the end of time." (160) Yet the very thought of Bhushan being conceived by the cave dweller suggests Bhushan's re-vision of the maternal as a formation through which tradition is upheld yet can be subverted at the same time. Further, Bhushan's mother is illiterate until he teaches her to read and write; from his perspective, his mother's "knowledge of the world depended on the slit between her carriage curtains." (41) Yet it is from Bhushan's acknowledgment that the revolutionary energy of his mother's dreams is part of his own history and maternal inheritance that the unique vision of *Mistaken Identity* emerges.

In my reading, one of the richest and most intriguing aspects of *Mistaken Identity* is its recovery, its re-creation, of a maternal history silenced by patriarchy, a system that reinforces its power through violence and silence. Bhushan recovers and re-interprets a silenced history of female infanticide, of the possible murder of two sisters, a recovery that not only functions as feminist resistance, but reinforces the destabilization of official histories and claims to static identity. This destabilization is repeated in Bhushan's discovery that his maternal lineage is also uncertain, unwritten, silenced:

> Wonderful how a study of the past, of ancestry, family, lineage, could give a young life a purpose, they said. I had discovered my duty. I knew who I was. Actually this was what I didn't know any more. Mother, I discovered, had been an identical twin. So devoted they had been, their parents couldn't risk parting them. Out of compassion they were both married to Father and as twin brides had refused to be separated. Then one of them had died. Which one, when, of what, the chronicle didn't say. Whoever wrote it skipped the details. What do flies die of? A swat, most likely. And they don't have names. (75)

"Official" history is thus as open to revision as is personal history, and it is in the fractures of such histories that Bhushan creates his revolutionary vision. It is in the re-visioning of the mother-son bond in particular, a relationship not traditionally associated with the subversion of patriarchal power, that *Mistaken Identity* is especially striking. Malashri Lal suggests that "the weakness in the novel *Mistaken Identity* is caused by Sahgal's decision to write on behalf of the male imagination" and that "the depiction of Bhushan's inner psychology is weak."[8] I suggest, however, that the very strength of the work lies in the radical unfolding and reconceptualization of the mother-son bond, a reconceptualization grounded in history as much as in dream, in desire. Bhushan's call to Razia, his declaration that "I am you, there is no other way" (129) is also a call to his mother, a voicing of desire and an acknowledgment of the interconnectedness of all identities—a recognition that social change must include the vision of women and the re-vision of their socially constructed roles.

The figure of Bhushan's mother appears early in the narrative, in Chapter Three. Significantly, her introduction includes a narrative shift from the past to the present tense, a strategy foregrounding cultural identity as interconnected, as a continual process of the past in the present, of constant "becoming." Bhushan's re-vision of his earliest memories of his mother are presented in the language of desire for maternal plenitude, for unity. Bhushan recalls: "I have a clear recollection of lying pinned against her ribs for years of afternoon naps, tracing the joins down her spine while she slept." (38) Further, he states, "Lying moulded against her narrow hollowed back until she turned over to clasp me close, I used to think she would melt goldenly as wax if sunlight ever touched her skin." (36) Bhushan's recollection, his memory and dream and desire, of being "cradled and cushioned and suckled by a soft, vast collective mattress of a breast," (36) seems in one sense to reinforce a Lacanian psychoanalytic paradigm of an infant's sense of unity, plenitude, with the mother. But whereas Lacanian psychoanalysis, like the Freudian Oedipal model that preceded it, posits a break from the maternal, the separation from and rejection of the maternal by the male child as necessary for "proper" psychological development, *Mistaken Identity* repudiates this model to theorize the necessity of the forging and maintenance of a continuing link between mother and son as the site of collective identity, feminist and secular resistance, and change.

In Bhushan's re-vision of his life and his re-connection with his maternal heritage, in Sahgal's radical vision, mother and son together are the catalysts for change. Bhushan recalls—dreams—that upon his birth it was not he but his mother who called out. Hers is a cry he has heard through his life. He symbolically recalls that upon his birth he "heard her first tormented cry" (36) and, he asks, "Had there ever been a time since her first cry that I had not grieved for her?" (136) In the revision of the mother-son bond as a site of political change, it is thus appropriate that Bhushan is born "the wrong way round" (36) and that he states that his mother was "the only person who didn't think there was anything wrong with me." (159) In turn, it is Bhushan who appreciates the energy, the transformative vitality of his mother, symbolized by her "look of violent, voluptuous joy," (68) her "black chaotic hair," (96) and "wild unearthly beauty." (96)

In memory, dream, and desire, mother and son here create a political vision of sexual equality; the mother's idealization of Rasputin as a Tantric sadhu is mirrored in Bhushan's obsession with Razia. This politicization and re-visioning of the maternal, finally, functions also as a refutation of the glorification of motherhood, of the image of "Mother India, bound in chains waiting for her children to free her," an image that, according to Ranjana Ash, became a highly charged metaphor for India's independence movement.[9]

Sahgal's *Mistaken Identity* thus reaches into the past, explores the potential of indeterminacy, the fluidity of cultural identities, to create a vision of political transformation. Yet the work's conclusion, in which the feminist secular vision of Bhushan and his mother is realized, disappoints. The marriages of Bhushan's mother to the Communist Muslim Comrade Yusuf and of Bhushan to Yusuf's daughter are too tidy, in fact a foreclosure on the rich potential the work explores. Jain, however, praises the ending: "At one level the ending is a flight of fantasy, makebelief and wishful thinking, the pursuit of a dream, and hence symbolical. At another level it is inevitable. It is the only direction which the story can take. And it is not as abrupt as it may appear. The whole narrative movement is towards this direction. Only so carefully are the clues hidden in the narrative that the reader is taken unawares." (263)

In my view, the ending of *Mistaken Identity* is not inevitable, not a last clue of a mystery story in which all the narrative threads instantly cohere. Neither, in my reading, is the ending "a comment on the nature of reality. Reality is elusive and multi-dimensional." (Jain, 264) While Jain locates in the work's conclusion a site of indeterminacy and, presumably, views the remainder of the work as in the realist mode, my reading seems diametrically opposed. It is, in my view, the ending of *Mistaken Identity* that is situated in a realistic mode, attempting as it does to control the indeterminacy and fluidity celebrated and demonstrated in the preceding pages. It is this intrusion of enforced and strained closure, of realism and linearity, that is not inevitable, but illogical, given the play of indeterminacy that precedes it. The tidy conclusion is a loss of the potential of that indeterminacy. It is an attempt to fix cultural identity—an attempt that is doomed to fail in the context of this work.[10] This attempt is the "mistake" of Sahgal's writing strategy in *Mistaken Identity*.

That there is, finally, such a divergence of critical perspectives on this conclusion speaks nonetheless to the richness of a text and its exploration of theorizing, from within Indian history and tradition, how the past informs the present and the future, how memory, art, desire, and the mother-son bond can be part of a revolutionary and feminist secular vision and politics. It is from this perspective that I would like to conclude by refuting Meenakshi Mukherjee's argument in her article "The Centre Cannot Hold: Two Views of the Periphery," her critique of post-colonial literary theories and their concentration on English-language writing and European theories. Mukherjee asserts: "In India, so long as the parameters of theoretical discourse are set by the available texts in English, nothing important will ever be achieved, because English texts, regardless of their literary and other values, have always been isolated phenomena in India unconnected with the network of pressures that determine the basic cultural design. These texts do not become points of intersection of larger social, political or historical forces. It is the Indian language texts that throw up theoretical possibilities."[11]

Nayantara Sahgal's *Mistaken Identity*, I hope to have demonstrated, is intimately connected with the pressures, the cultural design, and the social, political, and historical forces of India, past, present, and future. In my view, it powerfully theorizes such formations as gender, the "maternal," nation, "religion," "history," and "identity" in a manner that demonstrates not only the political dimension of all aspects of culture, but the very specificity and transformative power of Indian tradition, its perspectives on the nature of reality and power of the play of illusion, memory, and history in shaping the future. That *Mistaken Identity* theorizes the very absorption of this British layer within the complex Indian immensity as part of its secular and feminist vision, it seems to me, is not a capitulation to the imperial centre, but, like Bhushan's poetic dream, a transformative and revolutionary rejection of claims to power that do not emerge from within tradition itself. And if one of the strengths and enduring characteristics of Indian cultural tradition is its heterogeneity and multiplicity, surely there is a place for theoretical and political possibilities of the fluidity of cultural identity explored by Sahgal in *Mistaken Identity*.

NOTES

1. Nayantara Sahgal, *Mistaken Identity* (London: Sceptre; Heinemann, 1989), p. 49.
2. Stuart Hall, "Cultural Identity and Diaspora," *Colonial Discourse and Postcolonial Theory*, ed. Patrick Williams and Laura Chrisman (New York: Columbia University Press, 1994), p. 394.
3. Jasbir Jain, "Goodbye to Realism: The 'Ending' of *Mistaken Identity*," in Kirpal, p. 265.
4. Viney Kirpal, ed., *The New Indian Novel in English: A Study of the 1980s* (New Delhi: Allied, 1990), p. xviii.
5. Elsewhere Sahgal insists, in perhaps what is a resistant response to postcolonial theory, that this imagination is not concerned merely with British colonization of India and its effects, that the British merely "added one more complex layer to Indian immensity." Nayantara Sahgal, "Some Thoughts on the Puzzle of Identity," *The Journal of Commonwealth Literature*, 29.1 (1993), p. 7.
6. The critical impulse informing my use of this reference is not that of subscribing to the fallacy of authorial intention; rather, I draw attention to Sahgal's commentary in order to disrupt the problem-

atic theory-versus-practice distinction current in literary studies and to suggest that Sahgal's theory and practice are aligned, consistent, indistinguishable. Feminism in particular has demonstrated, for example, that theory is practice and vice-versa, a view I fully support. Sahgal's comment that she "cannot help being acutely aware of the dangers of this lethal combination of nationalism and religion" ("Some Thoughts") thus is consistent with the theoretical argument of *Mistaken Identity*.

7. Further, she writes, that she is "more interested in trying to trace in human terms the implications of what happens to us politically, the ideas and behaviour that religion breeds in us, and my on-going character has been India." (11) This comment thus casts light on the symbolic function of Bhushan.

Moreover, in her "The Schizophrenic Imagination," Sahgal has theorized not only the fluidity of cultural identity in general, but that of Indian identity in particular, emphasising the transformative power of the imaginative exploration of this process. The "schizophrenic imagination," she writes, "is a state of mind and feeling that is firmly rooted in a particular subsoil, but above ground has a more fluid identity that doesn't fit into any single mould. A schizophrenic of this description is a migrant who may never have left his people or his soil. We are all somewhat divided selves, but I'm referring to the divisions that history and circumstance impose on the complex creatures we already are. . . . It is not only inevitable, it is also perfectly natural for the inheritor of one of earth's oldest and most complex inheritances to feel fragmented. . . . The past is so much with us, in the beliefs and routines people live by . . . that no time is ever entirely past. . . . Where does one culture begin and another end when they are housed in the same person?" Nayantara Sahgal, "The Schizophrenic Imagination," *Unbecoming Daughters of the Empire*, ed. Shirley Chew and Anna Rutherford (Sydney: Dangaroo Press, 1993), pp. 115, 119.

8. Malashri Lal, "The Shift from Female Centred to Male Centred Narrative in the Novels of the 1980s: A Study of Anita Desai and Nayantara Sahgal," in Kirpal, p. 285.

9. Ranjana Ash, "The Search for Freedom in Indian Women's Writing," *Motherlands: Black Women's Writing from Africa, the Caribbean and South Asia*, ed. Susheila Nasta (1991; New Bruns-

wick, New Jersey: Rutgers University Press, 1992), pp. 152-73.

10. Professor Inder Nath Kher pointed out to me during a discussion on *Mistaken Identity* another of its textual knots, namely, that Bhushan's ranee mother is drawn as a revolutionary throughout her life. As a privileged woman with the zeal, it seems inconsistent that she does not leave her husband after his third marriage. While I agree this is an important point, I would respond in part by suggesting that, perhaps, the ranee's dependence on Bhushan as the catalyst for her ultimate revolution is consistent with the text's reconfiguration of the mother-son *bond* as central to change.
11. Meenakshi Mukherjee, "The Centre Cannot Hold: Two Views of the Periphery," *Kunapipi*, 11.1 (1989), p. 45.

A Search for Identity in Nayantara Sahgal's *Mistaken Identity*

D.K. SINHA and CHANDRA SHEKHAR RAJHANS

Nayantara Sahgal writes novels that mirror faithfully the contemporary Indian political scene. It is in this sense, that her novels are to be classed in the genre of political novel. She seeks to present in each of her novels a consistent point of view and moves from satire and irony to a positive constructive vision. She analyses and interprets the political themes/events with an intelligent and perceptive mind and reads the individual responses of the characters to these events with the unusual sensitivity of a mature artist.

Her novel *Rich Like Us* which echoes the dreadful sights of the emergency and the past, "is the climax of the series since the first novel *A Time to be Happy*."[1] Like *Plans for Departure*, her recent novel *Mistaken Identity* registers an important stage in her growth as a novelist and branches out in a new direction. Possibly, the writer is attempting to understand a country and its cultural-political life, the happenings and events, by adopting the technique of biography. The identity of India and a true Indian is to be searched and therefore like in *Rich Like Us* and *Plans for Departure*, in the novel under consideration, *Mistaken Identity*, the multiple vision and point of view of a political biography is at work. It is a narration of history-in-the-making with the advantage of hindsight. In choosing a context of vital significance and possibility, Sahgal assumes an ambitious position which has the danger of desertion as well as the possibility of synthesis and the novel is strikingly different from anything she has written before.

Sahgal appears to be treading in new and perhaps intense areas of experience, confronting with fresh insights and lyrical contents of human life. the central figure is Bhushan Singh, the only son of the 'raja' of the taluk of Vijaygarh. This novel focuses principally at the depiction of the life of Bhushan. In the year 1929, he returns to India after his long stay abroad. He is put behind the bars on conspiracy charges by the British government. Sahgal, with minute precision and utmost care, depicts the troubled and complex psychological mental make-up of Bhushan and in doing so, she fuses the history of politically charged up India artistically. She moves backwards and forwards in time, to create the life-story of Bhushan Singh.

The life of Bhushan Singh seems to have a triangular configuration, the three corners broadly mean his life—Sylla, Vijaygarh and poetry. Of these three corners, Sylla is the link with reality, the solid and soothing guiding force. Vijaygarh is seemingly a sleepy place, very much like the tortoise-cell for Bhushan Singh. For Bhushan, his country is Vijaygarh, he cannot be a revolutionary or nationalist. He was going back to Vijaygarh but is put into jail on conspiracy charges.

Bhushan Singh's third corner is his poetry. His poem "The Bridge" was published in a Soviet magazine. Though he has no public life and has no business, whatsoever, to do with politics, his poem is associated with revolutionary attitude. Bhushan's Bridge is intended to be a lovers's connecting bridge or link, but it is interpreted in an altogether different light. Why was this poem mistaken to mean differently, why was it published in the Soviet magazine, why was he arrested—these questions affect his life, yet they remain a puzzle for Bhushan.

Bhushan says categorically, "I'd never been able to resist a woman's beauty or the culture of Islam."[2] In Razia, Bhushan finds both these attractions. He develops sexual relationship with Razia, which satisfies him to the core of his soul. But lovers everywhere have to get away for one reason or another which isn't allowed," (47) and hence a bridge is needed. His desire to get a link to understand Islam and woman fail. Vijaygarh experiences a Hindu-Muslim riot, "claiming 15 Hindus, 10 Muslims and two policemen." (49) After this face-blackening incident, Bhushan's father sends this trouble-maker out of his taluk, and Bhushan comes out of his country, where he "had led the sort of life where things happen to you because someone knows your father." (36)

"All my poems are about Razia," (129) Bhushan Singh accepts boldly because through Razia, he opens up his innermost self. For this very reason, he feels the need to underline and experience the Hindu-Muslim unity, the sense of oneness. Unlike Nayantara Sahgal's earlier novels, *Mistaken Identity* speaks of Gandhi and his religious philosophy in a highly ironic tone. Bhushan feels:

> Gandhi makes no sense to me at all. Goes on bleating Hindu-Muslim marriage would send him on a fifty day fast. He's all for public brotherly embraces. . . . The unifiers take care not to let us blood-mingle. . . . I've never been able to interest myself in their treacherous politics. (46-47)

Later, Bhushan meets Sylla, a Parsee girl, who smokes and wears western clothes. She is a modern girl, full of enthusiasm. "Vitality has been always hard for me to resist. I am its natural follower. And Sylla was a natural leader," (126) Bhushan admits and naturally they develop healthy, satisfying and perfect love relationship. Bhushan is a man with no ambition, no occupation. He says to Sylla, "You are my nest from storm, plague, pestilence, not to mention the Hindu-Muslim love-madness that rages in my middle ear," (155) and that's why he needs her.

But Sylla needs him for she can come to him whenever she wants and Bhushan comes to the realization that "what women want more than success and ambition, seems to be a round-the-clock-lover." (129) Even in Bombay, the Hindu-Muslim love madness keeps on raging in Bhushan's mind, and he keeps on visiting the red-light areas in Bombay, in the hope of meeting his Razia to cool his madness. His visit to the immoral body market disgusts Sylla. Bhushan needs her love and company to come out of the Hindu-Muslim love-madness.

On being asked, Bhushan accepts that his religion is Hindu-Muslim and his mother-tongue poetry. He makes his answer more specified by adding that his mother-tongue is Hindi, and his father-tongue is Urdu. His mother is a traditional Hindu woman, for whom every great name is a saint or yogi, she can read only the Hindi script. His father has no knowledge of Hindi, he writes Urdu. In this family-background, Bhushan develops a composite culture-religion which is not accepted by common people, whether British or Indian.

Sylla tries to rescue Bhushan out of the Hindu-Muslim love-madness; and she suggests him to speak at the meeting on 'a beautiful theme' like Hindu-Muslim harmony. Though Bhushan is not in the habit of making speeches, he begins before the audience, constituting of pandits and ulemas. "In the prayerful stillness of an evening I had prayerfully put Razia on paper." (130) Bhushan marshals out his ideas. He pleads that fate meant they should love each other, not war or separation, and to roast their dogmas in the same bonfire. Bhushan represents his vision of Shiva temples with sprouting minarets and in the mosque, *Om*, flowing calm as a horizon along the muezzin's call to prayers. His interwoven life, the Hindu self mingled with the Muslim self, was presented to the audience, making a clarion call for Hindu-Muslim marriage. "Sexual unity was the acid test of unity," (133) Bhushan said.

But the whole meeting was not charmed by this vision of harmony, the audience approved only the harmony in public life. In utter noise and confusion, shouts and anger, the meeting ended before the thanksgiving speech of the chairman. To Sylla also, such a harmony was unexpected and she feels that the mental world of Bhushan had stopped in 1918 when he met Razia. But this was the wound Bhushan opened and closed, lived and died around, and Sylla had become a crab over it.

Sylla was a scab; she couldn't heal up the wound or cure Bhushan. Bhushan belongs to Sylla, because loving might be a vocation like medicine or the priesthood. Here in this novel Sylla is the real mistress and Bhushan waited at home for her visits. He loved to perform small services for her comfort and pleasure.

The situation here, may be said to have changed, in comparison with the earlier novels of Nayantara Sahgal. Sylla is not Saroj or Simrit, she is not even Sonali. She is an extended portrait of Anna (*Plans for Departure*) who is capable of making men wait for her approval and decision.

For Bhushan, she is his peace from his furies of Hinduism and Islam, because she is a Parsee, who believed in a God of light and Good, who pre-dated Islam in Persia. The realization 'peace be with you, all religions say, only Sylla means it; soothes and comforts Bhushan. People attach themselves to a Ganges or Mecca, but is there a possibility of a life without these affiliations—this seems the central thought of the novelist.

With Sylla, Bhushan does his utmost to sort out what being in love meant, bothering little for what percent of one's self could be put in the common pool. He strongly believes that lovers should enjoy what they can of each other. They did not want anything, no flirting with the idea of marriage. Such a relationship between a man and a woman can be lasting, crossing the isms, transgressing the boundary of creeds, castes and politics also. Bhushan says to Sylla, "I'm nothing but a tadpole without you. I'll never grow to maturity without you." (15)

After his release from the jail, Bhushan comes to Vijaygarh, he plans to go to Bombay to meet Sylla and marry her and live a carefree modern life, this was "one dream that was still within reach." (194)

At Bombay, Sylla thinks that they can't marry, because Sylla feels that Bhushan does not believe in any god or he had never "asked forgiveness, made amends or something." (196) She plans to marry Nauzer, the Parsee young rising star, the advocate. Bhushan's identity as a true lover is mistaken by Sylla also. She fails to pay heed to Bhushan's appeals to have mercy on him, she fails to accept the love-relationship, complementing each other. Bhushan, before wishing good bye to Sylla, kisses her gently on her "forehead," as a parent would do; for in many ways she was his child and he also had been her 'servant lover.' The novel reaches the climax here, and Bhushan Singh comes to reality from romance, "Outside Sylla's house there was Hindu-

Muslim madness. . . . And perfect love stayed out of reach." Bhushan further contemplates: "So men and women worshipped stones and clay instead and others smashed these with as perfect love." (197) He decided not to come in the way of Sylla again. He refuses to keep on moving like a shuttle from Vijaygarh to Bombay, from Hindu-Muslim love madness to carefree modern life.

He returns back to Vijaygarh in a state of awakened reality, with the identity he wishes to preserve, made aware of the rejection received from Sylla. Sylla is the guide, the life force to Bhushan.

At Vijaygarh, he meets Yusuf, his cell-mate in the jail and the communist social reformer. Bhushan immediately feels, "he had descended on me like a compass. I knew where north was again." (201) He feels the purpose in his life, with the arrival of Yusuf. Yusuf plans to start Profullo Sen Centres for the young, all over the province, and one is to be opened in Vijaygarh, and he has purchased the house of the imbecile. With the hopeful labour of Yusuf, the imbecile's house disappears and the monument of Sen rises.

Yusuf proposes Bhushan to write songs, inspiring revolution in Vijaygarh, but Bhushan, in the Hindu-Muslim harmony line, can write poems only about Razia, not the diesel engine poems. Yusuf stays on with his social purpose, he is helped by Bhushan's mother and father also. His father has recently returned to Vijaygarh after a trip abroad with his third 'ranee.' Once in reply to his mother's reaction to Sylla's western dress, Bhushan wanted to ask his mother "where did your beautiful bounteous bosom get you? What guarantees were your eyes, your glorious hair, your faithful womb? Did any of it save you from Damnation, even, the birth of a son?" (204) She is also like a typical Sahgal heroine, who leaps out of the bonds of the institution of marriage, to get her self-identity and one morning, she leaves the family mansion and goes to her communist lover Yusuf, caring little for the public approval. To Bhushan, his mother and Yusuf seem love-mad, unable to notice their notoriety. She, an illiterate ranee, knows nothing about communism but she knows a man when she embraces one.

Before this union of lovers, Bhushan met the young daughter of Yusuf, and married her. Here the Hindu-Muslim unity is finally achieved and this time 'the real Vijaygarh self' of Bhushan, wounded long time back and to which Sylla was simply a scab, is healed up. The final realization comes to Bhushan, "Great love is a serious, whole-time business," (160) as he sees his dream realized. One thing more is to be noted: this time there was no riot, none was killed either.

In *Mistaken Identity*, the story moves forwards and backwards in the stream of consciousness method as Bhushan Singh is in jail, facing the charges of attempts to overthrow the British rule. Though Bhushan has nothing to do with the revolution, his identity is mistaken and he is to undergo the trial and torments.

His stay in the jail brings him into close contact with Yusuf, Comrade Sen and Iyer and the true Gandhian Bhaiji. The comrades are greatly charmed by the Russian soil and the theory of revolution. The dethronement of the Tsars in Russia and the event of getting rid of the Caliph in 1925 have great impact on the socio-political and religious make up of the people in India. The people in Turkey, under the leadership of Mustafa Kemal Pasha, had dissolved the religious orders in 1926. They replaced the Sharia with a western civil code, a new constitution, and the use of European numerals in place of Arab numerals was adopted. The new situation in Turkey meant that there will be no Pope of Islam, and such changes did have direct or indirect relationship with Bhushan's Hindu-Muslim unity theory.

Bhaiji, the ardent follower of Gandhi, holds the juxtaposing position as against Yusuf and his comrades. Though their fight is unanimously against the British rule, they seem to have difference of attitudes. The worth and fame of Gandhi is presented in a new critical scrutiny, "the comrades make him sound like a comma in the middle of a sentence which would read a hell of a lot faster without it." (30) Sahgal, as an accomplished and mature writer, brings out the faded shades of Gandhism. The set of opposites help the growth of the novel and allow the characters to a better understanding of their selves.

Yusuf is a machine addict. He loves the perfume of factory

smoke and greese-oil. He says, "The future depends on machine." (80) Contrary to his views, Bhaiji favours the use of a few machines only, such as sewing machines that won't corrupt the economy or the moral libre. He is for cottage industries, his vision of freedom is "the dawn of an era washed clean of drink and lust." (81)

Between Yusuf and Bhaiji, Bhushan maintains the equi-distant stand because he is from a country called Vijaygarh and not India. The comrades and Bhaiji form a study circle with Bhushan as their topic. It is through the discussions between Bhushan and his jail-mates that the narrative of this novel progresses. The flow of language is the flow of relationships. Though none is able to understand the puzzle why Bhushan is in jail, they share ideas and ideologies.

Though Yusuf proves later to be the guide and the 'compass' to Bhushan Singh, because Yusuf lets him realize the 'harmony,' it is the Gandhian Bhaiji whose death leads him to meet his first love Razia. Bhaiji used to spin and send the thread to the fallen sisters, the prostitutes. Bhaiji once moved to the red-light area and tried to persuade the prostitutes to stop their immoral business. He called them his 'fallen sisters' and though they did not accept his theory, they accepted to spin 'takli' and promised to take part in the national movement.

It is at the time of claiming the dead body of Bhaiji that Bhushan is assigned to deal with the superior of the fallen sister. This superior of the fallen sister is none other than Razia, his teacher, who taught him the lesson of 'harmony.'

Bhushan, in his Hindu-Muslim madness, feels in the talk of comrades, a soviet style muezzin's cry echoing. The jail is the central situation, and the story grows in Bhushan's interaction with his cell-mates, his fancy and in his observations. In spite of all the recurring references to Lahore conspiracy case and Gandhiji's fruitless effort to save Bhagat Singh and his friends from hanging, to Jatin Das who wanted to die for the country, to the conditions in Andaman's jail and the speeches of Motilal Nehru and Amar Nath Das to save the convicts, this novel remains the life story of Bhushan and what is made of the life of Bhushan in the given situation. And thus, the characters build lives even outside the time and the political setting of the novel. This provides the novel its artistic beauty and literary charm.

Sahgal presents this novel as a political document of the period when concept of respectability mattered differently. Bhaiji said, "every Indian must get used to going to jail. Let it become our national profession." (80) We experience here the beauty of details, richly used by the author. The language is charming and absorbing, phrases like 'cooling anger' have refreshing artistic fictional charm. Herein, the emotionalized experiences, with the political events and situations, get the natural flow. In this well-crafted book, Sahgal writes a fine story, wherein the characters and situations not only amuse but also make the reader familiar with a fascinating period.

The genre of the political novel appears to have accentuated and intonated with natural integration of the new lyrical dimension of fictional art that Sahgal embraces at this stage. We have here, as in earlier novels, a documentary picturization of contemporary political reality, but what is remarkable, rather unmistakable in Sahgal's art is that it combines artistic portraits of life with the political history of contemporary India. History seems to speak the language of politics as it does in most of her novels, but at the same time distinct emotive life-pattern appears to be emerging as a powerful fictional force, in the conscious artistry, the texture and the contour of the world that she weaves.

One is tempted to remark that the story of the period becomes fascinating in *Mistaken Identity*, not simply because of the political potential of the period, but for the artistic reason of powerful story-telling also.

The documentary part of the political novel appears to be in clash with the artistic fictional effects that Nayantara Sahgal looks for in this novel. She seems to have discovered an artistic urge for fresher themes of life.

Sahgal appears to be inspired by an irresistible desire for assertion of fictional art and its aesthetic appeal as well, which is why in *Mistaken Identity*, some sort of artistic unity of impression is realized both in terms of content and form.

The story of the contemporary political life is narrated through the experiences of the protagonist Bhushan Singh and his cell-mates in the prison, Yusuf, Bhaiji, Comrade Sen, Iyer and Bhushan's love Sylla and others. These characters are allowed by the artist to live outside the recognizable point of the political period in which they live. They have an assigned role in telling or recreating the political situation and ethos of the period, through their interaction and confrontation with situation and conflicts they are in. At the same time, they breathe and live outside the prescribed political framework; they add wit, humour, wisdom and love, to the wholesome emotive world and its effect that the novelist aims at and achieves.

Sahgal presents successfully an India with all its religious and social contradictions, and depicts the political situation with all the ulterior undercurrents and succeeds in presenting the ideal and the real working against each other, the real undermining the ideal and the ideal resisting erosion. Thus *Mistaken Identity* shows her marked maturing development as a political novelist.

NOTES

1. Sahgal's letter to D.K. Yadav, L.N.M. University, Darbhanga (Bihar).
2. Nayantara Sahgal, *Mistaken Identity* (London: Sceptre, 1988), p. 205.

Marriage without Love and Love without Marriage: A Destructive Sexual Passion in Ruth Jhabvala's *Heat and Dust*

M.A. WAHEED

Ruth Prawer Jhabvala will be counted as a modern writer of contemporary India. She is neither brutally frank like Nirad C. Chaudhari, nor traditional in her themes like Mulk Raj Anand or R.K. Narayan. She has chosen for her a subject matter, the most vitally modern; the aspect of marriage without love and love without marriage in the contemporary Indian life. She has been writing for the past forty years but her eighth novel *Heat and Dust*[1] is the one with the Indian situations and settings. She won the famous Booker Prize for this novel in London in 1975. That's why H.S. Mahle considers her as the novelist "to the category of manufacturers of books rather than to that of growers of books."[2]

The issue of marriage without love and love without marriage that she has taken is one of the burning problems in India. Jhabvala dealt with the theme in her earlier novels. The theme of *Heat and Dust* is on a different plane in the sense that both the hero, and the heroine, Douglas and Olivia, are from the same culture, same religion, same social and educational background. Still, there is deficiency of love between wife and husband. The strong reason for this is Olivia's emotional dissatisfaction. They are married but they don't have psychological love between them. So, they are not made for each other. A woman's happiness is not just by providing everything in terms of comforts and luxuries. There is something beyond materialistic thinking and that is psychological affection. This affection she lacks, so there is dissatisfaction and that leads to their married life being loveless. Olivia's character cannot be compared with other characters of other novels of Jhabvala. In *Get Ready for Battle*, there were attitudal differences between Gulzari Lal and Sarala Devi and that resulted in total separation. Again, in *The Householder* and *A Backward Place*, there were attitudal differences between Prem and Indu and Bal and Judy respectively but at the end of the novel they developed the sense of coexistence. Again, in *Esmond in India*, the seriousness of dissonance takes place between Gulab and Esmond due to cross cultural conflicts. The separation was inevitable. In *Heat and Dust* the problem of marriage without love and love without marriage is due to emotional and destructive sexual desire with which the heroine of the novel, Olivia, becomes the unholy wife to her holy husband, Douglas, the Assistant Collector at Satipur town in Central India.

Olivia's India, as reflected in her diary and letters, is the India of the early thirties. Olivia, the wife of Douglas, eloped with the young Nawab of Khatm in September 1923. *Heat and Dust* is a novel of two women, Olivia, the heroine, and the narrator, whose name has not been mentioned anywhere in the novel. This story is about two English women and their life in India 25 years before and after independence. Mrs. Beth Crawford, the Collector's wife at Satipur is young narrator's aunt, and Miss Tessie, Beth's sister, is the narrator's grandmother. Tessie married Douglas after he got a divorce from Olivia. The young narrator is Tessie's granddaughter who comes to India with a bunch of Olivia's letters to unravel the mysteries of Olivia's existence and the dismal oddities of her life. The narrator wants to know about Olivia, her way of life, her friends, her parties, her escapades, finally culminating in her elopement with the young muslim Nawab. The young narrator visits India in the seventies to investigate the details related to Olivia.

The title of the novel symbolises the psychological state of the characters involved. The first reference to the title occurs in Olivia's way of life, in fact, the first phase of it when, as the wife of Douglas, she lives in a large and dull house. She feels bored and lonely in that spacious house: "The rest of the time

Olivia was alone in her big house with all doors and windows shut to keep out the heat and dust." (4) The heat and dust thus stand for an aspect of India. Olivia is bored in this spacious house. It is only on Sundays that she happens to meet a handful of stereotyped Anglo-Indian families in town. They are Mrs. Minnies, the wife of Major Minnies, the political agent to advise the Nawab, Mrs. Beth Crawford, the wife of Dr. Saunders, the British Medical Superintendent of Khatm town. In order to spend time, she used to read books or play the piano but she felt the days were long. Douglas was extremely busy with his work in the district:

> He always got up at crack of dawn—very quietly for fear of waking her—to ride out on inspection before the sun got too hot. After that he went to the court house and to his office and was usually too rushed to come home again till late in the evening and then always with files. By that time Olivia woke up, the servants had cleaned the house and let down all the blinds and shutters. The entire day was her own. In London she had loved having hours and hours to herself—she had always thought of herself as a very introspective person. But here she was beginning to dread these lonely days locked up with the servants who padded around on naked feet and respectfully waited for her to want something. (17, 18)

The hero of the novel, Douglas is always busy with the official duties. He has little time to spare for his wife who is all the time waiting for him. He is a work-conscious man. His superiors applaud him for his sincerity and honesty and the way he handles the administration in the district: "Douglas worked like a Trojan and never ceased to be calm and controlled, so that he was very much esteemed both by his colleagues and by the Indians. He was upright and just." (1) The fortitude with which Englishmen bear the heat while on duty in the plains is related to the strength, tenacity and moral uprightness of their character. This, in fact, is one aspect of the general image of an Anglo-Indian. Douglas is the prime example of such an image in the novel. His wife Olivia loves him very much "for his imperturbability, his English solidness and strength, his manliness." (116) But Douglas is worried very much about Olivia as for most of that effect of the heat and dust on Anglo-Indian women is such that they often become irritable and quarrelsome. "Douglas, for instance, blames the Indian heat and dust for increasing tension building up between Olivia and himself."[3]

Once there was an invitation from the young Nawab of Khatm for the dinner party to all the Anglo-Indian officials with their wives. Mr. Harry is a house guest to the Nawab Sahib. Douglas and his wife Olivia also attend the dinner party. For Olivia, all officials look dull and boring except her husband Douglas. "Only Douglas was different. She stole a look at him: Yes, he was right. As always he was sitting up very straight, so was his forehead; his evening jacket fitted impeccably. He was noble and fair." (16) Such a favourable view of Douglas's appearance is not restricted to Olivia who, being his wife, may be partial. Even in Nawab's personal friend Harry's opinion Douglas distinguished himself from others in the party. Surprisingly, the host Nawab's eyes rested on Olivia in the party. She allowed him to study her while pretending not to notice. She liked the behaviour of the Nawab, the style of his conversation, the way he received the guests, arrangement of the dinner with long tables decorated with flowers, candlebars, variety of the dishes, pomegranates, pineapples, crystallised fruits, little golden bowls etc. "She felt she had, at last in India, come to the right place." (15) Olivia liked the way the Nawab looked at her when she had first come in. "His eyes had lit up—he checked himself immediately, but she had seen it and realized that here at last was one person in India to be interested in her the way she was used to." (17)

The behaviour of Olivia after the party was different. She felt better about being alone in the house all day. She developed a sense of hope that the Nawab would visit and call on her as she experienced the soft and friendly behaviour of the Nawab in the dinner party. Now she started dressing in a different way "in one of her cool, pastel muslins and waited" for the Nawab. To her surprise, after four days of the dinner party, the Nawab Sahib visited her. She said, "'Why Nawab Sahib, what a lovely surprise.' She got up to greet him, holding out both hands to him in welcome." (18) That evening Douglas found Olivia not with much fatigue and boredom but so excited for the first time. Olivia reported to Douglas about the visit of Nawab. She laughed at him when she told his visitor, "he had his doubts but seeing how gay she was, how glad, he decided it was alright. She was lonely, and it was decent of the Nawab to have called on her." (19)

Jhabvala very scrupulously observes the behaviour of the Anglo-Indians and says that the effect of the heat and dust on them is such that they often become irritable and quarrelsome. The only escape for them is to go to some hill station like Simla. But the men posted often at far off places would not avail of such easy options. They would instead remain at their posts of duty and devote themselves to their work. Thus, Douglas, Saunders, Major Minnies and other Anglo-Indian officials don't think of going to such hill resorts. However, the option is open for the ladies and they generally make use of it to spend half the year at Simla. Douglas ascribes Olivia's irritability to the climate. Her cry at Douglas indicates this:

> He sucked at his pipe in rather a pleased way which made her cry out sharply: "Don't do that!" He took it out of his mouth and stared in surprise. "I hate you with that thing, Douglas," she explained. Although he didn't understand why, he saw that she was upset so he laid it aside. "I don't like it much myself," he said frankly. There was a pause. She stopped sewing, stared into space; her pretty lower lip was sulky. (39)

Douglas decides to send his wife to Simla with the other European ladies but Olivia's refusal to go to Simla is beautifully illustrated in the following passage:

He said "It'll be all right once you get to the hills. It's the heat, darling, that's getting you."

"I know it is . . . but when will you be able to get away?"

"Never mind about me. It's you we have to take care of. I was talking to Beth [wife of the collector] today. They're thinking of leaving on the 17th, and I said kindly to book a berth for you at the same time. It's the Kalka Mail—an overnight journey, but it won't be too bad, I promise you." He was so pleased with his arrangement that it didn't occur to him she could be anything else. "It's another four hours up the mountains but what a journey! You'll love it. The scenery, not to speak of the change of climate—"

"You don't for one moment think that I would go without you!"

"Beth Crawford will be there, and Mary Minnies. They'll take care of you." He gave one look at her face and said, "That's just silly, Olivia. Mother spent four months away from father every year for years on end. From April to September. She didn't like it either, but you're in a district, that's the way it has to be."

"I'm not going," Olivia said, sitting up very straight and looking at him very straight too. Then she said, "The Nawab wants to give a party for us."

"Very kind of him," Douglas said drily. He picked up his pipe again to knock it against the fender.

"Yes it is rather," Olivia said. "He sent Harry over specially to ask us."

"It's not everyday that royalty throws parties for junior officers."

"No but I expect he's as bored as we are with our seniors."

"We are?"

"I am." (39-40)

The conversation between Douglas and Olivia makes it clear that the situation of marital dissonance in them is at peak level. Douglas plans something and Olivia disagrees. He wants to provide comfortable journey facility for Simla but she is not ready and discusses with Douglas in a negative way. This lack of mutual understanding creates dissonance between them. Olivia tries to rationalize why she has been discussing and quarreling with Douglas.

> "Why are we quarreling?" she asked. He considered her question for a moment and then came up with his reasoned reply: "Because the climate is making you irritable. That's only natural, it happens to all of us. And of course it's much worse for you having to stay home all day with nothing to do. That's why I want you to go away." After a moment, he added: "You don't think I like it any better than you, do you?" Then she collapsed completely and could only be held up by his strong arms. She said she'd be bored, she'd be irritable, she'd hot, she'd quarrel with him—all right! But please not to send her away from him. (40)

Olivia does not like to go because of her growing involvement and interest with the Nawab. Thus she pleads with her husband not to send her to Simla. Her growing attraction towards the Nawab leads her gradually to a different plane. K.P.K. Menon rightly remarks: "The attraction is mutual and culminates in her elopement with him."[4] It is true that Douglas and Olivia are wife and husband but the way their life is passing is typical. Olivia is sentimental and emotional whereas Douglas is a man of practical bent of mind. They lack a mutual understanding. As Ramesh Chadha observes, "this dissonance may be owing to different attitudes towards life."[5] Douglas does everything for Olivia but the problem with him is that he is so busy that he does not have time to talk to his wife leisurely and pleasantly. He doesn't share his views in terms of personal life with her. He does the work mechanically. He does not take care of her views for making life more pleasant, more enjoyable by going for outings, picnics, and other activities.

Besides all these things, his routine and tight schedule for the day to day administration of Satipur province has disturbed the peace of life for Olivia. She develops an obsession against Douglas that he is for others and not for her. Douglas feels that his wife should be a conformist but Olivia feels that she is not an 'object' but a human being with psychological and emotional desires. Materialistically she is well off but emotionally and psychologically she is underfed. Douglas thinks that the closed bungalow without heat and dust, the servants to attend the orders of his wife, food to eat, books to read and piano to play are enough to stay at home and live happily. However, Olivia feels that there are certain situations where she wants her husband to sit comfortably without hurried programmes, talk to her without administrative worries, and move together. She feels that there must be a fixed time for administration and the rest of the time should be for her only. Somehow, the conservative mind of Douglas does not suit his wife. Therefore, she diverts her mind towards the Nawab and starts taking his help for the outings. During one of her secret visits to Nawab that she pays without knowledge and permission of her husband, she tells Harry that she doesn't want to see the Begum [Nawab's mother] but is interested in the Nawab. "I came here to be with you—and him of course. I mean, as your friend. Both of you." (102) She is charmed by the Nawab. His gay and courteous manner, his mellifluous voice in reciting Urdu poetry, his luxurious palace and its inscrutable interiors, his grand parties attract Olivia. As a European young girl, such Oriental aspects impress her much. As compared to the charming Nawab, the other Anglo-Indian officials appear quite boring to Olivia. "She kept asking herself how it was possible to lead exciting lives—administering whole provinces, fighting border battles, advising rulers—and at the same time to remain so dull." (15) Thus, Douglas's absence of feelings towards the psychological and emotional feelings of Olivia creates a gulf between wife and husband. Laurie Sucher opines that this "novel is rich in nature imagery. It contrasts the heat and dust of the plains—which signify at once an obsessive sexuality and the absence of feeling—with the life giving moisture of the Himalayas."[6]

There is another reason for Olivia's boredom. As India is not the motherland of Anglo-Indians, they are not rooted in the cultural heritage of India. The husband, Douglas is with his job, and the wife, Olivia gets bored in the spacious bungalow. Here love exists only at the physical level and not at the psychological level. She is a nonconformist and wants her own way of life. She didn't like the traditional way of life of her husband. She has an inquisitive mind and wants to know Indian culture and civilization. For this Olivia takes the help of Nawab. The Nawab acts as the guide and subsequently he develops friendship with Olivia.

Olivia is also disgusted with her life since she has not been blessed with a child. As a matter of fact, the Anglo-Indians are conscious of the need of procreating a race which would inherit the ideal British qualities. Since Douglas represents such ideals and qualities, a whole lot of Douglases is needed to people the world. Both Douglas and Olivia are keen to have children. Time passes but Olivia does not conceive. She herself is worried about it. Behind her worry is the assumption that the world would be poorer without the progeny of the Douglas couple dominating it. "She could not believe it. She was sure that a couple like herself and Douglas meant to have children, to be the founders of a beautiful line. He too was sure of it." (105) Curiously, Olivia does not ascribe her supposed infertility to any biological defect or physical incompatibility. She comes out with a psychological reason which itself gives a distorted picture of the country. She says that she could not conceive because "She had been so frightened by all the little babies in the graveyard, dead of small-pox, dead of cholora, dead of enteric fever." (105) Thus the rate of child mortality is exaggerated and the country is described as afflicted with terrible fevers and diseases. She is dissatisfied with her life besides these factors that she feels like Mrs. Kaul in *A Backward Place* 'a bird in a gilded cage.'

As a young bride, Olivia adores Douglas Rivers's gentlemanly idealism. She loves his English solidness and strength but with the passing of time and closer perspective of wifehood, her ardour fades. She suddenly thinks about him and says: "What manliness? He can't even get me pregnant?" (116) Then, she allows herself to be drawn into a liaison with a powerless minor prince of Khatm as that is the only option left to her. It is an option to her in the sense that between a wooden British official and a charming Nawab, she prefers the latter. There was no alternative left to her but to decide to go with the Nawab because she became "like the lovesick ladies of the Kangra miniature paintings, who toss on their lovely embroidered couches while dust storms gather threateningly overhead, she is racked by the delicate fire of a passion that her affectionate but unimaginative husband fails to recognise although he had seen a lot of Indian fevers."[7]

In terms of her decision to opt for an Eastern way of life, at the invitation of the Nawab, she goes to the Shrine of Baba Firdous. There she saw the gang of decoits armed with guns saluting the Nawab. She suspected their relationship with the Nawab but he clarified that they are good people. She believed and "he respectfully touched her arm with his finger tips." (134) In a gay mood, the Nawab described the situation how his ancestor, Amanulla Khan received with the British people and he in a gloomy mood termed them as very cunning people. He suddenly cried and became upset. Olivia could not tolerate his upset mood, so, "she put her hand and laid it on his chest as if to soothe him. And really he was soothed; he said 'How kind you are to me." He laid his hand on top of hers by a strength, a magnetism that she had never yet in all her life expected with anyone." (136) Later, "he led her away from the Shrine and they lay together under a tree." (137) So, she can't resist the temptation to love him. Thus, in Nirmal Mukherji's view, "Olivia is destroyed because she is the most vulnerable. She who is sensitive, passionate, human, and aesthetic is destroyed, whereas the 'tough old hens' like Mrs. Crawford and Mrs. Minnies survive."[8]

Olivia becomes pregnant. She first informs this to the Nawab Sahib and later to her husband, Douglas. Both the lover and the husband were happy over this news but Olivia worries more when she comes to fear that her would-be child might have black hair on the head because she knows that the Nawab made her pregnant and not her husband. So, she opts for an abortion under the supervision of Nawab's mother Begum and subsequently she is admitted to the hospital where Dr. Saunders declares that it is the case of an abortion. When everything becomes public, she straightaway goes to the palace of Nawab who in turn provides her accommodation at the Himalayas. She breathes her last there only.

Olivia's tragedy is due to her marriage with Douglas without love and her love with the Nawab of Khatm without marriage. Olivia's delusion of dissatisfaction, and emotional behaviour lead her towards destructive sexual passion for which she is responsible. Her obsession with the romantic Eastern view makes her a tragic victim.

NOTES

1. R.P. Jhabvala, *Heat and Dust* (London: John Murray, 1975).
2. H.S. Mahle, *Indo-Anglian Fiction: Some Perceptions* (New Delhi: Jaisons, 1985), p. 28.
3. A. Ramakrishna Rao, "Complex Racial Image in Jhabvala's *Heat and Dust*," *The Journal of English Studies*, 13:2 (April 1982), p. 66.
4. K.P.K. Menon, "Parallel Plots in *Heat and Dust*," *Littcrit*, 10:1 (June, 1984), p. 46.
5. Ramesh Chadha, "*Heat and Dust* and *Coffer Dams*: A Comparative Study," *The Journal of Indian Writing in English*, 10:12 (1982), p. 26.
6. Laurie Sucher, *The Fiction of Ruth Prawer Jhabvala: The Politics of Passion* (London: Macmillan, 1989), p. 99.
7. Yasmine Gooneratne, *Silence, Exile and Cunning: The Fiction of Ruth Prawer Jhabvala* (New Delhi: Orient Longman, 1983), p. 217.
8. Nirmal Mukherji, "*Heat and Dust*: A Tale of Two Women," *Kakatiya Journal of English Studies*, 3:1 (1978), p. 122.

Crossing Patriarchal Threshold: Glimpses of the Incipient New Woman in Manju Kapoor's *Difficult Daughters*

SEEMA MALIK

Taking into account the complexity of life, different histories, cultures and different structures of values, the Woman's Question, despite basic solidarity, needs to be tackled in relation to the socio-cultural situation. The impact of patriarchy on the Indian society varies from the one on the West and therefore, the Indian women novelists have tried to evolve their own stream of feminism grounded in reality. They have their own concerns, priorities as well as their own ways of dealing with the predicament of their women protagonists. Manju Kapoor's *Difficult Daughters*, recipient of the Commonwealth Writers' Prize for Best First Book (Eurasia region), is a significant contribution in this direction.

Set around the turbulent years of W.W. II and the Partition of India, Manju Kapoor realistically depicts women of three generations, focusing on Virmati, the difficult daughter of the second generation. The opening line of novel gives a jolt to the reader—"The one thing I had wanted was not to be like my mother."[1] This cryptic statement is made by Virmati's only daughter, Ida, a divorcee and childless perforce. She could not develop an understanding with her mother during her life time and after Virmati's death this realization engulfs her with guilt. Ida sets out on a journey into her mother's past by piecing together the fragments of memory in search of a woman she could know and understand. Virmati had been evasive about her past with Ida, and now she hoped to fill the critical gaps. The consciousness of the reader shuttles between the present and the past along with Ida who visits different places and meets her mother's relatives and acquaintances to know about Virmati, the woman.

Virmati, being the eldest, is burdened with family duties because of her mother's incessant pregnancies. Belonging to an austere and high minded Punjabi family, she grows up with the conditioning that the duty of every girl "is to get married" and a woman's "shaan" is in her home and not in doing a job. She is already engaged to a canal engineer, Inderjeet. However, seeds of aspiration are planted in Virmati when she sees Shakuntala, her cousin, tasting the "wine of freedom." She secretly nurtures the desire of being independent and leading a life of her own. She wants to shoulder responsibilities that go beyond a husband and children. She realizes that it is useless to look for answers inside the home as the "language of feeling had never flown" between Virmati and Kasturi, her mother. She had to look outside—to education, to freedom and the bright lights of Lahore College even if "she had to fight her mother who was so sure that her education was practically over." (17) Asserting herself, she not only clears her FA but joins A.S. College, "the bastion of male learning."

It is here that the Oxford-returned Professor, her neighbour, notices her, "flower like, against a back drop of male students" and forces himself into her mind and heart by spreading his anguish at her feet. Caught in the whirlpool of misplaced passion towards the already married Professor, she has the temerity to spurn marriage, attempts suicide and bears confinement. However, she does realize the hopelessness of her illicit love when she learns about the pregnancy of the Professor's wife. How could it be true? Man professing his love for her on one hand and making his wife pregnant on the other. At this juncture, decisively and brusquely, she cuts him saying: "You think you can do what you like so long as you go on saying you love" and goes to Lahore for further studies.

Thus far we see the budding of a "New Woman" in Virmati who does not want "to be a rubber doll for others to move as they willed." (85) Defying patriarchal notions that enforce a woman towards domesticity, she asserts her individuality and aspires self-reliance through education. She is not a silent rebel but is bold, outspoken, determined and action-oriented. She knows she cannot depend upon the Professor to sort out the domestic situation and proceeds to tackle it on her own. Later, she very decisively and coolly shuns the Professor, ignoring his plea and keeps the reins in her hand. She displays a marvellous strength of mind in overcoming her dejection. She is "strong to bear the pain, silently, without anyone knowing." (101) The determined and unperturbed manner in which she burns the Professor's letters show her resolution to close the chapter and look forward to a meaningful life in Lahore.

But does Virmati blossom into a "New Woman" in the real sense of the term? No. In spite of her initial revolt against the family and firm stand against the Professor, she succumbs to his implorations and passion in Lahore. Loss of virginity pricks her conscience but then she overcomes the guilt by rationalizing it as "outmoded morality." (114) She had come to Lahore to broaden her horizons but instead she gets involved in a useless love, doubtful marriage and unwed pregnancy. The initial tenacious and assertive self gradually wanes away into a pawn whom the Professor tells "just what to look for, what to admire, what to criticize." (119) She wants to spread her wings like Swarnalata, her roommate, who is committed to "meaningful activities" regarding the freedom movement and women's emancipation. But her emotional dependence on the Professor who constantly evades the question of marriage, stops her from doing any thing that he disapproves: "Maybe I could be like Swarna from the inside, secretly." (124) At the Punjab Women's Student Conference, she is amazed at "how large an area of life women wanted to appropriate for themselves." (132) But these larger spaces are not for her. She wastes her time awaiting the furtive meetings with the Professor in spite of the awareness that there were "myriad instances of where she felt she had been weak or wronged." (129) She is being used and the Professor wants to have the cake and eat it too. He enjoys the best of the two worlds and is not there even at the most crucial time when she undergoes termination of pregnancy. Even afterwards when the Professor eventually marries her very reluctantly, she is given a pariah status and faces exclusion from hearth etc. which is the sole domain of the Professor's first wife, Ganga. Virmati lives in a cramped space and is forced into submission though in a very subtle manner. "Indeed, any sophisticated structure today functions not by direct, visible exploitation but by making the victims willingly, freely and happily give in to its imperatives."[2] Professor Harish's attitude towards her is patronizing and demeaning. His interest in her is an extension of self-love—awakening her intellect and emotions inflates his ego. Undergoing a gradual process of self-effacement, her energies are directed towards pleasing him while she herself remains parched. She finds M.A. in Philosophy dull, abstract and meaningless but studying it was her only means of escape. She wishes "Harish had thought another subject suitable for her. She also wished it was not such an uphill task, being worthy of him." (237) In fact, she remains "difficult" only as a daughter—towards her grandfather who always championed her cause, her father who was very understanding and allowed her to study further and towards her mother who certainly had Virmati's good at heart.

Thus, though she dares to cross one patriarchal threshold, she is caught into another where her free spirit is curbed and all she does is "adjust, compromise and adapt." She could have put her foot down saying "she will be her own mistress and relate to him with dignity or not at all. Perhaps the words were at the back of her mind, teasing her tongue with their shadowy sounds" (236) but she does not. Maybe her mind had gone "soft and pulpy" with repeated complying. (236) Thus, in Virmati we see the incipient New Woman who is conscious, introspective, educated, wants to carve a life for herself, to some extent she even conveys a personal vision of womanhood by violating current social codes yet she lacks confidence, self-control, farsightedness and is psychically imprisoned with an underlying need to be emotionally and intellectually dependent on a superior force, Professor Harish, and it is precisely this knowledge through which the patriarchy works. She fails to break the "dependence syndrome"[3] and halts on the path to full human status.

Trampling patriarchal norms, Virmati defies societal expectation to assert her individuality and hopes to achieve self-fulfillment. But what does she really get? She is a loser whose acts totally alienate her from her own family and she fails to create a space for herself for which she had been striving all along. Perhaps it is this inability of Virmati to strike independent roots and grow that makes Ida remark "The one thing I had wanted was not to be like my mother."

It is possible to trace the feminism implicit in the novel through Ida's impatience towards her mother's weaknesses. When her Parvati Masi says that Virmati was a simple girl at heart, Ida says: "I hate the word 'simple.' Nobody has any business to live in the world and know nothing about its ways." (207) No woman, who dares to spurn patriarchal protection can afford to be ignorant, simple or naive. Surely, Virmati's unwed pregnancy and then its heartless termination is unpalatable to Ida who finally breaks up with her husband, Prabhakar, because he had forced her to have an abortion: "In denying that incipient little thing in my belly, he sowed the seeds of our break up." (144) And then, does passion so transform an individual that Virmati fails to see things in the right perspective? She not only disregards her filial duty but also becomes a victimizer by usurping what rightfully belongs to Ganga, the Professor's first wife, thereby giving a setback to the much-needed feeling of sisterhood among women. The concluding lines of the novel reiterate Ida's rejection of Virmati, not as a mother but as a woman. "This book weaves a connection between my mother and me, each word a brick in a mansion I made with my *head* and my *heart.* Now live in it, Mama, and leave me be. Do not haunt me any more." (258) Ida, who grew up struggling to be the model daughter, does not have the heart to reject Virmati, the mother, but her head, the rationale, rejects her as a woman after having an insight into Virmati's past.

Through Ida's admiration for Swarnlata, who enters into a wider socio-political sphere, the novelist seems to be saying that a woman can maintain her individuality and pursue her interest without threatening the family structures. Thus a woman should basically strive towards a fine interdependent partnership. But if she feels suffocated, then voice ought to be raised and there should be a total breaking away, like Ida. But merely transcending societal norms is not enough. A woman should be aware, self-controlled, strong-willed, self-reliant and rational, having faith in the inner strength of womanhood. A meaningful change can be brought only from within by being free in the deeper psychic sense. Thus Manju Kapoor's *Difficult Daughters* is a feminist discourse not because she is woman writing about women but because she "has understood a woman both as a woman and as a person pressurized by all kinds of visible and invisible contexts.[4] She presents feminism at its most sane, keeping in mind the Indian context.

NOTES

1. Manju Kapoor, *Difficult Daughters* (New Delhi: Penguin. 1998), p. 1.
2. Jaidev, "Problematizing Feminism," *Gender and Literature*, ed. Iqbal Kaur (Delhi: B.R., 1992), p. 57.
3. Chaman Nahal, "Feminism in English Fiction Forms and Variations," *Feminism and Recent Fiction in English*, ed. Sushila Singh (New Delhi: Prestige, 1991), p. 17.
4. Jaidev, p. 68.

Arundhati Roy's *The God of Small Things*: A Study in Abnormal Psychology and Consequent Behaviour Pattern

ALKA SAXENA

November 1962. Planters with their families started leaving Assam amidst rumours of Chinese occupation and India's defeat. A hair-raising bus ride to Shillong brought the heavily pregnant Ammu in a hospital for delivery. The windows of the hospital were blacked out and it seemed the insecurity of the outside world had made a severe impact on the newborn twins as they emerged—Wrinkled with the effort of being born, in the unfriendly and unsafe world. The dismal atmosphere of their birth, the detached uncaring father who lay drunk on the bench in the hospital, the total blackout and only a faint candle light—all these things become a part and parcel of the twins immediately. The candlelight symbolically stood for the love of Ammu—but even Ammu's life was as brief as that candle. She died at 31. "Not old, Not young. But a viable die-able age." (3) After they were born, Ammu had counted their eyes, noses, fingers, toes etc. to check for any deformities. Apparently she had counted everything, but she had failed to notice the SINGLE Siamese soul. The single soul was significant in the lives of Rahel and Estha, the twins. In a hopeless world, they managed to survive by the strength of this unique, rare, single soul. It seemed to bind them together, even to destruction.

When Ammu divorced her husband and came back to live in Ayemenem, she was aware of the "Constant, high whining mewl of local disapproval." (43) For the sake of her children, she learned to swallow this humiliation. The twins too felt that all was not well. The insecurity reflected in their faces. They seemed like a pair of small-bewildered frogs. But amidst the "highway of hurtling traffic they were engrossed in each other's company" (43) and could not imagine what 'trucks' would do to this pair of two-egg-twin. "In those early amorphous years when memory had only just begun, when life was full of Beginnings and no Ends, and Everything was for ever, Esthappen and Rahel thought of themselves together as Me, and separately, individually, as We or Us. As though they were a rare breed of Siamese twins physically separated, but with joint indentities." (2)

While the twins kept themselves together, Ammu found herself engulfed by the bitterness of her marriage and divorce. For women like Ammu, there was no happiness in either situation. With a drunkard as a husband who used to mercilessly beat her, she decided to divorce him. Life in Ayemenem was also not happy. She wanted to remove all things which associated her with her husband. She wanted to change her surname and revert to her maiden name, though she felt that "choosing between her husband's name and her father's name didn't give a woman much of a choice." (37) The bitterness of her marriage had spread in her entire body. This made her a dangerous and an unpredictable woman.

Rahul and Estha, the innocent children, had to bear the brunt of Ammu's personal trauma. Though she loved her children deeply, there was deep down in her heart a feeling that they were a burden on her soul. She had expressed in an agitated tone: "If it weren't for you I would be free. I should have dumped you in an orphanage the day you were born. You're the millstones round my neck." (291) Baby Kochamma, their great aunt, expressed her dislike for the twins openly. She spared no opportunity to criticize them. She considered them doomed, fatherless waifs. "Worse still, they were Half-Hindu Hybrids whom no self-respecting Syrian Christian would ever marry." (45) She made them realize that they had no right to live in their maternal grandmother's home. It angered her that despite her rebukes the twins sought happiness in childhood pranks and play. Though the mind of the twins was diverted by childhood games, Baby Kochamma's rebukes had caused damaging effect on their minds. The harsh words and lack of love and sympathy had managed to creep deep inside. The insides were wounded where the gashes were deep and never healed. Baby Kochamma was annoyed to see "the comfort they drew from each other." (46) She expected from them some signs of unhappiness. Under Baby Kochmma's evil designs, the kids blamed Velutha for the death of Sophie Mol. They were drugged so that vital information could not be conveyed to Ammu. It was Baby Kochamma once again who suggested that Estha be returned to his father.

As children, the temperament and behaviour of the twins was very unusual. The sense of insecurity, lack of parental love, the feeling of being unwanted was marked in their behaviour. Estha's state of mind can be measured from the way he messed up the front page of his school exercise book. On the front page, Estha rubbed his surname with spit and half the paper had been torn in that place. In the place of his surname, he had written Unknown. The name read Esthappen Unknown. While Ammu was still choosing between her husband's and father's surname, Estha had been caught up in the fear of not belonging to anyone and his emptiness reflected in the choice of the word Unknown. After Sophie Mol's death, the twins and Ammu were subjected to further humiliation. At the funeral, they were made to stand separately and not with the rest of the family. Nobody even looked at them. Ammu was cold and nervous, "Estha stood close to her, barely awake, his aching eyes glittering like glass, his burning cheeks against the bare skin of Ammu's trembling, hymn book holding arm." (6) Rahel on the other hand was "wide awake, fiercely brittle with exhaustion from her battle against Real Life." (5) The funeral was followed by the returning of Estha. The trio of Ammu, Rahel and Estha was broken. Estha went back to his father in Calcutta.

As a child, Estha has always been quiet. He had stopped talking altogether. It seemed as if he had run out of conversation. His silence was "the psychological equivalent of what lungfish do to get themselves through the dry season, except that in

Estha's case the dry season looked as though it would last for ever." (110) He seemed almost non-existent. It took strangers to notice his presence with them. At school in Calcutta, he was an average student. He never mingled with his class-mates. Due to the embarrassment of his father and stepmother, he refused to join college. He did some odd jobs to earn something for himself. He floated like a quiet bubble in a sea of noise. "Estha occupied very little space in the world." (10) The quietness spread in Estha: "It reached out of his head and enfolded him in its swampy arms. It rocked him to the rhythm of ancient, foetal heartbeat. It sent its stealthy, suckered tentacles inching along the insides of his skull. . . . It stripped his thoughts of the words that described them and left them parched and naked." (11-12) Gradually he got accustomed to the 'octopus' that lived inside him. He had no faith in people around him and his only companion was his beloved mongrel Khubchand. After the mongrel's death, Estha became even more lonely and forlorn. He was like a dead man, stripped of his soul. The unpleasant memories of the Orangedrinkman at Abhilash Talkies, the painful death of Velutha, the sense of guilt lay heavy on him. He carried many unknown secrets within his heart. He carried inside him the memory of what he had done to Velutha. Under pressure from Baby Kochamma he believed that he was responsible for Velutha's death. That affirmation was decaying him, corroding him. Even after twenty three years "it was lodged there, deep inside some fold or furrow, like a mango hair between molars. That couldn't be worried loose." (32)

When it was decided that Estha be sent back to his father, a twin expert from Hyderabad was consulted. She said that it was not advisable to separate monozygotic twins. She warned that they would definitely suffer the natural distress that children from broken homes underwent but at the time no one was interested in giving a secure future to the twins. It is an acknowledged fact that parents's splitting up affects the children for the rest of their lives. It is difficult for children from broken homes to lead happy normal lives both professionally and personally. The age of a child makes a big difference to how the break-up affects him. According to counsellor Julia Cole, "despite their achievements, the strain of their parents' divorce in their early years, and subsequent strained relationships with them, will have scarred them for life." (*The Hindustan TImes*, 17 Jan. 1980) Latest research points that divorce and other family strife can affect the child's chances of personal happiness.

Estha's childhood trauma and an analysis of his disturbed psyche has been thoroughly examined. Now let us consider the case of Rahel. After Estha was returned and Ammu died, Rahel drifted from one school to another. She was uncared and ignored by the members of the family. They only provided her with food, clothes and school fee but were not concerned about her emotional needs. In school, her behaviour was abnormal—she was a rebel. She was expelled thrice for her abnormal behaviour. She had taken to smoking and stealing. In the College of Architecture in Delhi, she was reckless. The five years's course remained incomplete even after spending eight years. She was shunned by boys and girls for her waywardness. "Rahel drifted into marriage like a passenger drifts towards an unoccupied chair in an airport lounge." (18) When she met Larry McCaslin, he had taken her very lightly—just like a jazz tune. After marriage, Larry noticed "the emptiness in one twin was only a version of the quietness in the other. That the two things fitted together. Like stocked spoons. Like familiar lover's bodies." (20) Soon, Rahel's marriage ended in a divorce. She spent the following years in an atmosphere of lust and violence. In the midst of turbulence in the personal life, Rahel received Baby Kochamma's letter saying that Estha had returned from Calcutta. Rahel left America and returned to meet Estha in Ayemenem.

Twenty-three years later when Rahel was going through Pappachi's books, the word 'returned' slipped out easily from her tongue. "Returned. As though that was what twins were meant for. To be borrowed and returned. Like library books." (156) She remembered vividly the incident when Estha and she were pushed from Ammu to Baba like billiard balls. After the divorce, Ammu had pushed Estha to Baba saying that he should keep one of them. Throughout their lives, they had been treated as inanimate objects. They kept moving from one place to another. They did not belong to anyone or any place.

The warning of the twin expert was correct. By separating the twins, the damage done to them was complete. They had never thought themselves as two different individuals. It was always us, they, them and we. When Ammu had once made the promise to always love each other, Estha and Rahel were unable to tell her that there was no each no other. When they were separated, Rahel could never write to Estha—"There are things you can't do—like writing letters to a part of yourself. To your feet or hair or heart." (163-64) At a very young age, the twins had learnt that worst things had happened and worse things kept happening. Sophie Mol's gift of two ball-point pens was also very symbolic. The top halves filled with water in which a cut out collage of a London-street-scape was suspended. Cops and people, a double decker bus propelled by an air bubble floated up and down the silent street. There was something sinister about the absence of noise on the busy ball-point street. The same danger was lurking in the silence of Estha and the emptiness of Rahel.

When Estha returned to Ayemenem, he just walked about the whole village quietly, without any interaction with anyone. But inside, the turmoil was great. His mind was flooded with the memory of childhood days. All had been quiet in his heart till Rahel returned. "The world locked out for years, suddenly flooded in, and now Estha couldn't hear himself for the noise. Trains, Traffic, Music. . . . A dam had burst and savage waters swept everything up in a swirling." (15) Even now, after a gap of twenty-three years, they still thought of each other as them but the two of them were no longer what they were or ever thought they'd be.

The re-union made Baby Kochamma feel very uneasy. She was curious to know what they were upto. She had always felt that together the twins were trouble—Satan in the eye. They had to be separated. Rahel and Estha did not look like each other and so there was no confusion as to who is who in childhood. But there was always a suspicion that "the confusion lay in a deeper, more secret place." (2) They were somehow unaware of the hint of doom which was there since their childhood. When the family had gone to receive Sophie Mol the twins had slept together in Chacko's room in the hotel. They slept with their arms around each other. A hot twin and a cold one. He and She, We and Us. Somehow not wholly unaware of a hint of doom and all that waited in the wings for them." (122) As children they had never been shy of each other's bodies and they had never together been old enough to know what shyness was. Even now after twenty-three years, "Rahel searched her brother's nakedness for signs of herself." (92) She watched Estha with the "curiosity of a mother watching her child. A sister a brother. A woman a man. A twin a twin." (93)

At a performance on stage, they had seen the kathakali dancers enact Bhima's role to fulfill his vow to Draupadi by ripping Dushasan's body and bathing her hair in that blood. Estha and Rahel recognized this play having been performed on another stage, in another kind of frenzy. They were reminded of the hideousness of the scene that changed the course of their lives some years ago. "Trapped in the bog of a story that was and wasn't theirs. That had set out with the semblance of structure and order, then bolted like a frightened horse into anarchy." (236)

After the performance, they walked home together. Silence hung in the air. There was the same old sinister silence as they watched each other. Estha did not look at Rahel when she came close behind him. In this silence Rahel could feel the rhythm of Estha's rocking, the wetness of rain on his skin. Both were so closely linked by the single soul that she could hear the raucous scrambled world inside her head. "It was time when unthinkable became the thinkable and the impossible really happened. The three members of a broken home were the worst transgressors. But it was not just that they crossed into forbidden territory. They tampered with the laws that who should be loved and how. And how much." (31)

History and Counterhistory: Reading Novels, Reading Politic[1]: Arundhati Roy's *The God of Small Things*

PRASENJIT MAITI

We would like to argue in this paper that Arundhati Roy's novel, *The God of Small Things*, is really an exercise in a couple of histories, one official and the other interpretative, resulting from the writer's sensitization to the realities of everyday life. So for a given politics there is yet another corresponding politics, and for one particular narrative there exists a counternarrative.

It can be mentioned here that a rejoinder issued by the late communist leader from Kerala, E.M.S. Namboodiripad's[2] daughter had originally induced this study. She was irked at the apparent distortions in Roy's rendition of Kerala's Marxist history. So we propose to study Chapters 5, 14 and 18 of this novel.

But a clarification is required before anything else. Our assumption here is: there is a history present in Roy's text and there is yet another history someplace else, and these are mutually exclusive.[3] We would rather address these as literary and hegemonic[4] histories respectively. The inquiry exactly how do these oppose or contradict one another comprise our universe of research.

We also assume that official history is informed by a certain complicity and tends to record only a particular version of events. We would, therefore, examine some generally accepted source materials to interrogate our notion of official history.

So our central objective is to discover, if possible, the different levels of fiction that allegedly distort the grand narrative of

Kerala's historiography. So we would really try and isolate the little stories of countercultures from the larger myths found in the political history of Kerala. This sounds bland only if the exciting possibility of the presence of intermeshed realities is ignored. But can we really pose a question about the innate structure of reality? Can we conscientiously allow notions of multiple realities i.e. literary reality as against official reality to invade the relative autonomy of our research universe?

Moreover, can we also conceive of a meaningful, evolving dialogue between a given reality and its doppelganger? Convenient, ready-to-serve-obsequious answers may not always be available. Still, let us for the moment try to grapple with Roy's work as a readerly text, and try to undertake an exercise in recognizing the patterns of history and counterhistory that have informed the craftsmanship of this novel.

We should explain here that our research design is not to follow either the elitist model or the subaltern one while trying to reinterpret India's not-so-recent colonial history. All we would be trying in this paper is to move away further from the critique of the subaltern theorists and try to build up an argument of our own.

While we are not quite convinced with the treatment of history as a mere collection of certain so-called grand narratives, we are also not entirely in consonance with the politics-from-below point of view that tends to examine history as an absolute discourse in terms of black and white. What we mean is we cannot possibly afford to discuss our categories of analysis in straitjacketed terms like either the subaltern or the elite. We do not feel very comfortable with such loud units and would rather prefer to interrogate these in order to explore other in-between areas of research as a more viable probability.

This is why we do not want to look at the subaltern as something that was without any further 'paraphernalia' of identity. There must have been intra-subaltern strife and tension, problems of sustaining a workable stock of social capital within the subaltern classes themselves. Moreover, can we at all afford to look at the subaltern as a class or rather as an actor as located in the little games for power and hegemony and legitimacy within the formidable framework of India's freedom struggle.

Chapter 5, 'God's Own Country,' has possibilities for content analyses. Let us first try to examine a few *vignettes* taken from some random lines and try to decode their signified meanings:

> Downriver, a saltwater barrage had been built, in exchange for votes from the influential paddy-farmer lobby. . . . Comrade E.M.S. Namboodiripad, 'Kerala's Mao-Tse-tung,' . . . History and Literature enlisted by commerce. Kurtz and Karl Marx joining palms to greet rich guests . . . smash the windscreen of a car that dared to venture out on the day of an Opposition bandh. . . . Comrade K.N.M. Pillai's son, Lenin . . . in order to allay any fears his [Lenin's] clients might have about his political leanings, he had altered his name slightly. . . '*Oower, oower, oower*. In Amayrica now, isn't it.' It wasn't a question. It was sheer admiration. . . . It occurred to Comrade Pillai that this generation was perhaps paying for its forefather's bourgeois decadence. . . . Perhaps this was the real revolution. The Christian bourgeoisie had begun to self-destruct. . . . It was curious how politics lurked in what children chose to stuff up their noses.

The above is an exemplar that indicates the kind of narrative we can reasonably anticipate while intercepting the deep text (or the politics of everyday life?) of chapters 14 and 18. Roy's portrayal of Kerala's communist Weltanschauung would apparently convince us of the different networks of patron-client relationships and the civil society's humdrum and pretentious ideological moorings. Half-baked children of a revolution that never did happen due to a time lag (!) or otherwise in the unlikely wake of an imperfectly mobilized political socialization, we may even venture to add.

As against such an engaging backdrop, let us return to the 'mainstream' (academic) literatures to find out what do these have in store for our research. Nagi Reddy, himself a communist radical, has written about a custody death[6] during the 'benign rule of Achuta Menon, the Chief of Kerala Communist Party (Revisionist) . . . the Revisionist-led government, as all other governments of other states, condoned this savagery.'[7]

Nossiter has described Kerala as 'India's problem state' but, however, has also argued that 'Probably the most lasting contribution made by the communist movement in Kerala is its politicization and mobilization of the propertyless and underprivileged. The 1987-89 government in particular did much to liberate the poor and free the society from the tyranny of caste and communalism. . . . At the same time it must be conceded that the beneficiaries of communist rule have been the peasants (in part by design) not the labourers and (unintentionally) the government employees not the workers in the traditional cottage industry sector such as coir, whose condition has changed little since 1945.[8] Partha Chatterjee has pointed out:

> There are numerous instances in Indian history, recent and not so recent, of peasant communities acting autonomously against the formally organized state, that is, against its agents or functionaries. . . . The language of organized politics often characterizes such forms of mobilization as an alliance of various classes or strata within the peasantry, but ideologically the notion of the alliance is hardly ever relevant in collective actions of this kind; it is always the concept of the community as a collective whole, a form of authority incapable of being broken down into constituent parts, which shapes and directs peasant politics vis-a-vis the state. The perceptual distance of the state—the absence of organic links with the everyday world of peasant life—also provides the analytical ground for explaining the sudden and unanticipated swings in popular opinion about the *sarkar*. Indeed, it is precisely this perceptual distance which, when favourable structural conditions prevail in the organized world of struggle between sections of the ruling classes, creates room for the manipulative operations of

> populist politics and charismatic politicians. . . .
>
> But whatever the variations in the specific social constitution of a peasant community, and hence of the specific set of cultural symbols and beliefs surrounding the relations of the community with feudal or bureaucratic state authority, when a community acts collectively the fundamental political characteristics are the same everywhere. . . . It is *the nature of the linkage of peasant-communal politics of this kind with the structure of organized politics* which designates one movement as 'Gandhian,' the other 'terrorist' and still another 'communalist.'[9]

Chatterjee, therefore, apparently treats a given actor as being quite (corporate and) monolithic in its personality make-up. This is not to suggest, however, that the battle lines between this particular actor and the state apparatus are quite well-defined. There is almost nothing about this confrontational relationship that suggests any ideas in absolute terms.

But movements acquire their various ascriptive statuses, according to Chatterjee, by virtue of an inner dynamic of cohesion; this reminds us of the process of identity formation that is so very important in the context of organizing and mobilizing social movements.[10]

We find this 'perceptual distance' (as conceptually formulated by Partha Chatterjee) quite interesting as it tends to increasingly draw us to the inevitable conclusion that the Indian crowds before and at Independence were merely the 'other' that was not at all 'hospitably'[11] incorporated into the principal format of the elite-determined Indian national liberal movement or even the process of building up of the Indian State-nation.

This distance was real in terms of everyday politics and was perceived in the sense of being deprived, even marginalized from the momentous process of decision-making that eventually shaped the future of the Indian polity.

It is true that without a sense of identity, a popular movement cannot even begin properly, let alone the possibility of its sustaining itself in the future. Such an identity is like a reference point that decides the level of efficacy of any particular movement.

We would argue here that whenever the Indian 'crowds' tried to identify themselves with any issue or institution whatever, they were generally manipulated by their elite leaders and diversified into channels of an abhorrent *otherness*.[12]

Paul R. Brass also confirms Nossiter's findings, at least partially, and has observed that "When they [the landless low castes] attempt to mobilize for political agitations for higher wages against the landed castes, however, they generally meet strong resistance and their movements usually fail except in . . . Kerala . . . at times when the ruling Communist parties there support their demands."[13]

Namboodiripad was convinced that the ruling Left and Democratic Front was an arrangement of leftist, democratic, secular and federal political forces.[14] The nuances of Roy's text would so appear problematic in such a composite context that is almost like a chiaroscuro background structured both by academic as well as activist source materials. Such a reality happens to inform our present odyssey. However, we can revisit the text once more to read Chapter 14, 'Work is Struggle':

> *Struggle is Work* . . . a framed photograph of Comrade Pillai garlanding Comrade E.M.S. Namboodiripad. . . . A jeep with a loudspeaker drove past, blaring a Marxist Party song whose theme was Unemployment. . . . The more people that were seen waiting to meet him [Comrade Pillai], the busier he would appear, the better the impression he would make . . . his straitened circumstances . . . gave him a power over Chacko that in those revolutionary times no amount of Oxford education could match. He held his poverty like a gun to Chacko's head. . . . Questions signified a vulgar display of ignorance. . . . 'Until then, struggle must continue' . . . trying to speak in the same idiom . . . '*Party worker*' . . . sly, misguided collusion . . . 'these caste issues are very deep-rooted.' . . . It is a conditioning they [the Paravans] have from birth . . . for Masses it is

> something different . . . 'it is a shameful matter for them [the workers] not to be unionized and join the Party struggle.' . . . 'They must launch their *own* struggle.' . . . 'Revolution is not a dinner party' . . . he [Comrade Pillai] deftly banished Chacko from the fighting ranks . . . to the treacherous ranks. . . . Comic book adversaries in a still-to-come war . . . ('Caste is Class, comrades') . . . the People's War joined the racks of broken airplanes . . . 'Party was not constituted to support workers' indiscipline in their private life.'

Arundhati Roy has sustained a certain kind of sarcasm throughout her text, and this aspect of her craftsmanship characterizes this narrative's inner identity of imagination. Whenever she employs the term Comrade, either to ascribe EMS or Pillai and the like, what she actually intends is derision that is packaged in an idiom symptomatic of the politics of language.[15] Roy would also like us to think that Chacko 'believed' in politics while Pillai 'used' it; only then are we allowed to draw our own inferences regarding these characters, keeping in mind the different 'days and works' of men.

Roy's terms of discourse, therefore, may well clarify those analytical categories we need to appreciate in the final section of this paper. These categories may facilitate our rather open-ended examination of multiple histories[16] and plural times. Such a disquieting flux of possibilities has already reminded us of the complications of art (and its expressions) as noticed in either the surrealist or even the 'stream of consciousness'[17] schools.

The politics of knowledge, and the resultant empowerment in real terms, is yet another concern of this Chapter. This is, however, not often reflected in Kerala's achievement in education or literacy. Nossiter has found out: 'By 1981 the general literacy rate [including babies] was 70 per cent, almost exactly twice the all-India figure. Still more striking was the general female literacy rate of 66 per cent as compared to 25 per cent for India. Excluding those five years of age, the effective literacy rates become: 87 per cent for males; 76 per cent for females; and 81 per cent overall.'[18]

Nossiter, however, confirms Roy's perceptions regarding the problem of unemployment.[19] We are also reminded of the Marxian notion of false consciousness while reading about caste ascriptions in Roy.[20] The distant reference to 'a still-to-come war' is pretty unnerving as history and speculation get fused here in quite an intriguing manner. We would now finally examine Chapter 18:

> The toy histories that rich tourists came to play with. . . . A History hole . . . the Touchable future. . . . It was human history, masquerading as God's Purpose. . . . History in live performance . . . abandoned by God and History, by Marx.

Roy's rendition of history and the kind of historiography we find in non-literary sources are not *quite* mutually exclusive. Perhaps that is all that can be observed about the different episodic treatments of 'time' we are concerned with in this section of the paper. To illustrate: how best can we reconcile Manoranjan Mohanty's analysis[21] with the memories of Rahel as an insecure child belonging to a religious minority in Kerala?

A sense of disenchantment is perceived in Chapter 2, 'Pappachi's Moth,' that outlines the beginning and the end of an euphoria attending 'the first ever democratically elected communist government in the world.' (1957) We almost have the feeling of reading official history in the pages that follow in this chapter.

An additional item of information is also interesting: we read about a demand 'that Untouchables no longer be addressed by their caste names.' This trend continues even in Chapter 4, 'Abhilash Talkies,' where Roy writes about the Naxalites.[22] Some more interesting phrases are also noticed in Chapter 14: "History's waiting glove . . . his blind date with history . . . Spring thunder."[23]

So our analysis would occasionally lead us into a labyrinth of conflicting or even skewed ideas. It is as if we have been overwhelmed by 'a History hole,' a warmhole in time and space that is both unrelenting and inexorable in its personal odyssey, pursuing the vistas of an ulterior reality. Our initial assumption regarding a couple of quite different histories appears to get vindicated here. But this is not to suggest, however, that EMS's daughter was entirely justified in her ire provoked by Roy's novel.

So it can be concluded that the reality of historiography and the reality of textuality are different in nature and scope. Still, we can afford to intellectually cohabit and make peace with the notion of intermeshed realities in the following sense: realities or renditions of a particular reality! This sounds puzzling enough, but the problem may soon be resolved if the narratology of Roy's text is discerned exclusively via the central character of Rahel. As it is, Rahel is engaged in a journey back to her roots. Chapter 1, 'Paradise Pickles & Preserves' states that "It was raining when Rahel came back to Ayemenem." The inchoate mosaic of history and counterhistory, all the versions that can and cannot be reconciled within the little and the metanarratives can finally be ignored when both space and time drop into an insignificant nothingness.[24] So far we have been up against Roy's humour, passion and cynicism; but now she also 'looks back in anger' and desperate helplessness to write:

> A band of children followed Rahel on her walk . . . twenty-five years too late. . . . Then someone threw a small stone at her, and her childhood fled, flailing its thin arms.

We addressed the *problematique* of 'two' histories in this paper, and tried to explore the deep text of reality from within these different renderings. It is difficult to pinpoint any given account of 'facts' as the hegemonic version as perhaps each and every exercise in historiography is informed by the 'choice' of the writer. "This is indeed the problem of 'the permission to narrate' discussed by [Edward] Said (1984). . . . Within the effaced itinerary of the subaltern subject, the track of sexual difference is doubly effected. The question is not of female participation in insurgency, or the ground rules of the sexual division of labour, for both of which there is 'evidence.' It is, rather, that, both as object of colonialist historiography and as subject of insurgency, the ideological construction of gender keeps the male dominant. If, in the context of colonial production, the subaltern has no history and cannot speak, the subaltern as female is even more deeply in shadow."[25]

But we are finally presented with a readerly text in a postmodern[26] context where it is fashionable to assume that the 'author is dead,' and what is available is only the reader's interface with the text. So we have to necessarily analyze the inner narratives from within the text if we are to catch up anywhere near with reality that, however, has its own flux and logic.

NOTES

1. I am grateful to Dr. Deb Narayan Bandyopadhyay of Burdwan University and Professor Amitava Roy of Rabindra Bharati University, for enthusing and kindly assisting me in writing this paper.
2. The first communist Chief Minister of Kerala during 1957-59. See Bipan Chandra, ed., *The Indian Left: Critical Appraisals* (New Delhi: Vikas, 1983), in this connection.
3. Cf. Ashin Dasgupta, *Itihas Or Sahitya* (Calcutta: Ananda, 1984; in Bengali), for an exposition of the critical relationship between literature and history.
4. "Hegemonic texts are authoritative accounts of reality." See Subrata K. Mitra, "Crowds and Power: Democracy and the Crisis of 'Governability' in India," in Upendra Baxi and Bhikhu Parekh, ed., *Crisis and Change in Contemporary India* (New Delhi: Sage, 1995), p. 242.
5. Cf. Samuel P. Huntington, *Political Order in Changing Societies* (New Haven/ London: Yale University Press, 1968).
6. This reminds us of an almost parallel incident of police atrocity found in Chapter 18 of *The God of Small Things*, 'The History House.'

7. See Tarimela Nagi Reddy, *India Mortgaged: A Marxist-Leninist Appraisal* (Anantapuram: Tarimela Nagi Reddy Memorial Trust, 1978), p. 357.
8. See T.I. Nossiter, *Communism in Kerala: A Study in Political Adaptation* (Delhi: Oxford University Press, 1982), pp. 371-72.
9. See Chatterjee, 'Agrarian Relations and Communalism in Bengal, 1926-1935,' in Ranajit Guha, ed., *Subaltern Studies: Writings on South Asian History and Society* (Delhi: Oxford University Press, 1982), vol. 1, pp. 9-38 passim. Emphases in the original.
10. It has been analyzed "that successful attainment of state sovereignty in the third world has so far been the burial ground, the graveyard, of social movements. We use the term 'attainment of state sovereignty' in the sense of national acquisition of political independence. The acquisition of that independence in most of the third world has often resulted in a rapid shrinkage of the arena of social movements." See Ali A. Mazrui, "The Frankenstein State and Uneven Sovereignty," in D.L. Sheth and Ashis Nandy, ed., *The Multiverse of Democracy: Essays in Honour of Rajni Kothari* (New Delhi: Sage, 1996), p. 51.
11. The *other* and *hospitably* are terms of discourse inspired by Jacques Derrida's hospitality thesis. See Prasenjit Maiti, "On Derrida, Marx and 'Hospitality,'" *Socialist Perspective* (with Panchanan Chattopadhyay), vol. 25, no. 3-4 (December 1997-March 1998).
12. See Asis Kumar Basu, "A Study in Leadership of the Untouchables: Gandhiji and B.R. Ambedkar," *Socialist Perspective*, vol. 25, no. 1-2 (June-September 1997), pp. 41-51.
13. See Brass, *The Politics of India since Independence* (New Delhi: Foundation Books, 1992), p. 308. Also see T.K. Oommen, *Social Transformation in Rural India: Mobilization and State Intervention* (New Delhi: Vikas, 1984); and Atul Kohli, *The State and Poverty in India: The Politics of Reform* (Cambridge: Cambridge University Press, 1987).
14. See Namboodiripad's article to this effect in the Fall Number of *Deshhitoishi* (Calcutta: Ganashakti, 1997; in Bengali), p. 19.
15. Cf. Bernard S. Cohn, "The Command of Language and the Language of Command"; and Gayatri Chakravorty Spivak, "Subaltern Studies: Deconstructing Historiography," in Ranajit Guha.
16. See Shashi Tharoor, *India: From Midnight to the Millennium* (New Delhi: Penguin, 1998), for other insights into contemporary

Malayali history.

17. Prominent exponents include Virginia Woolf and James Joyce.
18. See Nossiter, *Marxist State Governments in India: Politics, Economics and Society* (London: Pinter, 1988), p. 57. Also see Jean Dreze and Mrinalini Saran, "Primary Education and Economic Development in China and India: Overview and Two Case Studies," in Kaushik Basu, Prasanta K. Pattanaik and Kotsro Suzumura, ed., *Choice, Welfare, and Development: A Festschrift in Honour of Amartya Sen* (1995; New Delhi: Oxford University Press, 1999); and Myron Weiner, ed., *State Politics in India* (Princeton, New Jersey: Princeton University Press, 1968).
19. See Nossiter, *Marxist State*, p. 8.
20. See Dipankar Gupta, ed., *Social Stratification* (Delhi: Oxford University Press, 1998), in this connection.
21. See Mohanty, "Ideology and Strategy of the Communist Movement in India," in Thomas Pantham and Kenneth L. Deutsch, ed., *Political Thought in Modern India* (New Delhi/ London: Sage, 1986), p. 256. Also see D.N. Dhanagare, *Peasant Movements in India, 1920-1950* (Delhi: Oxford University Press, 1986), and N. Krishnaji, "Agrarian Relations and The Left Movement in Kerala: A Note on Recent Trends," in A.R. Desai, ed., *Agrarian Struggles in India after Independence* (Delhi: Oxford University Press, 1986).
22. Cf. Mohanty. Also see Biplab Dasgupta, *The Naxalite Movement* (Bombay: Allied, 1975); and Sumanta Banerji, "Naxalbari," in A.R. Desai.
23. An euphemism for the Naxalbari movement.
24. Reminds of Samuel Beckett's *En attendant Godot* (1952).
25. See Spivak, "Can the Subaltern Speak?" in Bill Ashcroft, Gareth Griffiths and Helen Tiffin, ed., *The Post-Colonial Studies Reader* (London/ New York: Routledge, 1995), pp. 24-28 passim. Edward W. Said has written in *Orientalism* (New York: Random House, 1978): "Orientalism expresses and represents that part culturally and even ideologically as a mode of discourse with supporting institutions, vocabulary, scholarship, imagery, doctrines, even colonial bureaucracies and colonial styles. . . . Taking the late eighteenth century as a very roughly defined starting point Orientalism can be discussed and analyzed as the corporate institution for dealing with the Orient dealing with it by making statements

about it, authorizing views of it, describing it, by teaching it, settling it: in short, Orientalism as a western style for dominating, restructuring, and having authority over the Orient. I have found it useful here to employ Michel Foucault's notion of a discourse, as described by him in *The Archaeology of Knowledge and in Discipline and Punish*, to identify Orientalism. My contention is that without examining Orientalism as a discourse one cannot possibly understand the enormously systematic discipline by which European culture was able to manage—and even produce—the Orient politically, sociologically, and imaginatively during the post-Enlightenment period. Moreover, so authoritative a position did Orientalism have that I believe no one writing, thinking, or acting on the Orient could do so without taking account of the limitations on thought and action imposed by Orientalism. In brief, because of Orientalism the Orient was not (and is not) a free subject of thought or action. This is not to say that Orientalism unilaterally determines what can be said about the Orient, but that it is the whole network of interests inevitably brought to bear on (and therefore always involved in) any occasion when the peculiar entity 'the Orient' is in question. How this happens is what this book tries to demonstrate. It also tries to show that European culture gained in strength and identity by setting itself off against the Orient as a sort of surrogate and even underground self." This has been cited in Ashcroft et al, ed., pp. 87-89 passim. See Francis Fukuyama, for a related comparison "Asian Values and the Asian Crisis," *Commentary* (February 1998), as well as Amartya Sen, 'Our Culture, Their Culture,' *The New Republic*, 1 April 1996, p. 34.

26. "As far as the deconstructive position staked out by Jacques Derrida goes, however, I think assessment has fallen short. If I may speculate a bit, it seems entirely possible that Derrida's philosophical approach will be superseded without the philosophical world's taking enough of a critical view of his work. The reasons for this may have to do with the combination of the 'Heidegger affair,' the 'De Man affair,' and a general uneasiness about the political commitments (or lack thereof) of deconstruction. Or it may just be that something else new comes along that goes better with cappuccino." See Todd May, *Reconsidering Difference: Nancy, Derrida, Levinas, and Deleuze* (University Park, Pennsylvania: The Pennsylvania State University Press, 1997), ch. 2, p. 77.

Dreams Re-Dreamed: A Study of *The God of Small Things*

SURENDRA NARAYAN JHA

Whenever a mega production of art touches upon "Nature's holy plan" through exceptionally "plaintive numbers," a sweetly tuned human being is rather made to "stop here or gently pass."[1] Really this striking feature of Arundhati Roy's *The God of Small Things* immensely moves the mind and heart of the reader. The novel is a superb graphic picture of "human history, masquerading as God's Purpose, revealing herself to an under-age audience."[2] Still, the yarn of the thematic texture is remarkably "spun from the ungodly, human heart." (230) Besides, the mystery and magic of "the Great Story" of this novel records "things that had been out of bounds so far, obscured by history blinkers." (176) Of course, Roy greatly excels in creating a splendid dream world wherein "dreams are captured and re-dreamed." (306)

The narrative of *The God of Small Things* hinges on or around the Ayemenem House and at times peeps into the misty atmosphere of the History House to delicately explore "the Big Things lurked unsaid inside." (173) This is rather the pliable and complete track through which Roy significantly drives the main points home. For it features "the very worst sort of war, a war that captures dreams and re-dreams them." (53) Altogether, the novel reiterates how "it really began in the days when the Love Laws were made. The laws that lay down who should be loved, and how. And how much." (33) This manifests almost like the guiding motif of this novel.

On the whole Arundhati Roy's *The God of Small Things* is

a major breakthrough in Indian fiction in English. Especially in typical Indian setting, the depiction of an engaging tale of cross caste forbidden love between a Paravan boy and a Syrian Christian girl has been treated in a superb manner with the theme of love chiefly with a view to establishing the eternal state of love with respect to the present Indian social scenario. It has been suggested philosophically that "the truth of art lies in its power to break the monopoly of established reality . . . to define what is 'real.' In this rupture, which is the achievement of the aesthetic form, the fictitious world of art appears as true reality."[3] In fact, fiction is supposed to be such a suitable vehicle that can deliver the truth of, or the truth behind the world we live in. D.H. Lawrence asserts that the novel "can inform and lead into new places the flow of our sympathetic consciousness, and it can lead our sympathy away in recoil from things gone dead."[4] Indeed, the truth of art signifies its power to imaginatively inscribe hitherto unknown dimensions of reality. Therefore, Roy's certain technical innovations of modernism and the linguistic deviations are but the definite design to fathom the deeper meaning behind the superficial framework. Similarly, the very essence of *The God of Small Things* reads as follows: "Little events, ordinary things, smashed and reconstituted. Imbued with new meaning. Suddenly they become the bleached bones of a story." (32-33)

The God of Small Things focuses on one family—the Ipes—and employs a narrative that traces a generational progression. With respect to the genealogical table of the family, Arundhati Roy mainly concentrates on the three most recent generations, stressing upon the second and third. The central character, Ammu, belongs to the second generation. The dominant narrative voice is that of her daughter, Rahel. The narrative unravels through the eyes of seven-year-old Rahel, one of the twins of Ammu. The novel opens on a wet monsoon day in Kerala, with Rahel coming back from America to her childhood home at a remote village, to meet her two-egg twin brother, Estha, who, like her, has also re-returned to Ayemenem after an interval of twenty-three years. Her return actually sets off a flow of memories covering up their own childhood and the past and present of others too. Thus, we come to know that all the inmates of the Ayemenem House consider themselves the privileged descendants of Reverend E. John Ipe, a priest of the Mar Thoma Church and a celebrity in the Christian community for being blessed personally by the Patriarch of Antioch, the sovereign head of the Syrian Christian Church." (22) He was widely recognized as Punnyan Kunju—the "Little Blessed One." (23) We find a brief account of the marital life of John Ipe. The focus shifts to Baby Kochamma and Pappachi, the two out of the seven children of their parents. These two belong to the first generation and enjoy elaborate reference in the novel. The writer notes down the relationship between Father Mulligan and Baby Kochamma in the following words: "The young girl and the intrepid Jesuit, both quaking with unchristian passion. Using the Bible as a ruse to be with each other." (24) When Father Mulligan returns to Madras, she displays her stubborn single-mindedness in defying her father. She becomes a Roman Catholic and goes to Madras as a trainee and enters a convent hoping that she would spend as much time with Father Mulligan as she could. But, because of the superior nuns and heavy engagements of Father Mulligan, she is rather convinced that she could hardly succeed in her mission. However, this frustration of the young lady turns her all the more restless and love crazed. At this juncture, her father realized that his daughter by now developed a "reputation" and was unlikely to find a husband. He decided that since she couldn't get a husband, there was no harm in having an education. So he made arrangements for her to attend a course of study at the University of Rochester in America. (26) In spite of her education abroad and exposure both to native and American culture, Baby Kochamma grows more and more angry and resentful and peevish. Arundhati Roy has remarkably observed Baby Kochamma's anger and hate in the following words: "Baby Kochamma resented Ammu, because she saw her quarrelling with a fate that she, Baby Kochamma herself felt she had graciously accepted. The fate of the Wretched Man-less woman. The sad, Father Mulligan-less Baby Kochamma." (45)

A fine mesh-design of characters and incidents of the novel

further narrates the story of a high-ranking government official, Rev. Ipe's son Pappachi, the entomologist. Despite his long official stay in Delhi and a brief stint abroad, he remains all along an orthodox, jealous husband. There are many references in the novel enumerating his maniac capabilities and his methods of terrorizing his own family. He is a compulsive wife beater, thrashes his wife mercilessly either with a brass vase (50) or his "ivory handled riding crop." (181) Even though Mammachi suffers a lot of her husband's cruelty, she does not look repulsive against her husband. Rather she adapts herself "properly into the conventional scheme of things." (122) However, the author adds that Mammachi cries at her husband's funeral because "she was used to him, (not because) she loved him." (50) "With her eyes she looked in the direction that her husband looked. With her heart she looked away." (30) Mammachi's physical abuse is finally stopped by Chacko's superior physical might. One day "he twisted his father's hand" and said, "I never want this to happen again." (48) But, this incident hurts Pappachi's pride so deeply that he does not speak to her until his death. He has nothing to do with her pickle making. To him, her job is too low to tell upon the dignity and status of a respectable "high-ranking ex-Government official." (47) What irks him most is the sudden attention that Mammachi enjoys from her flourishing business: "He had always been a jealous man, so he greatly resented the attention his wife was getting." (47)

Chacko is "Mammachi's only son. . . . He devastated her." (65) He is the youngest male member in the Ayemenem House. During his undergraduate days in Delhi, he develops a taste for communism, what he carries wherever he goes. Still, he has a "Marxist mind and feudal libido." (168) His colonial obsession takes him to Oxford and then to the English girl, Margaret, whom he marries. Chacko's feudal libido had been active long before his marriage. For Margaret, Kochamma is not "just the first woman that he had slept with." (245) She satisfied Chacko's inherited Anglophilia for a brief period. The Oxford-educated Rhodes scholar Chacko is, in fact, discarded by his English wife for a "better man," Joe. His blue-eyed daughter,

Sophie Mol, informs him that "even though he was her Real father, she loves him less than Joe." (189) The little girl insists "Joe's my dad." Adult Chacko becomes the saviour of Mammachi and the owner of the pickle factory established by her. But, he soon joins the team of exploiters. So, he registers the venture into a "partnership" and his mother is informed that she is the "sleeping partner." (57) Chacko displays abundant love for his fair-skinned blue-eyed daughter. While his feelings for his own niece and nephew, two-egg twins, Rahel and Estha, are well within the limits of discipline and formality. He treats them as have-nots and thinks that they should be grateful for the small mercies.

Pappachi's treatment of his daughter highlights how intensely his brutish violence has affected Ammu's psyche. Daughter of a Syrian Christian family, she is compelled to have an early taste of male chauvinist brutality and hypocrisy through her own father. (180-82) Ammu is forced to drop her education the year her father retires. He believes that a college education is "an unnecessary expense for a girl." (38) Pappachi and Mammachi look quite unconcerned, rather the most casual, with respect to Ammu's marriage. "Her eighteenth birthday came and went. Unnoticed, or at least unremarked upon by her parents." (38) Being so terror-stricken with this "cold, calculating cruelty," Ammu evolves "a lofty sense of injustice and the mulish, reckless streak that develops in Someone Small who has been bullied all their lives by Someone Big." (181-82) At Ayemenem, she felt like a captive lady but to assist her mother in relation to household chores. She gradually begins to grow desperate. Roy notes:

> All day she dreamed of escaping from Ayemenem and the clutches of her ill-tempered father and bitter, long-suffering mother. She hatched several wretched little plans. Eventually, one worked. Pappachi agreed to let her spend the summer with a distant aunt who lived in Calcutta. (38-39)

It is there that Ammu accepted the proposal of a man whom she had known so little and for such a short time simply because, in a fit of desperation, "she thought that anything, anyone at all, would be better than returning to Ayemenem." (39) But she soon discovered in her husband a full blown alcoholic and an outrageous liar. (40) The fellow scarcely hesitates to barter even his wife in order to safeguard his job. Ammu had no alternative but to divorce him and come back with her twins, Estha and Rahel, "to her parents in Ayemenem. To everything that she had fled from only a few years ago. Except that she had two young children. And no more dreams." (43) Her reception was awfully cold. Her father did not believe that an Englishman, any Englishman, would covet "another man's wife." (42) While, her mother, Mammachi, thought "what her grandchildren suffered from was far worse than Inbreeding. She meant having parents who were divorced." (61) Moreover, the society treats her as a juicy topic. All these so conditioned her that "Ammu quickly learned to recognize and despise the ugly face of sympathy." (43) At this stage when she sensed that she was "already damned," she became an "unmixable mix" combining the "infinite tenderness" of motherhood and the reckless rage of a "suicide bomber." (44) Further, Ammu knew that she enjoyed no "Locusts Stand I" in her parents's house even. Thus, at the age of twenty-four, she was rather made to realize painfully that "Life had been lived" since she had spoiled her "only one chance" by making the irrevocable mistake of choosing the wrong man. Then, she was virtually an "untouchable" in her family and the society as well.

At this point, Velutha, the son of Vellya Pappen—a low caste Paravan—returned to Ayemenem after his years away from his native place. He was a talented young man, "an accomplished carpenter" and later developed "a distinctly German design sensibility." (75) His fiery spirit of protest, which she herself wanted to articulate but could not, forcibly drew her towards him, "she hoped that under his careful cloak of cheerfulness, he housed a living, breathing anger against the smug, ordered world that she so raged against." (176) He is "the God of Small Things" who emanates from the pitch-black wave of a dark sea in her dream. She felt herself "drawn towards him like a plant in dark room towards a wedge of light." (248) On the basis of this discovery, they were longing to offer gifts to each other. Being the representatives of the oppressed and the marginalised, both tried to seek solace in each other's warmth. Thus, they longed and ached for each other with the whole of their biology. Whenever "a liquid ache spread under her skin," (44) Ammu stepped out like a witch to a better, happier place, "It was this that grew inside her, and eventually led her to love by night the man her children loved by day." (44) Though being convinced that they have no future in a society deliberately hostile to individuals who violate its "Love Laws" and enter into forbidden territory, they remain sticking to small things, small but unaccountably valuable pleasure. Thus, they continued their fragile, transient happiness for thirteen nights with their firm belief that "things could change in a day." (339)

As their nightly trysts are disclosed by Velutha's father, all hell breaks loose heavily on the lovers. The price that the lovers paid is decidedly high: "Two lives. Two children's childhood. And a history lesson for future offenders." (336) Subsequently, Velutha becomes an easy victim of "the boundless, infinitely inventive art of human hatred." (266) It is the "Man's subliminal urge to destroy what he could neither subdue nor deify" (308) that really caused his death in the police lock-up of the Kottayam Police Station. Since the accidental death of their English cousin, Sophie Mol, made Estha and Rahel take refuge at the back of the History House, they also watched, in fact, "a clinical demonstration . . . a human nature's pursuit of ascendancy. Structure, order, complete monopoly." (309) While Ammu was separated from her twins and at the age of thirty-one she breathed her last all alone in a grimy room in the Bharat Lodge in Alleppey, (161) haunted only by her familiar fears. Further, the Church also refused to bury Ammu on several counts. As a result, Chacko and Rahel carried her dead body to the electric crematorium where "the whole of her crammed into a little clay pot, Receipt No. Q498673." (163)

The lovers's punishment further engineered the separation of the two-egg twins too. Thus, Estha was returned to his father residing in Calcutta. Theirs is quite a different sort of childhood.

Roy affirms: "While other children of their age learned other things, Estha and Rahel learned how history negotiates its terms and collects its dues from those who break its laws. They heard its sickening thud. They smelled its smell and never forgot." (55) They always remind themselves that "Worse Things had happened. That Worse Things kept happening." (55) All these wrecking elements of childhood experiences ruin Estha's life completely. Due to sexual abuse by "the Lemondrink Man" (101) in the Abhilash Talkies, he gradually lapses into silence from partial to total. He starts living "with sea secrets in him." (13) However, his sister, Rahel, anyhow manages to salvage something from nothing. Rahel grows up into a young woman. Being an educated and modern girl, she violently protests to accept the fate of her mother and grandmother. Having a greater confidence and a clearer perception of life, Rahel acknowledges the marriage as a brief arrangement for the fulfillment of one's self. Hence, "Rahel, dark woman in a yellow T-shirt, turns to Estha in the dark" (327) in order to enjoy the game of incest, the very terrifying practices which usually bring about the destruction of mankind. Naturally, the twins "once again broke the Love Laws." (327) Therefore, Roy observes: "Perhaps, Ammu, Estha and she were the worst transgressors." (31)

Then, though bearing somewhat a short reference, there follows the account of one of the most instrumental characters, Comrade K.N.M. Pillai, the self-proclaimed Marxist leader of the workers. Quite unseemingly to his Maoist slogans—"Annihilation of the Class Enemy," "Caste is Class," (287, 281) he showed the least concern with Velutha against their common class enemy, Chacko. It is his hypocritical approach that makes him denounce "Chacko-the-management," while he willingly allures "Chacko-the-client" at his printing press. (275) His are rather new revolutionary ideas of social change: "Change is one thing. Acceptance is another." (279) It is he who helps Baby Kochamma with respect to the forged F.I.R. lodged by her at the Kottayam Police Station to intentionally feed his evil political impulses. For, Velutha's removal would certainly ascertain for him the electoral votes of the workers of the pickle factory and, thereby, ensure him a seat in the Legislative Assembly.

Lastly, it is Inspector Thomas Mathew, the decisive element that ruthlessly says, "It is a little too late for all this." (7) Similarly, he insists: "the Kottayam Police didn't take statements from Veshyas or their illegitimate children." (8) Indeed, the officer, through his brute manners, represents the society's treatment of a woman who dares to love outside the rules of "Love Laws." Undoubtedly, he is portrayed as one of the "history's henchmen, sent to square the books and collect the dues from those who broke its laws." (308) Roy says:

> I have to say that my book is not about history but biology and transgression. And, therefore, the fact is that you never understand the nature of brutality until you see what has been loved being smashed. And so the book deals with both things—it deals with our reality to be brutal as well as our ability to be so deeply intimate and so deeply loving.[5]

Altogether, the novel makes some poignant references of typical setting and striking images. Thus, Roy depicts the Ayemenem House as a unique house "but aloof-looking. As though it had little to do with the people that lived in it." (165) This reveals the writer's sole intention to adequately examine how the power of money operates in the House and in the pickle factory and how far it was responsible for the family's downfall in recent years. Pappachi's Skyblue Plymouth bears the token of his revenge on everyone. In similar spirit, the History House symbolises the Heart of Darkness that truly suggests the recent history of exploitation, violence and strife. The English occupant of the house committed suicide "when his young lover's parents had taken the boy away from him and sent him to school." (51) In fact, this house has been recorded as a symbol of India's current communal divisions and conflicts, what is very much reflected in the Anglophilic heritage of the Ipe family. Again, the recurring motifs in the novel are those of the "rose" and the "river."

When Estha and Rahel noticed Velutha smashed and broken, they sensed: "It smells though, Sicksweet. Like old roses on a breeze." (310) It looks like the symbol of guilt, fear and terrible grief. It is the deathly smell that forces Estha "steeped in the smell of old roses," (12) stopped talking "altogether." (10) It also monitors Rahel's drifting in an entirely indifferent world, whereas the river stands for the unexpressed emotional sensibilities of the human world. So, when Ammu left Velutha to cross the river "she had a dry rose in her hair." (338) No doubt, the "river" and the "rose" elaborately outline the fragile world of "their Love, their Madness, their Hope, their Infinite Joy." (339) Besides, we have many other images and numerous references to Christian and Hindu myths and rituals that obviously exemplify the sordid affairs regarding the human relationships of various nature. The symbolic suggestiveness of the images used openly paints a social scenario that propels the ideal and the real intermingle to rear a world wherein "The God of Small Things" often appears "the God of Loss." John Updike, in his famous review of the book, which he termed as "a Tiger Woodsian debut" has elaborate explanation for his fellow readers: "Roy manages to catch, in the skein of the Ipe's haunted history, a sense of India's deep past, the mingling of dark inhabitants and light invaders going back to the Aryan authors of the Vedas, the roads of Hinduism, she brings us, in her ecstatically written last pages, into the heart of human love and the mythic past: Krishna as it were, couples with Radha on the riverbank, and when the lover makes the beloved dance, it is the dance of kali, of death and coming destruction."[6]

The God of Small Things is immensely replete with the vivid descriptions of the sexual act. However, it barely dips low to touch the level of vulgar writing. To her, the act of sex is "not a furtive reality that is difficult to grasp but a great surface network in which the stimulation of bodies"[7] and the ecstatic pleasures serve the purpose of self-exploration. She never considers sex as a hush-hush matter. On the contrary, all her references to sex in the novel seem to be the most suitable device to probe: "Everything that might concern the interplay of innumerable pleasures, sensations and thoughts which through the body and the soul had some affinity with sex."[8] Thus, Ammu and Velutha continue their amorous game of good sex. "Even later, on the thirteen nights that followed this one, instinctively they stuck to Small Things. The Big Things ever lurked inside. They knew that there was nowhere for them to go. They had nothing. No future. So they stuck to the small things." (338) Moreover, the virus of incest is projected almost genetically coded in the case of Pappachi's profession. He was a celebrated Imperial Entomologist who spotted a rare moth. Of course, the genetic moth embodies the Insect of Incest. This is the driving force that Estha and Rahel, the two-egg twins, "had never been shy of each other's bodies, but they had never been old enough (together) to know what shyness was. . . . Rahel searched her brother's nakedness for sign of herself. In the shape of his knees. . . . Rahel watched Estha with the curiosity of a mother watching her wet child. A sister a brother. A woman a man. A twin a twin." (92-93) Indeed, Rahel and Estha's relationship bears the foreshadowing semblance in the apparent incestuous love of Mammachi for her only son, Chacko: "Mammchi packed her wifely luggage and committed it to Chacko's care. From then onwards he became the repository of all her womanly feelings. Her Man. Her only Love." (168) A renowned French anthropologist, Claude Levi-Strauss, affirms that the incest taboo is the most primitive and universal taboo. He argues that its imposition duly regulates the transformation of a state of nature into a state of culture: "The prime role of culture is to ensure the group's existence as a group, and consequently, in this domain as in all others, to replace chance by organisation. The prohibition of incest is a certain form . . . of intervention over and above anything else; even more exactly, it is the intervention."[9] This sort of distinction between nature and culture clearly indicates that the significance of incest taboo is its regulatory status; that modifies it almost synonymous with culture. Though Rahel and Estha look all out to break a law which is culturally so deep-rooted, their act delicately justifies that they have definiteiy been hurt to the core of their beings. That is why Arundhati Roy's *The God of Small Things* is marked as "one of our protest novels, radical and subversive and attacks several holy cows. In its taboo-breaking too, it goes farther than what has been attempted."[10] So, Roy emphatically notes down: "They had known each other before Life began. There is very little that anyone could say to clarify what happened next. Nothing that [in Mammachi's book] would separate Sex from Love or Needs from Feelings." (327-328) It further grows so powerful "that for them there was no Each, no Other." (225)

All these whats of the novel indeed enthuse one of finer sensibilities so intensely that he can scarcely help but be swayed into the realm of corresponding whys—the very area of my study. It is exactly the overpowering, all-pervading dream world that wholly monitors, operates and governs the entire activities of worldly life and *The God of Small Things* as well. Roy is convinced "that the whole of contemporary history, the World Wars, the war of Dreams, the Man on the Moon, science, literature, philosophy, the pursuit of Knowledge—was no more than a blink of the earth. Woman's Eye." (54) Of course, this element of dream ipso facto proves to be the primum mobile that artistically fashions all the intricacies and subtleties of *The God of Small Things* which abounds in "big dreams and little ones . . . an Old Bihari Coolie . . . used to say of dreams." (89) Thus, Chacko believes: "Our dreams have been doctored." (53) The central character of the novel, Ammu, also launches her tumultuous life history purely in accordance with her fond dreams: "All day she dreamed of escaping from Ayemenem." (39) But, she soon returns to her parents's house with "no more dreams." (42) In similar psychological state of mind she finds "something restless and untamed about her. As though she had temporarily set aside the morality of motherhood and divorcehood." (44) Later, she grows so preoccupied with her dreams that "that afternoon, Ammu travelled upwards through a dream in which a cheerful man with one arm held her close by the light of an oil lamp." (215) Further "Ammu, resting under the skin of her dream observed, ached, with her love for them." (218) Rather, she stresses, "It wasn't a mare. . . . It was a dream." (218) It is through her dreams alone, Ammu "sensed that a pact had been forged between her Dream and the World. And that the midwives of that pact, were, would be, her sawdust coated two-egg twins." (220) Similarly, "After that, for four years Rahel would dream this dream: a fat man, faceless, kneeling beside a woman's corpse. Hacking its hair off. Breaking every bone in its body." (225) With a view to justifying and voicing its wide ranging appeal, Roy earnestly goes on telling "Foreign Returnees would be trapped outside the History House, and have their dreams redreamed." (149) Taking it almost as the throbbing content of the go of worldly life, the novelist clearly states: "It is after all so easy to shatter a story. To break a chain of thought. To ruin a fragment of dream being carried around carefully like a piece of porcelain." (190) Surely all these elaborately furnish the writer's "attempt to instil order into a world gone wrong" (260) so that even a commoner may be capable enough of rendering "the unthinkable thinkable and the impossible really happen." (256)

No doubt, Roy expresses: "When you recreate the image of man, why repeat God's mistake." (301) Still, the whole skin of the narrative employed in Arundhati Roy's *The God of Small Things* remarkably accommodates its sublime deeper thought only when it traverses through the fanciful realm of dreams of all the major characters. Had there been no dreaming and redreaming in the novel, the tragic tale of love between Ammu and Velutha might have appeared merely the sinful act of flesh trafficking and signifying nothing particularly in the literary sense. As a matter of fact, it superbly entails upon the individual's cherished vision of life or life wish which greatly moulds his or her life history and also promotes profound human feel. It also looks like the writer's own commanding earnestness that compels Arundhati Roy to admit: "I will write a book because I have a book to write, not otherwise."[11] Again, she observes: "If you are looking for me, you'll find me in there. For better or for worse."[12] Above all, it invariably suffices the writer to strike a unique rhythm divine melodiously tuning the eternal state of love that magnificently signals foolproof panacea for all the ills of worldly life with "the sweet smell of authenticity, tranquillity and triumph"[13] that "fulfills the highest demand of the art of fiction."[14]

NOTES

1. Quotes from the poems of William Wordsworth.
2. Arundhati Roy, *The God of Small Things* (New Delhi: IndlaInk, 1997), p. 309.
3. Collin Falck, *Myth, Truth and Literature, Towards a True Post-Modernism* (Cambridge: Cambridge University Press, 1989), p. 113.
4. *Ibid.*, p. 114.
5. "For me language is a skin of my thought," *The Week*, 26 Oct., 1997, p. 46.
6. Madhusudan Mukherjee, "Why *The God of Small Things* Sells," qtd. *Arundhati Roy, The Novelist Extraordinary*, ed. R.K. Dhawan (New Delhi: Prestige, 1999), p. 28.
7. Michel Foucault, *The History of Sexuality* (Harmondsworth, 1984), p. 106.
8. *Ibid.*, p. 20.
9. Claude Levi-Strauss, *The Elementary Structure of Kinship*, qtd. Kaja Silverman, *The Subject of Semiotics* (New York, Oxford: Oxford University Press, 1983), p. 179.
10. Ranga Rao, "Booker of the Year," *The Hindu*, Sunday, Nov. 23, 1997.
11. Arundhati Roy in Interview with Sheila Maharani, *The Times of India*, Oct. 25, 1997, p. 15.
12. "I had two options—writing or madness," Arundhati Roy interviewed by Urvashi Butalia, *Outlook*, April 9, 1997, p. 75.
13. Binoo K. John, "The New Deity of Prose," *India Today*, Oct. 27, 1997, p. 23.
14. Jason Cowley, "Why We Chose Arundhati," *Ibid.*, p. 28.

The Small God Made Big: Arundhati Roy's *The God of Small Things*

K.M. PANDEY

Arundhati Roy's *The God of Small Things*[1] is a polysemic novel, which can be interpreted at several levels. It may be said that the novel is a satire on politics attacking specifically the communist establishment. It may be tested as a family saga narrating the story of four generations of a Christian family. It may also be treated as a novel having religious overtones. One may also call it a protest novel which is subversive and taboo-breaking. It may also be treated as a love story with a tragic end. The novel gives good dividends if studied from the viewpoint of childhood experience. In terms of stylistic experimentation it is the boldest novel of the nineties as *The Midnight's Children* was of the eighties.

The present paper aims at studying the novel as a love story whose dimensions are touched by caste, creed and other socio-political realities existing in the regionally contextualised boundaries of the south Indian state of Kerala. It is the story of two Christians Ammu and Velutha. Ammu is a divorcee having two small children Estha and Rahel; Velutha is an untouchable working in the Paradise Pickles factory belonging to Ammu's parents.

Typical themes in Indian English fiction are said to be "the caste system, social attitude, social and religious taboos, superstitions, notions of superiority and inferiority."[2] *The God of Small Things* deals with most of the mentioned themes along with the most elemental of human emotion i.e. love. It is true the story of love is never complete; recounted many times, it has never been told to the end[3] because it has been as Melville says, "the endless flowing river in the cave of men."[4]

To make the running of society smooth, all societies make their own rules. Hinduism in India developed the *Varna* system based on the nature of work people did. But in due course of time it was overtaken by the caste system based on birth and this resulted in several kinds of disparities. The *Bhakti* cult of 16th century, the Indian Renaissance of the 19th century and the freedom movement of the country did much to eliminate this evil from the society but it has not been completely eradicated. A number of Indian English novelists have paid attention to this theme. Mulk Raj Anand selected his heroes from the downtrodden people in novels like *Untouchable* (1935) and *Coolie* (1936). S. Menon Marath's *The Wound of Spring* (1961) depicts the affair of an upper caste Hindu boy Unni and an untouchable girl Cheethu resulting in the tragic retribution inflicted on them. In Roy's novel the untouchable lover is killed by the touchable police and the beloved dies from the shock.

The hero's name is Velutha which in Malayalam means "white." He is a carpenter who can create wonderful things with perfect craftsmanship. He is introduced in the very first chapter when he is shown sitting on a plank "bare bodied and shining." (6) The expression immediately suggests that he is an untouchable though his colour is not black. Two pages later, Ammu while coming back from the police station mutters "He's dead and whispers 'I've killed him.'" (8) This arouses the reader's curiosity in the relationship of Ammu with Velutha, which is unfolded in the coming pages of the novel which oscillates between past and present.

The second chapter shows Velutha as an activist of the Travancore-Cochin Marxist Labour Union which has three demands—an hour's lunch break in between a non-stop eleven and a half hour's work, increase in the labourer's wages and the removal of caste names showing the labourer's untouchability. It is here for the first time that we have an overt reference to the untouchables who do not want "to be addressed as Achoo Paravan, or Kelan Paravan, or Kuttan Pulayan, but just as Achoo, or Kelan, or Kuttar." (69) The untouchables cannot enter the house of the touchables. Living together in close proximity with each other, there is hardly any worthwhile human interaction between them:

> As a youngman, Velutha would come with Velya Paapen to the back entrance of the Ayemenem house to deliver the coconuts they had picked from the trees in the compound. Pappachi would not allow Paravans in the house. Nobody would. They were not allowed to touch anything that Touchables touched. Caste Hindus and Caste Christians. (73)

Mammachi, Rahel's grandmother, remembers that in her childhood the position of untouchables was still worse. They "were expected to crawl backwards with a broom, sweeping away their footprints so that Brahmins or Syrian Christians would not defile themselves by accidentally stepping into a Paravan's footprint." (73-74)

To save themselves from this humiliation they converted to Christianity but this did not bring any change in their social life. The new religion which claimed to be casteless and free from unjust hierarchy, did not do justice to them. "They were known as the Rice Christians. It did not take them long to realize that they had jumped from the frying pan into the fire. They were made to have separate churches, with separate services, and priests." (74) Thus they were doubly cheated: they were torn between two worlds—one rejected by them and the other not ready to accept them. Even the Independence of the country went against them as they were not entitled to enjoy any government benefits like job reservations or bank loans at low interests. The caste consciousness continues in the Christians converted from the upper caste Hindus. Thus "Kochu Maria could not stop wearing her kunukku because if she did, how would people know that despite her low cook's job (seventy five rupees a month) she was a Syrian Christian, Mar Thomite? Not a Pelaya or a Pulaya, or a Paravan." (170)

It is Mammachi who recognises Velutha's "remarkable facility with his hands." He is like a magician who can make intricate toys—tiny windmills, rattles, and minute jewel boxes out of dried palm reeds. After being trained by Johann Klein, a carpenter from a carpenter's guild in Bavari, he attains "a distinctly German design sensibility." (75) He has also a way with machines. According to Mammachi, he might have become an engineer, had he not been a Paravan.

Velutha is a new generation Paravan and has a "lack of hesitation," "an unwarranted assurance" which begets fear in his father Velya Paapen, an old world Paravan who had seen the "Crawling Backward Days." (76) His fear is well represented by the novelist:

> Velya Pappen feared for his younger son. He couldn't say what it was that frightened him. It was nothing that he had said. Or done. It was not *what* he said but the *way* he said it. Not *what* he did, but the *way* he did it. (76)

Out of his love and concern for his son, Velya Paapen continuously cautions him to mend his *ways* which results in a general air of unpleasantness between the father and the son. And one day he disappears and does not come back for four years, The rumour was that he was working on a building site for the Department of Welfare and Housing in Trivandrum. Another rumour was that he had become a Naxalite.

When he comes back, he is hired by Mammachi as the factory carpenter and in charge of general maintenance. It causes much resentment among the touchable workers who claim that Paravans were not meant to be carpenters. To appease them Mammachi pays Velutha less than she would pay a touchable carpenter.

Ammu comes from a poor family. Since her father does not have enough money to raise a suitable dowry, no proposals come for Ammu. However, she gets a husband who works on a tea plantation in Assam. She somehow adjusts with her drunkard husband and gives birth to the twins Rahel and Estha. When her husband wants to exchange her honour for a handful of rupees from the English manger of the tea plantation Mr. Hollick, she leaves her husband and comes back unwelcome to her parents in Ayemenem, "To everything that she had fled from only a few years ago. Except that now she had two young children. And no more dreams." (42) She is a woman torn between different roles At one moment she calls her children the millstones because of whom she has to suffer agonizing loneliness.

Living in Ayemenem with her twins, she sees her daughter Rahel playing with Velutha and sharing the innocent joy of his company. She too longs for his company. The four eyes meet and they enter the love knot immediately:

> Ammu saw that he saw. She looked away. He did too. History's fiends returned to claim them. To rewrap them in its old, scarred pelt and dragged them back to where they really lived. Where the Love Laws lay down who should be loved. And how. And how much. (177)

The physical attraction leading to physical union symbolises the victory of love over the power of law and the lovers start meeting in the dark. Ranga Rao rightly says: "In Ammu the novelist has presented with compassion, a woman, a feminist locked in a struggle with her family, its 'hidden morality,' with society and tragically with herself."[5] One day Velya Pappen sees them and is "torn between Loyalty and Love." (255) Loyalty ensuing from fear wins over love and he tells Mammachi what he had seen: "The story of the little boat that crossed the river night after night, and who was in it. The story of a man and woman, standing together in the moonlight. Skin to skin." (255)

It is ironic that the love affair between Velutha and Ammu is disclosed by Velutha's own father who is terror stricken to see "what his untouchable son had touched. More than touched." (78) The only thing he can do is to rush to the Ayemenem House and inform Mammachi about it. She wonders how her granddaughter could stand the particular smell a Paravan has. She immediately contrasts it with the Irish-Jesuit smell she had experienced in the company of Father Mulligan, an Irish monk whom she wanted to marry but could not.

The revelation of the affair makes the power of the law active and it does not take long to have its revenge over love. Baby Kochamma calls Velutha and dismisses him from the service. He does not know that his affair with Ammu has been disclosed by his father. He maintains his restraint and composure throughout the time Mammachi abuses him. She says she'll have him castrated like a pariah dog. He quietly responds that he would see about that and leaves the place. She rushes to the police station to explain why Velutha has been dismissed and adds that Velutha had given threats of murder and abduction.

Being a party cardholder, Velutha goes to Comrade Pillai's house to explain his position and get his support but he refuses to help him saying: "It's not in the Party's interests to take up such matters. Individual's interest is subordinate to the Organization's interests. Violating Party Discipline means violating Party Unity." (287) Pillai knows that his refusal to help Velutha would result in the latter's death yet he wants this to happen because of his thinking on the caste line. When Velutha dies, he uses this opportunity to take over the Paradise Pickles factory by insinuating the party workers against Baby Kochamma and Chacko. Thus the communism which claimed to be the substitute of religion fails in the case of Velutha. The novelist aptly makes the comment: "And there it was again. Another religion turned against itself. Another edifice constructed by the human mind, decimated by human nature." (287)

Sophie Mol, Ammu's niece, dies from drowning the same night and the simple case of accident is fabricated into a brutal murder done by Velutha. The police standing for Politeness, Obedience, Loyalty, Intelligence, Courtesy and Efficiency go to Velutha's house and he is awakened by the thud of boots. He is brutally beaten unto death and his dead body is duped in the pauper's pit marking the tragic end of the life of the untouchable lover. The clinically perfect details of the inner injury show Roy's capacity to give such minute heart touching details. Ammu, too, soon dies out of the shock received by her. She dies alone in a grimy room in a lodge where she goes in search of a job. At the time of death she is "thirty-one. Not old, not young, but a viable-die-able age." (161) It is ironic that the church refuses to bury her "on several counts," (162) so Chacko has to hire a van to transport the dead body to the electric crematorium.

That the Ammu-Velutha relationship is not going to be a lasting one is already suggested by the dream Ammu sees. She sees a cheerful man with one arm holding her close by the light of an oil lamp. He has no other arm with which to fight the shadows that flicker around him on the floor. "If he touched her, he couldn't talk to her, if he loved her, he couldn't leave, if he spoke he couldn't listen, if he fought, he couldn't win." (215) Obviously, he is this God of Loss, the God of Small Things whose relationship with Ammu is bound to be broken. And this is what happens eventually.

Thus the novel is a love story with a tragic denouement. In such stories love is always portrayed as the passionate longing of the soul of lover for the beloved which culminates in the physical union. More often than not, it challenges the social order and "challenging the keepers of the social order and guardians of its taboos, we tremble at the punishment fitting the crime, emasculation, or more generally a pervasive unsexing."[6] In fact, there is no such thing as 'love without fear.' Naturally, tales of love are bound to be tales of terror and torment, and herein lies the most elemental of love's paradoxes—the core of love's exhilaration and terror.

The God of Small Things observes this dialectical cosmology of suffering and sublimity. In fact, in every culture, love is presented as an emotion of subversion and conventions are always challenged by love. If Romeo end Juliet meet their tragic end, it is the family authority which is responsible for it. Laila and Majnu, Sohini and Mahiwal, Heer and Ranjha—all die for just one cause—longing lingering desire that refuses to follow man-made boundaries. In all these cases, love can be interpreted as madness which leads to the ultimate destruction of the lovers but it also provides them the reward—"the promise of the immortality attained in becoming ensconced in the pantheon of love's legendary goddesses."[7]

It is also worth remembering that Ammu is a Malayali woman and Malayalis are the only society in India where matriarchy prevails. But the women of even such communities adopt different standards for men and women giving priority to the former. Thus Baby Kochamma's hypocrisy is exposed as she takes proper care of fulfilling her son Chacko's "Man's Needs" by secretly allowing lowly women to enter his room and the same woman condemns her daughter for her affair with Velutha.

Thus the Ammu-Velutha relationship is portrayed as a protest against the existing laws of society. It attacks the institutions of family, religion, politics and public administration but in doing so it touches the bounds of sentimentality oscillating between a personal tragedy and an archetypal symbol.

NOTES

1. Arundhati Roy, *The God of Small Things* (Delhi: IndiaInk, 1997).
2. Braj B. Kachru, *The Indianization of English: The English Language in India* (Delhi: OUP, 1983), p. 87.
3. Sudhir Kakar and John M. Ross, *Tales of Love, Sex and Danger* (1986; Delhi: OUP, 1992), p. 237.
4. Qtd. Kakar and Ross.
5. *The Hindu*, Sept. 23, 1997.
6. Sudhir Kakar and John M. Ross, p. 5.
7. *Ibid.*, p. 63.

Arundhati Roy's *The God of Small Things*: A Study in Feminine Sensibility and Aspects of Style

PRATIBHA VERMA

In *The God of Small Things*, there is substantial exploration of female experience, yet there is a wider view of society as other ideas have been combined with this essential theme. Much in the novel has a bearing on how female characters live their lives and their relationships with men who mostly control them. It is observed that they are repressed; denied basic amenities that naturally fall to the lot of men. This unequal relationship has been characterized as patriarchy: "a system of social structures, and practices in which men dominate, oppress and exploit women."[1]

Roy has a strong social concern like Drabble. Having an enduring passion for equality and fairness she is insistent on what she sees. There is scrupulous accuracy for her analysis of ordinary experiences. Ammu, the female protagonist is uncared for. Her education is neglected; it finishes after school though Chacko, her brother, is educated in Oxford. When money is not enough, her mother Mammachi secretly pawns her jewellery to send him. Her ill-tempered father, Pappachi, in bouts of anger, snips off her gum boots and beats his wife with a brass vase. Needless to say, they suffer meekly. Since no dowry is arranged for Ammu, she rushes into marriage. Her maternity, full of vitality, is ignored by her parents. When her husband coerces her to stay with his English boss during his absence, she returns to Ayemenem to her parents with her twins, a boy named Estha, and a girl, Rahel. As a divorcee, she is shattered; her life finished at 27. The problem is to choose between the name of her father and husband. Unwelcome in Ayemenem, she ridicules the self-deception and folly of Chacko in regarding himself as brilliant, and breaking the myth of mothers like Mammachi who believe in the cleverness of their sons. Alienated, her distress is diverted to her children, "You're the millstones round my neck." (291) She wants to hurt them for their helpful nature. Though taut in nurturing and domestic roles, it also confers peace. Baby Kochamma, her aunt, hates her for, in her view, there is no place for a woman in her parents's home after marriage. Ammu desires to leave her maternal home, take up a job and stay with her kids. In the preparation of an interview for it, she dies alone in Bharat Lodge in Alleppey. The church refuses to bury her. Wrapped in a dirty bedsheet she is disposed off in the electric crematorium, witnessed only by Chacko and Rahel.

Even Ammu's children are not spared from discrimination against their cousin, Sophie. In their trip to the airport to receive her and her English mother, Margaret boils water for them while the twins have to be content with tap water. In the pickle factory, the workers ceremoniously honour Margaret and Sophie while the twins are ignored. Mammachi plays Welcome Home Our Sophie Mol tune on her violin.

Except Ammu and her twins, the other members of the extended family and staff are very ingratiating to the incumbents. .Sophie is considered an angel and the twins devils. She is "Loved from the Beginning." (135) At supper, the conversation centres around Margaret and Sophie with Ammu and her children left out to drive home the point of their place in the joint family. Sophie patiently explains to her cousins how they are bastards. She is adulated while the twins are belittled. In her obsequies, grandly celebrated, the twins stand aloof. Though deeply attached to one another, they are mostly separated since Chacko is of the view that he can keep only one in the house, the other 'Returned.' He regards the twins and Ammu as a burden. That they don't belong to the core of Pappachi's family is known even to the maid Kochu who utters that Estha can break as many beds in his father's house but not in Ayemenem House. Estha, off and on, is packed to his father's house where he grows painfully shy and unobtrusive.

Rahel drifts from school to school, uncared for. She is expelled from a school for colliding with girls to find the truth about her breasts whose existence was never acknowledged. The convent instead of producing an aura of the religious encourages patriarchal values. On decorating cowdung, she is unjustifiably punished. In the hotel, Rahel doesn't eat anything since she became aware her mother loves her less due to her behaviour but Chacko overeats. He is insensitive to Rahel, tells her bluntly he loves Sophie more than her whereas Rahel adjusts her instinct of love with duty. She doesn't acknowledge to Sophie that she loves her brother more than her or Mammachi for he might turn out to be a male chauvinist, and because they don't count in the scheme of things.

When Ammu calls them a millstone round her neck, the children deduce she doesn't love them anymore. So with toys they escape. Sophie joins them only to be drowned.

Gender-domination is also evidenced between Ammu's parents. Her father, a research officer is disgruntled for he cannot get the moth he has discovered named after himself. But after 12 years, the credit unfairly goes to his successor whom he has hated. His cruelty to his wife is probably due to the credit not falling to him. He is jealous of his wife's profiteering pickle-factory and expert violin-playing. Though oppressing his wife, he gives the signal to the public as if she is neglecting him by stitching buttons on his clothes himself. In contrast, his wife's stance towards him has been respectful. She cries copiously after his death and pastes flauntingly the clipping of *Indian Express* about him below his photo.

Even regarding property, gender-priority is obvious. Until Chacko returns from Oxford, the factory is owned by Mammachi. It is a small profit-giving business. When he registers it in his name, Ammu and Mammachi continue persevering for the factory; still it is, "my factory, my pineapples, my pickles," (57) and it starts incurring losses. Legally Ammu, being a woman, has no claims on the factory. Chacko believes that women are unfit to wield power though problems related to the factory are solved by Mammachi.

Another unequal couple is Baby Kochamma and Father Mulligan, and Irish Jesuit priest. She converts to Catholicism and enrolls herself as a nun to be physically close to him. But since he is monopolized by other nuns she leaves the nunnery, remains a spinster and Roman Catholic till death. Everyday she writes in her diary, "I love you." Father Mulligan goes to Hardwar and gets converted to Vaishnavism in the course of training in Theology in Hinduism. He remains so till death. From Hardwar, he sends her a greeting card every Diwali. Though she has a sacrificing attitude towards her lover, she is grossly malicious towards Ammu and the twins. Her sad and defeatist life tortures others weaker than her. She initiates Chacko to lock up Ammu, holding her responsible for Sophie's death. She tries to salvage the family honour through finesse i.e. by lodging a false F.I.R. to implicate Velutha, an untouchable in a case of rape and abduction of the twins. She even cajoles Estha to become a false witness in the F.I.R. But intrepid Ammu goes to the police station to report the truth about her willing participation in the affair. Meanwhile Inspector of Police, Thomas Mathews, prods her breasts with his baton, an instance of molestation by the so-called saviours of society.

Another couple delineated in the novel is Chacko and his English wife, Margaret. Shown as immature lovers, their love flounders. She fell for his irresponsible, quaint and optimistic ways but soon grew tired of the same, leading to a divorce. She and Ammu rushed into marriage like Lydia of *Pride and Prejudice*. Margaret later marries Joe who dies in a car accident. Even immediately after his death she retains her equanimity as a mother for she coaxes her daughter to have eggs and do homework. But after Sophie's death driven by hysteria, she slaps Estha. Thus we observe that women have various pressures, interests and obligations.

As a husband, Chacko isn't a good provider, and he likes Margaret for not being dependent on him. Even as a son, he is a taker and not a giver. The mother-son relationship is a complex one, he never reading the whole of her letter or replying to it. He even marries without informing them though Ammu informed them of her marriage that was ignored. When he returns to India, he demands his mother's adoration but despises and punishes her for it. She is possessively in love with her son, denying he has ever loved Margaret. Callous, he pains her the most when he praises Margaret with pride as though he admires her for divorcing him. Chacko is a representative of the exploitative male who oppress women.

Ammu's inter-religious marriage is spoken of scornfully by Baby Kochamma but Chacko's promiscuity with women of different castes is accepted as 'Men's Needs.' Ammu's affair with Velutha, an untouchable Christian, is resolved to be terminated by the machination of the accusation of rape. Her physical yearning for sex is accepted as natural by the author. Ideal lovers are Ammu and Velutha who accept each other as they are. Sensitive and bold, they don't conform to the demands of society; they perish. The idea of freedom proves as ephemeral as natural surroundings like the peace-giving river Meenachal which turns turbulent, drowning Sophie. In this novel, marriage is a trap for all.

Kalyani and Pillai are a Hindu couple. Kalyani is subservient to her husband, the master of the house who gives orders. Her mother-in-law is a neglected, old woman of ill-health. Gender disparity is not the only problem in society. Insanitation, pollution, old age, ill-health, the plight of prostitutes (whose hair is deliberately cut), the evils of caste-system, crass commercialization of the arts, oppression of the poor, child abuse, untouchability, political manipulation of labour, political-criminal nexus, and other injustices have been dealt with adroitly in *The God of Small Things.* Mere feministic idealism cannot solve the evils of society but a co-ordinate approach towards its eradication may. Roy deals incisively and devastatingly with ways in which women are abused in a patriarchal society.

To bring out effectively the feminine sensibility and moral life of the characters in the fragmented text of the novel, Roy uses language that is very fresh. The description of events involves the visual, aural and imaginative seizing of the emotions of the people—and she does it with a panache. At this point it would be pertinent to bring in a definition of style as, "deviation from the norm, style as recurrence or convergence of textural pattern and style as a particular exploitation of a grammar of possibilities."[3] Applying this interpretation to Roy's work, we find it very meritorious. Words chosen are near the spoken medium. Most of the language is stark, bereft of musical phrases. The essential style is the high proportion of short sentences, and on the frequent use of dramatically short paragraphs. The effect is clear cut and incisive. In the use of elision, language is without implicature so that readers become onlookers as in Abhilash Talkies, "The back-inside smell. Fan shadows. Backs of heads. Necks. Collars. Hair. Buns. Plaits. Ponytails." (110) The juxtaposition of words sick and sweet into 'sicksweet' adds an extra dimension to the anguish of the destruction of human beings.

Pronouns are the linguistic conditions of identification. In a moment of fictional unity the interchangeability of pronouns is established: "On the next bed, his niece and nephew slept with their arms around each other. A hot twin and a cold one. He and She. We and Us." (122) In the above passage, capitalization of pronouns displays pre-logical sensibilities since the twins were fused in their mother's womb, and spiritually one in the world. Capitalization can also be used for emphasis: "Sophie Mol. Hatted, Bell-bottomed and Loved from the Beginning." (328)

Images can be very effective as that of the moth, a symbol of torment: "The moth on Rahel's heart lifted a downy leg. Then put it back. Its little leg was cold." (136) The similes are of a practical kind as her wedding is like being taken to the gallows. The twins apprehend things by spelling them backwards e.g. 'ecneidebO' (313) in the police station to focus the young awareness in opposition to the adult one that has false perceptions and delusions. Chacko sometimes speaks in a Reading Aloud voice indifferent to anyone listening or understanding his words.

In this novel, elements of realistic narrative are blended with non-naturalistic material by making use of resources of legends and myths and fairy tales as in Carter's novels. Folk tales that endorse patriarchal values have been rewritten from the perspective of women. In Roy's version of the Three Bears papa bear beats mother bear with a brass vase, and mother bear suffers in resignation. The plight of children, separated from their father and denied advantages accrued to them, has been highlighted through the Indian myth of Karna, performed by Kathakali dancers. In *The God of Small Things* a new method is made to portray what flits across the mind. Thoughts jump from one thing to another in association as when Pillai asks Rahel about Estha: "How is he?" she answers, "He's fine." Her thoughts jump to "Fine Flat and honey-coloured. He washes his clothes with crumbling soap." (131) Roy seems to love living in words, as in "Locusts Stand I." (57) Some of her work is bewitching: much of the phonetic renderings are local, Roy being a Keralite. The abstractions of untouchability and war have been personified as History House where map-breathed ancestors whisper. Silence is more expressive than speech: "Silence filled the car like a saturated sponge." (70)

Language is also expressed below the level of consciousness whence all impulses to act have their origin; it is made tangible in dreams, songs, essays, stories, myths etc. In dreams, we have the whole life experiences of a person concentrated into a night's dream. Ammu dreams of the family living together and going to their own school where punishments are meted according to the action. Margaret's hysteria on her daughter's death reveals her innermost aspirations in distress. But the subconscious thoughts give hope that prove illusory. In this novel mass mind of the audience in Abhilash Talkies is expressed like newspaper headlines: "Shutup or Getout. Getout or Shutup" (100) when Estha is singing aloud. An attempt is made to follow not so much as what goes on in the mind as what flits across it. In this endeavour the structure of thoughts may be eliminated. When Rahel comes to Ayemenem after many years, in Estha's mind: "Trains. Traffic. Music. The Stock Market. A dam had burst and savage waters swept everything up in a swirling. Comets, violins, parades, loneliness, clouds, beards, bigots, lists, flags, earthquakes, despair were all swept up in a scrambled swirling." (15)

Her language has a hypnotic effect due largely to repetitions and refrains. She patiently follows the echo of a thought: "She had no plans/ No plans/ No Locusts Stand I." (188) The refrain of the river Meenachal is in the minds of the twins: "Greygreen. With fish in it. The sky and trees in it. And at night, the broken yellow moon in it." (203) The sudden starts of the mind are helped by the very marked, very short rhythm with hardly any structure. In Estha's mind in the train: "Rain. Rushing, inky water. And a smell. Sicksweet. Like old roses on a breeze." (32)

Much of the novel's charm is in the use of poetic prose: "It was a boat. A tiny wooden vallom. The boat that Estha sat on and Rahel found. The boat that Ammu would use to cross the river. To love by night the man her children loved by day./ So old a boat that it had taken root. Almost. A grey old boatplant with boatflowers and boatfruit. And underneath, a boat-shaped patch of withered grass. A scurrying, hurrying boatworld." (202) A method of poetry is in leaping from one thing to another, leaving out the intermediate steps[4] "They left: Six princes, their pockets stuffed with toys. A pair of two-egg twins. And the God of Loss. He couldn't walk. So they dragged him. Nobody saw them." And after the possible intervening steps, "Bats, of course are blind." (312)

Considering Roy's deep interest in feminine sensibility, and an explicit concern with the nature of art, we are enormously impressed by her huge talent, and are patiently awaiting her next fictional work.

NOTES

1. S. Walby, "Theorizing Patriarchy" *Sociology*, 23 (2), p. 214.
2. Arundhati Roy, *The God of Small Things* (New Delhi: IndiaInk, 1998).
3. Donald C. Freeman, "Linguistic Approaches to Literature," in Freeman, ed., *Linguistics and Literary Style* (New York: Holt, Rinehart and Winston, 1970), p. 4.
4. Bonamy Dobree, *Modern Prose Style* (Oxford University Press, 1964).

From Frustration to Suffering: A Recurring Pattern in Arundhati Roy's *The God of Small Things*

PRAHLAD A. KULKARNI

Arundhati Roy bagged the Booker for her novel *The God of Small Things* and once again the whole panorama of Indian Writing in English came into limelight. In fact, Indian Writing in English has a long tradition of great achievements.

The God of Small Things deals with a Syrian Christian family in Ayemenem. Pappachi, the head of the family, comes from Delhi to his ancestral house to spend the years of his retirement. He is accompanied by his wife Mammachi "almost blind," (5) Baby Kochamma "living her life backwards," (22) Chacko, the Rhodes Scholar and the only son of Mammachi, and Ammu, a school-girl. Further in the course of time, Ammu marries a man of her own choice and gives birth to the twins: Rahel and Estha. Chacko marries Margaret. Margaret gives birth to a girl, Sophie Mol. An opportunistic leader of the local communist party K.N.M. Pillai "walked through the world like a chameleon." (14) Vellya Pappen—the Paravan, his son Velutha and the Police inspector Thomas Mathew figure in the novel.

It seems that Arundhati Roy uses a particular pattern in the novel. Her characters have their weaknesses and have their distinct personalities. Their unquenched desires, unfulfilled assurances, broken marriages, shattered faiths, unreasonable hate, planned revenge—all these form the crux of the novel. These complex and complicated problems bring them nothing but frustration which, later, culminates in a perpetual suffering.

Pappachi, prior to the Independence, works as an imperial Entomologist and retires as the Joint Director, Entomology. He becomes restless and angry to see that his important discovery of moth has been named after an Acting Director in the Department of Entomology. His is a multi-faceted personality. It is a queer mixture of love and hate; kindness and anger, selflessness and selfishness. He has generously donated his money to orphanages and leprosy clinics. "He worked hard on his public profile as a sophisticated, generous, moral man." (180) But he turns to be "a monstrous, suspicious, bully. With a streak of vicious cunning" with his wife and children. During the years of his retirement, he slowly withdraws himself from other activities and prefers to live in isolation. He buys a Skyblue Plymouth for himself. His pride makes him strong. It seems that he lives like a king—a defeated king who hesitates to accept his defeat. Obviously his death makes no difference to anyone.

Mammachi's life seems to be sandwiched between inhuman cruelties of her husband, Pappachi and her responsibilities. Probably the slender income of the family constrains her to start a business of pickles on a smaller scale. She is not a miser in appreciating Velutha's skill as a carpenter, though he is a Paravan (untouchable). But when she learns about the secret of Velutha-Ammu affair, she becomes angry and warns Velutha not to step in the campus of the factory. Mammachi has learnt to tolerate things. Her silent suffering articulates more, giving meaning to her suffering.

Baby Kochamma's real name is Navomi lpe but everybody calls her Baby Kochamma. She, a romantic creature in her youth, now tries to live her past in the present. Her passionate love affair with a Roman Catholic Father Mulligan still haunts her. He was a frequent visitor to her house as her father was much respected all over the Parish. The handsome, youthful Irish Monk, Father Mulligan realises, "sexual excitement that rose like a tide in the slender girl" (23) and remains passive. He does not respond nor does he encourage her. She becomes a Roman Catholic for Father Mulligan. Still all her efforts to win Father Mulligan fail.

She goes to America and obtains a Diploma in Ornamental Gardening. Anyhow, she feels everything meaningless. She becomes nervous. She withdraws herself from the other activities and keeps herself in-doors. She prefers isolation and the world of dreams. Probably her aloofness has given rise to hate, anger, jealousy and revenge in her. She dislikes Ammu's running away from her husband's house, nor does she like her affair with Velutha, the paravan, either. She hates Ammu and so when she learns about the accidental death of Sophie Mol, she plans to utilise it to defame Velutha. She rushes to the police station and files a false complaint against Velutha accusing him as an abductor of small children, and killing one of them. She ultimately succeeds in getting Velutha behind the bars where he dies later. She tries to protect the status of the Ayemenem house at the cost of Velutha's life. It seems that the snake of her unquenched desires and unfulfilled expectations moves everywhere searching for a prey.

Chacko, the Rhodes Scholar, studies in Oxford. His frequent visits to the cafe where Margaret works, give an opportunity for them to come close. His youthful, charming body tempts Margaret and she begins to love him. In spite of her parents's objections, she marries him and gives birth to a girl, Sophie Mol. Slowly she finds that Chacko is missing something that she wants to preserve and finds another friend, Joe. After taking divorce from Chacko, she marries Joe. Chacko, as a divorcee, returns to India like a "helpless exiled prince." (244)

Further, this self-proclaimed Marxist cultivates his interests in his mother's business of pickles. He develops it into a factory: 'Paradise Pickles and Preserves.' Chacko assures his labourers of their rightful wages. Being politically motivated and instigated, they do not listen to him. It results into closing down the doors of the factory.

K.N.M. Pillai, the communist party leader, tries to take his personal revenge against Chacko. As an aspiring politician, he dislikes the decision of appointing a Paravan, Velutha, as a factory carpenter. He openly suggests to Chacko to remove Velutha from the factory. He tells him that "workers do not accept the change easily. You better send Velutha away from the factory. He is a Paravan. People do not like him to be with them." Chacko turns down his demand. On the contrary he says that Velutha runs the factory. K.N.M. Pillai takes it as a personal insult and takes revenge by instigating the workers for strike.

K.N.M. Pillai blames Chacko as a man of management and infuses workers to overthrow the regime of oppression, exploitation and slavery. It seems that Chacko's rationality has no place anywhere. Pretensions become more effective than reasonable thinking. Unfortunately, opportunism has become a powerful way of life. Chacko's idealism shatters into pieces and he becomes frustrated. He is constrained by the condition to leave India for Canada for a job.

Velutha, a Paravan, is brought up by his father in a house that is socially hated, economically neglected and culturally barren. Through his humiliations, he has learnt to control his anger. Sometimes he bursts like a volcano. At early age he had learnt carpentry and mastered the art skilfully. Unlike his father Vellya Pappen, he does not like to be meek always. He becomes the cardholder of the communist party expecting it would give him justice. His only fault is that being a Paravan, he loves Ammu. It brings many difficulties for him. When he approaches K.N.M. Pillai for his support, he flatly refuses and tells him that organisations are formed for common interests and not for private indiscipline among the workers. Velutha becomes a tool in the hands of K.N.M. Pillai.

Velutha falls a victim to the planned conspiracy against him. His suffering begins from his birth and ends with his death. He is always made aware of his caste by people. In fact, he is not at all concerned with the death of Sophie Mol but is brought into it by Baby Kochamma. He finds that justice is denied to him. He suffers a lot. He accepts death in order to escape reality. Velutha incarnates the perpetual suffering. He is nothing but "The God of Small Things. He left no footprints in sand, no ripples in water, no image in mirrors." (265)

Ammu feels the death of Velutha intensely but remains helpless. Ammu has "a delicate, chiselled face, black eyebrows angled like a soaring seagull's wings, a small straight nose and luminous nutbrown skin." (45) Realising her father's difficulties in raising the money for her marriage, Ammu prepares herself to find a life-partner on her own. She meets a man who happens to be an assistant manager of a tea-estate in Assam. He is twenty-five, "a small man, but well-built. Pleasant looking." (39) She plainly admits that she is not in love with him. Only she wants to escape from the house and so "she thought that anything, any one at all, would be better than returning to Ayemenem." (39) After her marriage, she goes to Assam. Her beauty and charm attract lustful eyes of the members of the Planter's club and especially Mr. Hollick becomes restless. He is the Manager of a tea-estate. Ammu's husband, Baba works there. In order to get her, Mr. Hollick contrives a plan and tells Baba about innumerable complaints he has received against him. When he finds his plan working, he further adds that he can protect him only if he sends Ammu to his bungalow for a week or so. It shocks Ammu. She is not a fallen woman. She feels sorry for the inability of her husband in protecting her self-respect and decides to leave him. She returns to Ayemenem with the twins with her. She returns to the same dark cellar from which she wanted to run away. Fate brings her back to the place of perpetual suffering.

The story of frustration and suffering seems to have no end. It continues even to the next generation of Rahel, Estha and Sophie Mol. After Sophie Mol's accidental death, Estha was sent to his father in Calcutta. Baba—Ammu's husband—has resigned his job as an assistant manager in the tea-estate and returned to Calcutta. He marries again and lives in Calcutta. After twenty-three years, Estha returns to Ayemenem with a letter from his father. In this letter Baba says, "he had retired from his carbon black job and was emigrating to Australia . . . he couldn't take Estha with him." (9)

Rahel, Ammu's daughter, is a mischievous girl in her school. She was expelled thrice from school for her bad behaviour by the school authorities. First for her behaviour, second for smoking and third for setting fire to her Housemistress's false hair bun. She is very slow in studies and takes eight years to complete five years's course in a mediocre college of Architecture in Delhi. Rahel is bold enough to face problems. During her college days, she comes in contact with Larry McCaslin and their love culminates in marriage. "She drifted into marriage like a passenger drifts towards an unoccupied chair in an airport lounge. With a Sitting Down sense." (18) She goes with her husband to America but soon she gets frustrated. Her experiences may have created an urge for Home in her. She expected it for her. Even in the company of Larry McCaslin, she expected it. Probably Fate looms large over her desires and keeps her away from that pleasure. She is unable to understand the reason behind this: "She wondered why it was that when she thought of home, it was always in the colours of the dark, oiled wood of boats, and the empty cores of the tongues of flame that flickered in brass lamps." (73) Probably her longing for material pleasures takes her to the land of hollowness. She experiences meaninglessness in her marriage and takes a divorce. When she listens to the news that her brother Estha has returned to Ayemenem, she resigns her job in New York and returns to India. Probably with lost hopes and unsatisfied desires. Rahel represents the contemporary man representing the waste land—culturally barren, morally empty, socially inimical.

Arundhati Roy seems to be influenced by her profession of a newspaper writer. She keeps curiosity aroused in portraying her characters. All these characters come with their own problems and try to seek solutions. The pattern misses to achieve artistic effect as a whole.

She talks about the God of Small Things. If God means pity, kindness, love, fearlessness, then He is nowhere. There are many small things in the narration like Chacko's lecturership, Baby Kochamma's love for Father Mulligan, Mammachi's business of pickles, etc. Arundhati Roy devises a pattern that shows how frustration sustains perpetual suffering in the life of the characters in the novel.

Dark of Heartness Tiptoed into the Heart of Darkness: Arundhati Roy's *The God of Small Things*

A.K. MUKHERJEE

"A posse of Touchable policemen" (Dark of Heartness) with their "Politeness, Obedience, Loyalty, Intelligence, Courtesy, Efficiency" (POLICE) tiptoted into "The Heart of Darkness" where Velutha and Ammu met, had their secret romance; where their body spoke to each other; where they stood "Skin to Skin": "Her brownness against his blackness. Her softness against his hardness. Her nut-brown breasts (that would not support a tooth brush) against his smooth ebony chest."[1]

It was an act of sacrilege on the part of Velutha, an untouchable, a paravan, whose father was a servant working at Ammu's parents's place, Ayemenem, in a Syrian Christian family which was no less orthodox than any Hindu family. It was also an act of sacrilege on the part of Ammu, a divorcee and widow, living with her twin-eggs, 'Dizygotic,' Rahel and Esthappen at her parents's place, Ayemenem. These things are small things, but they could demolish, once and for all, the prestige of Mammachi's family (although her younger sister Baby Kochamma still turned over the yellow pages of her diary where in each page she wrote "I love you" to commemorate her love for father Mulligan.) So things should be hushed up; Ammu should be locked up in her room and Velutha should be entangled in a rape case, kidnappping of the children (Rahel, Esthappen, Sophie Moll) and ultimately jailed, booted, and if possible, killed. And he was killed. He broke the Love Laws that lay down "who should be loved.

And how. And how much." (328) The same law was broken by Rahel and Esthappen when they were "Not old. Not young. But a viable die-able age." (327)

The title of this paper is taken from one of the lines of the novel: "Dark of heartness tiptoed into the heart of darkness. The sound of stridulating crickets swelled." (306) There is something rotten in the state of Denmark. Nature as understood and mapped out by man has been violated and human machinery must be employed to bring it into order. Who is that human machinery? The police, a combination of six alphabets and each alphabet is given an attribute by the novellist as P stands for politeness, O stands for obedience, L stands for loyalty, I stands for intelligence, C stands for courtesy and E stands for efficiency, walks on its toe, not touching the ground into the Heart of Darkness whose area is beyond the contour of human imagination and its laws are above human laws, and demolish it. This "Heart of Darkness" is not what Kurtz was confronted with in Conrad's *Heart of Darkness*; it is rather what Lawrence tried to fathom in his *The Rainbow* or *Lady Chatterly's Lover*, it is the primal world, the eternal primitive instinct, the abode of love and sex that makes its inmates "lay translated in the peace of satisfaction."[2] It is the world where Skrebensky seemed to Ursula "like living darkness upon her" and she was in the embrace of "strange Darkness" (446) and "Darkness cleaving to Darkness" and their kisses "knitted them into one fecund nucleus of the fluid Darkness"—"it was bliss. It was the nucleolating of the fecund darkness." (447) But this abode of peace and satisfaction is very often invaded by men, and to quote Roy, "Man's subliminal urge to destroy what he could neither subdue nor deify." (309) It is because "feelings of contents born of inchoate, unacknowledged fear—civilization's fear of nature, men's fear of women, power's fear of powerlessness." (308) This is the world that Paul Morel was frightened of; Clifford tried to demolish to which Connie and Mellor, Ursula and Skrebensky without fearing the consequences entered. Ammu and Velutha, though poles apart in their social status, entered this world without thinking of "tomorrow":

> Ammu, naked now, crouched over Velutha, her mouth on his. He drew her hair around them like a tent, like her children did when they wanted to exclude the outside world. She slid further down introducing herself to the rest of him. His neck. His nipples. His chocolate stomach. She sipped the feet of the river from the hollow of his naval. She pressed the heat of his erection against her eyelids. She tasted him, salty in her mouth. He sat up and drew her back to him. She felt his belly tighten under her hard as a board. She felt her wetness slipping on his skin. He took her nipple in his mouth and cradled her other breast in his calloused palm. Velvet gloved in sandpaper. (336)

This is how Velutha "left behind a hole in the universe through which darkness poured like liquid tar." (191) This long passage from the text is not quoted to titillate the readers or support some of the critics in their opinion of the novel as a 'porno.' I quote it to substantiate the thesis of my paper that how the Heart of Darknesss is ruptured, raped and demolished by the Dark of Heartness. How small things are booted out by big things. So Ammu and Velutha "stuck to the small things." (338) These small things, however, matter and are recollected by Rahel and Estha after twenty-three years. The beauty of the novel is that the sad and fond memories (OrangeLemonDrink man in the chapter Abhilash Talkies); their mother's affair with Velutha; her death; Sophie Moll's death by drowning in the river Meenachal; Baby Kochamma's affair; K.N. Pillai's point of view which is always mixed with grin and derisive laughter. This reveals the author's power of empathy to understand the helplessness of man against the tailor-made society. It is again in the tradition of R.K. Narayan's Malgudi stories, but here Rahel and Estha are much more sensitive than Swamy, and their reality is different from that of Swamy.

The novel is, then, a major breakthrough in Indian literature in English. It is much more than even the novels written by Indian writers in English like Rushdie, Amitav Ghosh, Vikram Seth, Alan Sealy and Upamanyu Chatterjee.

It is a postmodern novel in its use of technique. Arundhati Roy herself confesses this in her interview to Alix Wibur: "For me language is a skin on my thought and I was thinking about it as a story, and was thinking of the way of telling it."[3] So the "telling" of the book is what is emphasized by Roy. The telling is carried out by twin-eggs, although the novel gives an impression that an omniscient author is narrating the tale from shifting points of view and frequently with authorial comment.

But what is more striking than this is its structure and chronology of the narrative which makes this novel a postmodernist text. In this novel, Roy weaves four incidents in a Syrian Christian family which extends to three generations living in the Ayemenem House in Kottayam, what Binoo K. John would say "a saga, microscoped in time which irreversibly moves towards its doomed love between Ammu and Velutha; Sophie Moll's death by drowning; traumatic experiences of Rahel and Estha, and the last is Rahel's unsuccessful marriage and return to Ayemenem and join her re-returned twin Estha. The first, second and third strands of action form the main action and constitute the major part of the narrative, and take place in the past. The fourth story of the grown-up twins happens in the present and occupies a little space of the narrative action. The narration of the past can be considered a micro-narrative whereas the present action (the fourth level) makes up a micro-narrative of sorts.

So far as structure is concerned, the novel appears different from Rushdie's *The Moor's Last Sigh*. Arundhati Roy tells in her interview with *The Week*: "For me the structure of my story, the way it reveals itself was so important—I really took a lot of care in designing the structure of the story, because for me the book is not about what happened but how what happened affected people." (46) Roy breaks away from the conventional plot with a beginning, middle and an end. Rather the main action of the novel takes place in December 1969 describing the seven-year-old twins, Estha and Rahel. Sophie Moll's arrival, her sudden death and their mother's affair with Velutha. The novel begins with Rahel's returning to Ayemenem after twenty-three years. The novel proceeds to narrate the main action, but not chronologically. Even most of the important things are mentioned in the first chapter "Paradise Pickles and Preserves." This makes the author's task difficult and challenging as she has to keep up the interest of her readers. But readers are on their toes to know how and why such things happened. Even this 'how and why' is not narrated in a logical manner. Sometimes the action moves forward, sometimes flashback, almost cinematic technique, and sometimes rapid editing, a word or half a sentence. There is no linear progression of events, not in just the story of the novel but also within the individual streams of narrative. The text almost plays with space and time. For example, Ammu's death which follows quite sometime after Velutha in custody, is narrated in chapter 7, whereas Velutha's death is described in chapter 19, almost towards the end of the book.

In the same manner, the account of Ammu's death precedes the narration of Estha being returned to his father (when his uncle Chacko orders Ammu and the twins out of his house following Sophie Moll's drowning) in chapter 20—"Madras Mail."

The time sequence is, thus, obliterated in the novel. There is a constant slipping back and forth between several different time frames. Roy employs a circuitous narrative so that events emerge elliptically and out of chronological sequence. This is quite in keeping with the new Indian novel starting in the 1980 in which the narratology has altered. The change in narratology and the break with the time-frame allows freedom to the story to move freely both in past, present and future. It annihilates time and, at the same time, the book time and again makes its readers aware of all time—time present and time past, both present in time future. This also gives freedom to the novelist to insert texts within the text anywhere. While transposing the texts, the future time sequence is brought earlier and the past takes place later than the future: "Sorrow, however, was still two weeks away on that blue cross-stitch afternoon, as Margaret Kochamma lay jet-lagged and still asleep." (266) The transposed text makes future memory possible. Jacques Derrida speaks of memory in advance that offers "a rear view vision of a future."[4]

In its technique *The God of Small Things* is a major breakthrough in Indian fiction in English. Arundhati Roy is no less than Iris murdoch, Toni Morrison or Margaret Atwood. She is an Indian writer using Indian English or what one would say 'Indish.' She has broken all the rules of pedagogic English and all norms of English grammar. For example, she describes the activities on a railway platform where there is no punctuation mark, and only a conglomeration of some words that give a better picture of a railway platform activities than any other description by an English author:

> Scurrying hurrying buying selling luggage trundling paying children shitting people spitting coming going begging bargaining reservation checking. (300)

Not only in language but in handling the story, Roy reveals her craftsmanship. She is a conscious artist. She said in her interview to *The Week* that she was not like an architect who designs a building, taking care of the beginning and its ending. Rather, "I would start somewhere and I'd colour a bit and then I would deeply stretch back and then stretch forward. It was like designing an intricately balanced structure." (46)

The ending of the novel is as striking as its beginning. The book ends with the word "Tomorrow." The lovers as well as readers know what this "tomorrow" means. It is not the "tomorrow and tomorrow" of Macbeth but something frightening, something terrible. There will be no change in the world. The Dark of Heartness will always tiptoe on the Heart of Darkness. Nevertheless, it is a wonderful experience. It is the romance of living. It is larger than life. Roy comments on the ending of her novel, "even though it's terrible, it's wonderful that it happened at all." Nothing happens in Joseph Heller's *Something Happened*.

Indian literature has gone a long way to establish an identity of its own. The dream of Raja Rao has come true. Rao writes in his foreward to *Kanthapura*: "We cannot write like the English. We should not. We cannot write only as Indians. We have grown to look at the large world as part of us. Our method of expression therefore has to be a dialect which will some day prove to be as distinctive and colourful as the Irish or the Americans. Time alone will justify it." It is time for us to look at Indian literature in English as Indian literature. It has at last freed itself from the colonial hangover and language imperialism. *The God of Small Things* is undoubtedly a postcolonial text, both in form and content.

NOTES

1. Arundhati Roy, *The God of Small Things* (New Delhi: IndiaInk, 1997).
2. D.H. Lawrence, *The Prussian Officer and Other Stories*, ed. John Worhten (Cambridge: Cambridge University Press, 1982), p. 19.
3. Arundhati Roy, Interview to Alix Wibur, *The Week*, p. 46.
4. Jacques Derrida, "Racism's Last Word" in *Race, Writing and Difference*, ed. H.L. Gates (Chicago University Press, 1986).
5. John K. Binoo, "An Epochal Chronicle," *India Today*, 15 March 1997.
6. Raja Rao, *Kanthapura* (Delhi: Hind Pocket Books).

The Crisis in Human Values in *Coolie* and *The God of Small Things*: A Comparative Study

ROSY MISRA

Throughout the ages, literature has always explored human values and their relevance in moments of crisis. This is especially evident in Indian writing in English, which from its very beginning has focused on social issues. In this context a comparison between Mulk Raj Anand's *Coolie* and Arundhati Roy's *The God of Small Things* is of particular interest, for the two writers are very different. Not only is one a male, the other a female, they belong to different socio-historic periods and areas of interest. Anand established himself in the first half of the twentieth century, he is one of the pioneers of Indian fiction writing in English, being classed with R.K. Narayan and Raja Rao as the founders of the Indian novel in English. But Roy is a contemporary novelist—young and volatile. Anand has been greatly influenced by Marxism, Roy is emphatically not a Marxist. Nevertheless, their novels are comparable on various levels. Both are revolutionary novels and depict the social reality of conflict between the powerful and the powerless, and treat the downtrodden humanistically. Both are social reformers.

When I was reading *The God of Small Things*, the picture of Munoo came to mind again and again. Coolie is what one might call a character novel with the focus on one person being victimised by society. But in Roy's novel, all the characters are victimised in some way or the other, in a perpetual repetition of what has been happening through time. In Munoo's story, amorous love is almost absent whereas in *The God of Small Things* the main thread of the story is a love-affair between a high-caste Christian woman and an untouchable. In spite of these differences, the novels are comparable on various levels. They are sagas of conflicts between the powerful and the powerless. This paper attempts to compare the encroachment upon human values and the resultant crises which lead to the tragic deaths of the main characters of both the novels.

Coolie (1936) portrays the yawning gap between the haves and have-nots, the exploiters and the exploited, the rulers and the ruled, the powerful and the powerless. It is a veritable saga of unending pain, suffering, and prolonged struggle punctuated only occasionally by brief moments of relief and hope. Beginning his journey from the house of his loveless uncle and aunt, Munoo passes through diverse situations—as a domestic servant in an urban middle-class family in Sham Nagar, as a worker in a small pickle factory and as a coolie fighting for work in the city market in Daulatpur, as a labourer in a cotton mill in Bombay and as a rickshaw coolie in the employ of an Anglo-Indian woman of no morals. Before he dies, Munoo is subjected to exploitation at the hands of various exploiters in four different places.

In *The God of Small Things* (1997), Roy presents the tragic plights of several characters being exploited in the hands of various exploiters. It is all about, how the human values of children, youth, women, and the untouchable have been encroached upon, and how they have been victimised, and, unwittingly, some of them victimise each other. It tells us the story of an intense, but doomed, love affair between a high-caste Syrian Christian woman Ammu and an untouchable Paravan Velutha. We can hear the voices of various victimised characters: the voice of Mammachi, the bitter, long suffering mistress of the household who was being regularly beaten with a brass flower vase by her husband; the voice of Baby Kochamma, who had been denied love by Father Mulligan, with whom she fell in love; and the voice of Margaret Kochamma the English woman whom Chacko had married. We also hear the voices of the small children, Estha and Rahael, who had been forced to become false witnesses against their friend

Velutha. But the voices of Velutha and Ammu, the protagonists, end in their tragic deaths. There is nobody to help Velutha in his crisis. The whole of humanity turned against him. It was Ammu who had initiated their love affair. The inevitable had happened and Velutha's father Vellya Pappen dutifully informed Mammachi what he had seen. Instead of protecting his son, he asked God's forgiveness for having spawned a monster and even offered to kill his son and thereby destroy what he had created. The "Man-less, Father Mulligan-less Baby Kochamma"[1] was actually jealous of the young lovers's physical union and wondered how Ammu could stand the smell of a Paravan. The crisis was triggered by the drowning of Sophie Mol. On the pretext of saving the family reputation, Baby Kochamma locked up Ammu in the Ayemenem house and informed the police "a few days ago he [Velutha] had tried to, to . . . to force himself on her niece" (259) and kidnapped her children. Velutha was informed by a communist comrade that the police had been searching for him. He directly went to Comrade K.N.M. Pillai for help. Pillai was more worried about the reaction of the people. He told Velutha to his face that Party was not constituted to support workers's indiscipline in their private life. He made it clear that the individual's interest was subordinate to the organisation's interest. Velutha did not get any support from the party of which he had been a sincere worker. He was also denied justice in the hands of his employer Mammachi, who instead spat on his face. Ultimately he was arrested by the police and died in the police custody.

Ammu is portrayed as a tragic figure, a woman struggling against her family, her motherhood and society and with herself. Her broken marriage, her unwantedness in her parental family, her love for his children and her womanly desires, lead her to her untimely death. The right to love a man of her choice is a woman's birth right and this birth right of Ammu is encroached upon in the name of caste. Hers is the story of the helplessness of the powerless against the powerful.

The two novels under consideration have epic qualities. The four tragic episodes which make up Munoo's tragic life—as a servant in bank clerk's household, as a worker in a pickle factory in a feudal city, as a factory worker in an industry in Bombay, and lastly as a servant of a half-caste woman at Shimla—present a sequence of events suggestive of the poor conditions of a helpless illiterate Indian. In a sense, he conforms to the archetype having mythic significance for humanity as a whole. *Coolie*, epical in sweep and panoramic in purview, pictures the effects that pervasive evil of class system has on a poor little boy. The novel is remarkable for the largeness of its canvas, the multiplicity of its characters and variety of its episodes. However, the focal point is always Munoo and pathos is sustained by the emphasis on the innocence of Munoo against the merciless, mechanical rhythm of society. Anand humanises the 'coolie'—as in Bakha he humanises the 'untouchable'—and gives him feelings, a mind, a heart, a soul and raises his dignity as a trembling piece of flesh and blood, worthy of commemoration in serious literature. By raising an ordinary wretched creature to the level of a hero, perhaps for the first time in Indian-English literature, Anand proves that the struggle of a waif could be as good a subject for a work of art as the Trojan war itself.

In *The God of Small Things*, Roy, with a master-stroke of reversal, draws a parallel between the murder of Velutha in police custody and the murder of Dushasana and Duryodhana at the hands of Bhima. "Another morning, another stage, another kind of frenzy." (235) With this parallelism between Bhima and Velutha, the novelist raises the latter to the status of an epic hero. As far as the theme of crisis of human values is concerned, the parallelism has great significance. In both the stories, there is a struggle between good and evil. In the *Mahabharata*, Dushasana and Duryodhana represent evil and Bhima 'represents good. Good is able to destroy evil. In *The God of Small Things*, in the struggle between good and evil, evil turns out to be victorious. Velutha who represents good is defeated by the police who represents evil. In ancient India, human rights of the weak were always protected. But in modern India, human values are encroached upon. The police who are servants of the State of democratic set up, the police who stand for Politeness, Obedience, Loyalty, Intelligence, Courtesy and Efficiency killed an innocent man without even probing the real facts only because he belonged to the downtrodden class. Velutha is, as his name signifies, as white as whiteness itself. Even when he knows that his end is imminent, he remains a true apostle of non-violence. The story of Velutha can be interpreted as an extended allegory of Christ's life. Like Christ, he was a very good carpenter, like Christ he remains non-violent. And, again, like Christ, he dies saving other people—saving the reputation of Ammu and her family. Like Christ, he knew that sacrificing his life was too big a cost for this purpose. But he embraces it willingly. When he was taken to the police station, Rahael notices that the nail of his right thumb was painted red. This symbolises the blood of Christ which was shed for others. In this extended moral allegory of struggle between good and evil, Baby Kochamma plays the role of Judas who betrayed Christ. According to this allegory, Velutha achieves the status of an epic hero.

There are many other themes in the novels which are comparable; for instance, the themes of incest, child abuse and Oedipus complex are common to both the novels. In *The God of Small Things*, incest is between the twins who meet after twenty-three years. "Only that once again they broke the Love Laws. That lay down who should be loved. And how. And how much." (328) In *Coolie*, we find that Mrs. Mainwarring is sexually attracted towards Munoo, who is as young as her son. When Munoo met with an accident under the car of Mrs. Mainwarring, he was physically and mentally broken and felt sad, bitter and defeated, like an old man. The novelist comments: "But to Mrs. Mainwarring, he was not the old man he felt himself to be, otherwise she would have had no use for him and would perhaps have left him where she had found him. . . . He was to her a young boy with a lithe, supple body, with a small delicate face and with a pair of sensitive eyes." She appointed him as a page, for a boy of fifteen was just what she wanted. There are many passages in the novel which proclaim Mrs. Mainwarring being incestuous or even a child abuser.

The child abuse near the beginning of *The God of Small*

Things in the Abhilash talkies by a cold drink vendor is disgusting. This physical abuse is later parodied in the mental seduction of the children by Baby Kochamma which is blood-curdling.

Similarly, the Oedipus complex can also be traced in both the novels. In *Coolie* between Munoo and Parbati—the wife of Seth Prabha Dayal. When Munoo falls sick and is laid up with fever, she nurses him tenderly like a mother and never ill-treats him. But later the warmth of Parbati's body as he nestled against her aroused the confused feeling of son and lover. "He pressed her close to him. He felt quivering. And for a moment, he forgot himself in her warmth. . . . And his blood boiled with love that crushed him with a torture." (135) In *The God of Small Things* the son-lover relationship is between Mammachi and her son Chacko, a divorcee. Mammachi is the Jacosta of *The God of Small Things*. "The day that Chacko prevented Pappachi from beating her, Mammachi packed her wifely luggage and committed it to Chacko care. From then onwards, he became the repository of all her womanly feelings. Her man. Her only love." (168) The narrator also emphasises several times how Mammachi takes special care for her son Chacko's room for the "objects of his Needs," (169) "a Man's Needs." (168)

The mingling of fact and fiction is another comparable element in both the novels. All the places through which Munoo moves are geographically traceable. More than that, Anand "took for his hero his childhood playmate Munoo, who was consigned to labour in a pickle factory and who accepted his lot with a fatalism peculiar to the Indian peasantry."[3]

Likewise, in *The God of Small Things*, Roy took the liberty to change Aymanam—a village geographically a ten-minute drive from Kottayam city—to Ayemenem. The Booker prize has unleashed a torrent of interest centering on Ayemenem and the media has been preoccupied with identifying the novel's characters with real life counterparts. The character of Ammu is apparently modelled on Mary Roy—Arundhati's mother. Mary Roy explains: "I am not Ammu. Arundhati has created a character called Ammu, using my biodata on her bare bones."[4] Similarly Arundhati's brother, Lalit Kumar Christopher Roy, has been mistaken by critics as Estha of the novel.

The fusion of history and fiction is another similarity between the two novels. The plight of Munoo and his kind is the direct result of British rule, and of the industrial revolution, their rule initiated without consideration for socal reforms. One of the highlights of *Coolie* is the Hindu-Muslim feud. Munoo is the horrified witness of communal murder and senseless killings. Cowasjee writes, "In Indo-Anglian fiction *Coolie* perhaps is the first novel to touch on this subject; and it foreshadows the murderous riots that followed the partitioning of India in 1947." (65) Further, the episode of the invitation of Mr. W.P. England to Nathoo Ram's house for tea illustrates Anand's conviction that the British Government not only exploited the country's natural resources, but also debased the characters of those Indians who were in its service. It created a body of sycophants, looking upto the English, fawning, cringing, becoming a ready tool of exploitation in the hands of their masters. Nathoo Ram, Dayaram and Todar Mals have been dehumanized in the service of English. This is best seen from the way they bully and abuse Munoo. The police is shown more as a symbol of British oppression than British justice. Their world is a world of hysteria, one without restraint or self-respect. When Prabha goes bankrupt, the police yell, shout abuses, fight among themselves for what little might still be got from auctioning the property, and then together fall upon their victim.

In *The God of Small Things*, there is similar hysteric unrestrained and even more cruel attitude being adopted by the police, even several decades after India had achieved independence. This is proved from the way they torture Velutha like animals fall upon their prey. "If they hurt Velutha more than they intended to, it was only because any kinship, any connection between themselves and him, any implication that if nothing else, at least biologically he was a fellow creature—had been severed long ago." (309) There are references of Communism in the chapter "Pappachi's Moth," Rahael recognises Velutha who was taking part in a march which had been organised by Travancore-Cochin Marxist Labour Union to present a Charter of Peoples

Demands to Comrade E.M.S. himself. The main demands were an hour's lunch break for the paddy workers, increase in women labourer's wages from 1.25 to Rs. 3.00 and men labourer's from Rs. 3.50 to Rs. 4.50 a day. They were also demanding that untouchables no longer be addressed by their caste names. Instead of Achoo Paravan, or Kelan Paravan or Kuttan Pulayan, they should be addressed as Achoo, or Kelan or Kuttan (69). These are references to the facts of political history of Kerala. There are also references to Kathakali being performed. Some of the characters like Chacko and Baby Kochamma are representatives of Indian people who were over influenced by western culture.

In *The God of Small Things*, a number of characters are victimised by society. Velutha and Ammu are denied the right to choose their own life partners. Ammu had been ill-treated and deserted by her Bengali husband and afterwards by her own people. Velutha's human right to 'relive' as a touchable was encroached upon and he was denied protection of his family, his employer and the political party he belonged to. He was denied justice at the hands of the police although he was innocent. They both met with their tragic end. The twins were forbidden love even by their own mother. Estha was treated as a football being returned to his father and re-returned to his mother. Apart from this, his unlucky experience with the cold drink vendor reduces him into a dumb boy. Mammachi had suffered all the evils of a patriarchal family set-up. Love was denied to Margaret Kochamma and even to Baby Kochamma. Thus, in Roy's novel, the crisis is caused because human values of several individuals are encroached upon and they unwittingly encroach upon the human values of others.

In *Coolie* also, we come across scores of characters but as far as the breach of human values is concerned, Munoo is the focal point. What he wished for was minimal; to live, to know and to work. But even these basic human rights were denied to him. Like the twins of *The God of Small Things*, Munoo became an orphan at an early age and was denied by fate the right to be loved. Like Estha he had to face child abuse at the hands of Mrs. Mainwarring. Instead of caste struggle as in the case of

Velutha, he had to face class struggle. In Munoo's case, it is only the exploiters that change, the exploited remains the same. Thus as far as suffering is concerned, the character of Munoo is an amalgamation into which several of Arundhati Roy's characters like Velutha, Estha, Rahael and even Ammu culminate.

Both Anand and Arundhati are social reformers in their own way. Munoo's tragedy seems to be Anand's plea for reform, "beneath this pervasive pessimism, there is an essential undercurrent of optimism in that the protagonist's death poignantly establishes the rotten state of society and the consciousness of the need for its drastic reform."[5] Similarly, Roy also emerges as a prophetess of the new millennium—prophetess of gender and social equality. She seems to plead never to forget about the small things in life: the insects and the flowers, wind and water, the outcaste and the despised.

NOTES

1. Arundhati Roy, *The God of Small Things* (Delhi: IndiaInk, 1997), p. 45.
2. Mulk Raj Anand, *Coolie* (New Delhi: Arnold, 1988), p. 285.
3. Saros Cowasjee, *Studies in Indian and Anglo-Indian Fiction* (New Delhi: Harper Collins, 1993), p. 50.
4. Venu Menon, "Sleepy Ayemanum," *Outlook*, Vol. III, No. 44 (New Delhi, 1997), p. 126.
5. K. Venkata Reddy, *Major Indian Novelists* (New Delhi: Prestige, 1990), p. 12.

Arundhati Roy's *The God of Small Things*: A Novel of Poetic Narratology and Lawrentian Ecstacy

UDAY SHANKAR OJHA and GAJENDRA KUMAR

Arundhati Roy, the Booker prize winner, is, indeed, superb in exploiting and exploring the linguistic competence, pliancy, resilience and mobility in English language. Her creative work is psychologically and culturally rooted in Indian soil through the medium of English. It capitalizes the fact that Arundhati Roy like a nightingale does not afford to forget the roots, even when it flies to heights hitherto unknown. Her magnum opus *The God of Small Things* is a shining and scintillating example of a native genius which prefers to communicate in a language other than her mother tongue. *The God of Small Things* is imbued with a large number of poetic phenomena like intensity of situation, moments of crisis, strange emotions, extensive use of symbols and images, imaginative scenes and situations, intensely emotional and imaginative moods of characters which Virginia Woolf calls 'persuasive mood.'

Like Virginia Woolf, Arundhati Roy conceives the novel as one bright book of life which is more than philosophy, science or any other book and life for her is a coin which has both obverse and reverse. Her extraordinary art lies in her dazzling potency to illuminate and illustrate both the sides simultaneously. The vision and variety of life she presents, her understanding and analysis of circumstances, her insight and intensity into the characters and her knack of investing mundane and morbid events crystallize her novel into poetic odyssey. Artistically, *The God of*

Small Things is characterized as 'fine web of poetry.' It is worthwhile to suggest that aesthetic evaluation, to a great extent, is dependent on a logical interpretation of its phonetic, grammatical and lexical constitution. An excellent analysis of literature depends on the indispensable and vital linguistic studies plus other semantic, aesthetic and emotive values. In the linguistic interpretation of the text Beth Yahp considers it, "Verbal Wizardry"[1] for its non-conventional and unacceptable grammatical expressions.

In the structural schematisation of the novel, the novelist enjoys poetic licence and scrutinizes her 'speech level' and 'pre-speech level' expressions in the tradition of stream-of-consciousness novels. *The God of Small Things* syntactically breaks the "conventional rules of grammar and syntax, abandons orthodox punctuation, coins neo-logism, imports typographical devices, runs sense impressions together with synaesthetic richness."[2] The rich and resourceful unconventional verbal tapestry, very innovative in nature, captivates the ebb and flow of emotions. The commanding poetic mode finds full rhythm through the resonance of words. Her poetic passages are powerfully packed with present participle words emphasizing the contour of consistency and are elegantly juxtaposed with words that stand in binary opposition in content. M. Adhikari examines linguistic narratology of *The God of Small Things*: "the choice of words loaded with meaning with a rise and fall of notes produces fine rhythm, metaphors and similes become the integral part of the prose. Roy begins the novel by following the rules of conventional grammar but very soon, she moves into the sphere of arbitrary or so-called ungrammatical sentences. . . . By creating new nouns and names, she is not only projecting the psychology of children but also constructing arbitrary siginifiers that present situational meanings for Estha and Rahel."

A fundamental facet of narrative technique is the point of view from which the story is told. The presiding point of view of the story telling is that of the twins Estha and Rahel plus unconventionality of the structure, scope and sphere of the narrative which fairly recognizes Roy's book as daringly postmodernist.

The book convincingly weaves the saga of a family, of three generations living in the Ayemenem House in Kottayam, a memento microscoped in time, which irrevocably moves towards its doomed destiny. The narrative strategy of this work of art nullifies time and invests a poly temporal scheme of time where there is a constant shift from the past to the present and to the future. It problematises chronology and history. Actually what the text purports is not the reality of history but the reality of human sensibility between Ammu and the untouchable Velutha culminating into their separate and sad demise. The woman's point of view exposes the very roots of an authoritative exploitative socio-economic-political structure that victimizes both man and woman and ties both to its stakes. The second is the sad drowning of the Anglo-Indian girl Sophie Mol in the Meenchal river during holiday. There has been a correlation between the first and the second. The third strand of action constitutes traumatic childhood of the Siamese twins Estha and Rahel. The novelist adequately focuses on the coming back of young Rahel from America to Ayemenem and her incestuous and immoral encounter with Estha, the twin.

Structurally and thematically, the book is designed to be eye-catching and challenging. The novelist herself reveals her approach. "For me the structure of my story, the way it reveals itself was so important. . . . I really took a lot of care in designing the structure of the story, because for me the book is not about what happened but how what happened affected people."[4]

It has been widely acknowledged that the perspective is basically directed at the very character of the society and culture, the deeply held beliefs, thought patterns, substantive values and relations. Thus the free flow of love and sex takes the turbulent and tormenting turn in the ultimate effect of the novel. Most of the chapters of the novel are pregnant with the chain of actions like Sophie Mol's funeral, the twins's birth, Baby Kochamma and her past, Velutha's death, Rahel's marriage and divorce, the twins's early education, Ammu's death, comrade Pillai's role, Ayemenem House—all are introduced in the first chapter itself.

In the Introduction of the well-received book "Orientalism,"

Edward Said has illustrated the inclusion of native words in a foreign language text which points out not only the mastery of the author but also the device to suggest the typical nuances of words and profound reactions of a culture. Said rightly suggests that "The images, themes, motifs that circulate in the text can be useful indicators of its ideological underpinnings."[5] In her novel, Roy creates images which are primarily based on Indian experience like the drowned child's skin being as wrinkled as the "dhobi's finger"[6] or Estha's feeling of betrayal of Velutha "like a mango hair between the molars." (32) Stylistically her crisp and racy language, similes and metaphors are very accurate and illuminating. For example, "Rahel's new teeth were waiting inside her gums, like words in a pen." (37)

"The Indian-English novelists are conscious of the significance of the novel's time structure and have been successful in integrating either the cyclic or the linear concept of time with the oral or the mythological narrative modes."[7] There is no linear structuring of events not in just the story of the novel but also within the individual streams of narrative. On both the planes of style and theme, Aurndhati Roy bears a comparison with D.H. Lawrence. In Lawrentian works of art, the lyrical ecstacy and spontaneity comes out from tenderness in human relationships and phallic consciousness.

Lawrence's *Lady Chatterley's Lover* is the hallmark of narrative tenderness and the genuine and profound sex relationship. Connie Chatterley, like Ammu, is the central figure of the novel. When she marries Clifford, her love is based on 'all the passion of mental attraction. With the passage of time, she thinks of her life with Clifford as years of suffocating and suffering and the singular reality about its 'nothingness.' Similar is the case with Ammu when she gets herself united in wedlock with the assistant manager of Assam tea garden and finally returns to Ayemenem House by deserting her husband. As Ammu attracts towards Velutha, Connie falls in the game of love with the gamekeeper Mellors. In a state of ecstatic compassion, the keeper takes Connie to the hut and their love bursts forth with the sexual intercourse which justifies 'nothing' to her but it imparts perennial peace. This ecstatic pleasure of sex and love vivify and vitalize their life-force.

In the poetic description, Arundhati Roy evinces her craftsmanship in explaining erotic and emotional scenes in the last chapter "The Cost of Living" where man-woman relationship finds full consummation. Ammu, the mother of the twins, has been depicted as a day-dreamer, an abandoned woman, she remains unrequited biologically. Roy, in weaving the character of Ammu, is more woman-like, more attached, mere earthy, more natural. The intense passionate affair between Velutha and Ammu inside the river Meenachal is described in terms of Lawrentian flavour and fragrance. Biologically Ammu's responses to Velutha's muscular, well-built body is spontaneous because her suppressed womanhood is aroused after a long span of time. But the caste-ridden male chauvinistic set up does not provide such relaxation for human considerations. Her elopement with him for thirteen days under the threat of incessant heavy downpour due to cyclonic disturbances gives her sexual saturation. The stolen hours of the night simultaneously satiate and further sharpen her desire for sexual assuagement. Ammu to some extent is nymphomaniac in her relationship with Velutha. The novelist describes this Lawrentian explosive sexual encounter in tantalizing details. The writer says:

> Ammu, naked now, crouched over Velutha, her mouth on his. He drew her hair around them like a tent. . . . She slid further down, introducing herself to the rest of him. His neck. His nipples. His chocolate stomach. She sipped the last of the river from the hollow of his navel. She pressed the heat of his erection against her eyelids. She tasted him, salty, in her mouth. . . . She felt his belly tighten under her, hard as a board. She felt her wetness slipping on his skin. He took her nipple in his mouth and cradled her other breast in his calloused palm. Velvet gloved in sandpaper. (336)

Both Arunthati Roy and D.H. Lawrence in their works of art use remarkable poetic language, their medium of communication approximates to that of a poet. They find the common language as if it were their own invention, and employ words and their sound patterns to suggest the meaning poetically. In the *Lady Chatterley's Lover*, Connie has nothing to pay for her free and fearless game of sex owing to the socio-cultural-ethical morality of the west but in Indian perspective the situation is diametrically opposite and Ammu has to pay with her life.

She is forced to vacate Ayemenem house by Chacko and she also gets separated from her affectionate children, to die unwept, unhonoured, unsung and unremembered. Actually, she is more sinned against than sinning. No doubt, sadness, sorrow, gloom and grief sound too much in the novel. Ammu and her Siamese twins have to suffer the traumatic experience of separation and self-alienation. 'The History House' has connotations of a bizarre, haunted place where heart-rending scenes of police atrocity, socially prohibited sexual assuagement between Velutha and Ammu and the tragic drowning of Sophie Mol occur.

The brother-sister physical reunion after a considerable gap of twenty-three years in Ayemenem suggests an unusual, socially impermissible, incident on a rainy, wet night. What prompts them to this act is not "happiness but hideous grief." In the heart of this artistic framework, four women characters are shown grappling with problems and plights of life and being repeatedly defeated. Among these four women characters—Ammu, Margaret, Rahel and Baby Kochamma—some succumb, suffer and finally die in the deplorable condition and some live death in life. Arundhati Roy focussed on this endless suffering of the women characters in the following words at Frankfurt World Book Fair in October 1997: "*The God of Small Things* is indeed a poetic yet sad book, and somehow the sadness of the book is what stays with me."

Technically *The God of Small Things* stands close to *The Guide* of R.K. Narayan, especially in the use of flash forward and flashback technique. In the time scheme, *The Guide* also moves backward and forward like *The God of Small Things*. Arundhati Roy herself explores the poly temporal theory of time which has been used in the thematic structure of the novel. She says:

> The way an architect designs a building . . . it was not as if I started at the beginning and ended at the end. I would start somewhere and I'd colour in a bit and then I would deeply stretch back and then stretch forward. It was like designing an intricately balanced structure.[8]

A number of sympathetic critics have explained the greatness of Roy's novel in terms of her ability to display contradictory social and psychic elements which, when perceived in terms of deep structure, attain a unity. This becomes feasible due to the twisting capacity of the novelist—twisting the word or words in such a remarkable manner that it loses its place and identity.

Throughout the novel, there is a unique experimentation of words and images. Both manner and matter are grandiose, superb and befitting to the theme of the novel. Arundhati Roy justifies the Lawrentian approach that the closest human intimacy is possible only through sexual intercourse, an experience that is marked by a momentary but complete unity of man and woman and of the two with the very soul of life. The novel is highly poetic not only on the plane of theme, words, language and style but also in the selection of the title which is elegantly suggestive. As the text points out: "The God of less? The God of Small Things? The God of Goose Bumps and Sudden Smiles?" (217)

This God is undoubtedly associated with Ammu's dreamland. The little dreams constitute an integral part of 'Small Things.' Hence Ammu dreams of the one-armed man. Who is he? Is he Velutha, the Paravan? The questions are directly related with 'The God of Small Things.' Ammu craves for this man feverishly and aches for him with the whole of her biology. Evidently, the title purports that these two lovers in life exercised 'small things' secretly because society would not permit them. The novelist says: "They stuck to the Small Things. The Big Things ever lurked inside. They knew that there was nowhere for them to go. They had nothing. No future. So, they stuck to the small things." (338)

The title of the book itself is pregnant with poetic poise where the 'small things' denote the sublimation of sexual desire. The title is also complementary to the poetic design of the novel, a hint to the palpable love of Ammu and Velutha. This is the He-Man Velutha, a love-light and 'The God of Small Things' for Ammu.

NOTES

1. Beth Yahp, "Larger than Life," *The Australian Review of Books*, May 1997, p. 5.
2. Cynthia vanden Driesen, "When Language Dances: The Subversive Power of Roy's Text in *The God of Small Things*," *Arundhati Roy: The Novelist Extraordinary*, ed. R.K. Dhawan (New Delhi: Prestige, 1999), p. 365.
3. M. Adhikari, "Language through Literature and Literature through Language: A Study of Arundhati Roy's *The God of Small Things*" *Points of View*, Vol. III, No. 1, Summer 2000, pp. 71-72.
4. Arundhati Roy, "Interview: For me language is a skin on my thought," *The Week*, 26 Oct. 1997, p. 46.
5. Edward Said, *Orientalism* (Victoria: Penguin, 1991), p. 21.
6. Arundhati Roy, *The God of Small Things* (New Delhi: IndiaInk, 1997), p. 14.
7. Gajendra Kumar, *Indo-Anglian Novel Criticism: Tradition and Achievement* (Patna: Novelty, 1999), pp. 12-13.
8. Arundhati Roy, Interview, *The Week*, p. 46.

Arundhati Roy's "The Greater Common Good": A Poignant Ode on the Dalit and the Deserted

AMAR NATH PRASAD

"The Greater Common Good" is a thought provoking revolutionary article (now it is in the form of a book) by Arundhati Roy, the author of the famous Booker Prize-winner book, *The God of Small Things*. It deals with the author's rational and progressive attitude to the dam projects of the government; her sympathetic talks with the sufferers of the Narmada Valley Project; her harsh and rugged satire on the faulty decision and adverse attitude of the political parties and above all, her Wordsworthian nostalgia for the natural scenes and sights of nature. The book reminds us of what Wordsworth, the great poet and philosopher of Nature, observes:

> The world is too much with us, late and soon
> Giving and spending we lay waste our powers
> Little we see in Nature that is ours
> We have given our hearts away to a sordid boon.[1]

The book opens with an innuendo: "I stood on a hill and laughed out loud."[2] Here the laughing is not the general laughing but it is full of sarcastic irony on the resettlement of the sufferers of the Sardar Sarovar Dam. The author laughed loud because the sons and daughters of the displaced tribal people are not happy at all in the resettlement colonies which have seesaws and slides and swings in every park. Why? Because the homes of the tribal people are not the big buildings or great mansions in the polluted and populated cities, but an open sky, far from the madding crowd, saturated with age long myths and traditions, songs and dances, fruits and flowers. In other words, to quote Shakespeare, the tribal people "find tongues in trees, books in the running brooks, sermons in stone and good in everything."[3] And perhaps this is what made Arundhati Roy 'laugh out loud' on a hill. The excerpts from a letter from Bava Mahalia of Jalsindhi village in Jhabua district to Madhya Pradesh Chief Minister Digvijay Singh in 1994, very clearly answers the laugh of the Booker Prize-winner author, Arundhati Roy. The letter says: "We have lived in the forest for generations. The forest is our moneylender and banker. In hard times we go to the forest. We build our houses from its wood. From its rushes and splints we weave screens. From the forests we make baskets and cots, ploughs and hoes and many other useful things. . . . We get various kinds of grasses; and when the grasses become dry in summer, we still get leaves. . . . If there is a famine we survive by eating roots and tubers. When we fall sick, our medicine men bring us back to health by giving us leaves, roots, bark from the forest. We collect and sell gum, tendu leaves, bahera, chironji and mahua. The forest is like our mother; we have grown up in its lap. We know how to live by suckling at her breast. If we were made to live in a land without forests, then all this knowledge that we have cherished for generations will be useless and slowly we will forget it all." (14)

So, according to Arundhati Roy, to give modern facilities and other materialistic advancements to the displaced tribal people is not to show sympathy to them but to deprive them of their natural instincts and nostalgic coherence. As a matter of fact, it is the psychology of human mind that however poor and miserable the man's home may be, he is so much emotionally tagged to it that all through his life the memory of his birthplace always haunts him and compels him to come back to his home. A house may be a place of all the facilities but it lacks love and affection, affinity and happiness. But, on the other hand, a home (though without any wall and roof, just under the shade of a tree) is always made of love and dreams. And the forests and the rivers, the hills and the mountains of the tribal people are their real homes which provide them love and affection, livelihood and nourishment. This shows that the tribal people cannot adjust in the society full of pollution and corruption; the society which seldom harbours a sense of co-operation and intimacy among its people these days; the society in which the ceremony of innocence is drowned in the "blood-dimmed tide"[4] of aberrations of several kind. J.B.S. Haldane, in his famous essay, "The Scientific Point of View" points out that common man is more interested in the emotional and ethical side of a problem than its facts. For instance, the segregation of the American Negro is more of an emotional and ethical problem than a biological one. He observes: "In the country districts of the southern states, the birth-rate of the Negro population exceeds the death rate. In the southern towns, and all through the north, more Negroes die than are born. Their high death rates are due to the fact that, in environments suitable to a white man, they die of consumption and other diseases, just as the white man dies on the West coast of Africa, the Negro's original home."[5]

It is to be noted that in America there is a public debate over the possible dismantling of dams built fifty years ago. Today it is proved there that dams have done more harm than good. But in India, we continue to build more and more. There is sufficient evidence to show that good watershed management is a much more effective and economical way of storing water. In conjunction with water harvesting and drip irrigation, it conserves water and leads to much higher agricultural productivity with far less danger of salinisation—one of the results of large dams and extensive irrigation systems. The other important thing which always goes beyond our notice is that by watershed development, as suggested by the Narmada Bachao Andolan, rather than increasing the heights of the dam, the tribal people could be gainfully employed where they live. Arundhati Roy rightly observes:

> The fact that they do more harm than good is no longer just conjecture. Big dams are obsolete. They're uncool.

> They're undemocratic. They're a government's way of accumulating authority. They're a guaranteed way of taking a farmer's wisdom away from him. They're a brazen means of taking water, land and irrigation away from the poor and gifting it to the rich. Their reservoirs displace huge populations of people, leaving them homeless and destitute. Ecologically, they're in the doghouse. They lay the earth to waste. They cause floods, water logging, salinity, they spread disease. There is mounting evidence that links Big Dams to earthquake. (6)

So, big dams, these days, are no longer the monuments of modern civilization, emblem of man's ascendancy over nature. Monuments are generally unaging, timeless and are full of worship and devotion. But the recent havoc caused by the big dams all over the world is a testimony to the fact that big dams do the opposite of what people say about them. Perhaps this is why the building of a dam is not the first priority of a developed country. The dam building industry in the First World is in great trouble and out of work. It has been transported to the Third World where poverty and malnutrition, unemployment and population are widely prevalent. The First World encourages the poor world to make more and more dams only to become more and more poor and destitute. Consequently, they provide the Third World developmental aid with their other waste like old weapons, superannuated aircraft carriers and banned pesticides. The author thinks that aid is just another praetorian business enterprise. It is just like colonialism. Yet, in India, our leaders welcome the strategy of the First World with slavish smile. It is astounding that the government of India has detailed figures for production of food grains but hasn't a figure for the number of people displaced by dams or sacrificed in other ways at the altars of "National Progress." The author holds the view:

> The millions of displaced people in India are nothing but refugees of an unacknowledged war. And we like the citizens of White America and French Canada and Hitler's

> Germany, are condoning it by looking away. Why? Because we are told that it is being done for the sake of the Greater Common Good. That it's being done in the name of Progress, in the name of National Interest. Therefore gladly, unquestioningly, almost gratefully, we believe what we're told. We believe that it benefits us to believe. (8-9)

Arundhati Roy also makes a difference between the city and the village, She seems to fling a mild irony on those who say that India lives in the villages. But to Arundhati Roy, India doesn't live in her villages but dies in her villages. India gets kicked around in her villages. Truly speaking, these days India lives in her cities and the country's villages live only to serve her cities.

The other problem associated with the dam projects is the heavy loan India has taken from the World Bank for the development aid given to the sufferers of the said project. But the irony is that India is in a situation where it pays back more money to the bank in interest and repayments of principal than it receives from it. We are forced to create new debts in order to be able to repay our old ones. The author is of the view that "the relationship between us is exactly like the relationship between a landless labourer steeped in debt and the local Bania—it is an affectionate relationship, the poor man loves his Bania because he's always there when he's needed. It's not for nothing that we call the world a global village. The only difference between the landless labourer and the Government of India is that one uses the money to survive. The other just funnels it into the private coffers of its officers and agents, pushing the country into an economic bondage that it may never overcome." (11-12)

It is to be noted that water is an important source of irrigation and power, necessary for the agricultural growth and industrial production of the country. Water is channelised for irrigation of agricultural fields. It is also controlled and regulated by means of dams, to produce hydro-electricity. All these projects are already having deep beneficial effect on India's economy. In short, they provide power to the industries, water to agriculture and electricity to villages and cities for better living. The government says that Sardar Sarovar Projects have multiple purposes like irrigation, power production and flood control, and will produce 1450 Mega Watts of power. But according to Roy, the fact is just the otherwise. She observes: "Irrigation uses up the water you need to produce power. Flood control requires you to keep the reservoir empty during the monsoon months to deal with an anticipated surfeit of water. And if there is no surfeit, you're left with an empty dam. And this defeats the purpose of irrigation, which is to store the monsoon water. It's like the riddle of trying to ford a river with a fox, a chicken and a bag of grain. The result of these mutually conflicting aims, studies say, is that when the Sardar Sarovar projects are completed and the scheme is fully functional, it will end up producing only 3 per cent of the power that its planners say it will." (13)

The other great drawback which Roy points out is the earthquake caused by the reservoir of the dam. Activists protesting against the construction of dams on the Narmada (in Gujarat and Madhya Pradesh), the Tehri (in Uttar Pradesh) and Bedthi (Karnataka) argue that dams would lead to R.I.S. (reservoir-induced-seismicity) and subsequently earthquakes. The Uttar Kashi and Jabalpur earthquakes are often cited to support their arguments. But the fact is somewhat different as observed by the recent research in the field of Seismology. We should also not forget that despite all these scientific and technological developments, an element of seismic risk could haunt a dam and cast a shadow on its construction. But this anticipation of risk shouldn't stand in the way of progress, particularly in a country like India which needs water and electricity to provide its people good living standards. Hydropower is the solution to the country's requirements, and this can be achieved by storing water in dams. Now the question is: Can electricity or other facilities be generated at the cost of a number of poor people of the villages or the forests? Is it not wrong to displace a large number of tribal people from their homeland—the forests and the rivers to which they are nostalgically attached? Certainly it is an inhuman, brutal and callous act on the part of the government if its concerned authority doesn't pay any heed to the demands of the displaced people.

It is this inhuman treatment to the Dalit and the deserted, the poor and the defenseless that compelled Arundhati Roy to visit the site of the dam and made her to write this poignant ode on the trials and tribulations of the fate of the sufferers. Perhaps this is why, the author calls upon all sections of society to come and think over this giant and universal problem. She thinks; "The war for the Narmada Valley is not just some exotic tribal war or a remote rural war or even an exclusively Indian war. It is a war for the rivers and the mountains and the forests of the world. All sorts of warriors from all over the world, anyone who wishes to enlist, will be honoured and welcomed. Every kind of warrior will be needed. Doctors, lawyers, teachers, judges, journalists, students, sportsmen, painters, actors, singers, lovers. . . . The borders are open, folks! Come on in." (17)

The state Governments of Madhya Pradesh and Maharashtra are very harsh, as pointed out by the author, to their dealings with the displaced people. On paper, the Government of Gujarat has a lot of things for the welfare of the displaced people. It has a goon rehabilitation package which offers land for land to the sufferers. But in point of fact, the Government of Gujarat hasn't even managed to rehabilitate people from its own 19 villages slated for submergence. The people of these villages are scattered to separate rehabilitation sites. In practice, it is seen that the people of the resettlement sites have to face so many obstacles and hurdles. Some people have been given land, others haven't. Some have lands that is stony and uncultivable. Some have land that is always waterlogged. Some have been driven out by landowners who sold land to the government but haven't been paid yet. The picture of the resettlement site was well painted by Arundhati Roy in a poetic language:

> In several resettlement sites, people have been dumped in rows of corrugated tin sheds which are furnaces in summer and fridges in winter. Some of them are located in dry riverbeds, which during the monsoon, turn into fast-flowing drifts. I have seen some of these sites. I've seen film footage of others: shivering children, perched like birds on the

> edges of Charpais, while swirling waters enter their tin homes. Frightened, fevered eyes watch pot and pans carried through the doorway by the current, floating out into the flooded fields, thin fathers swimming after them to retrieve what they can. (20)

To crown the effect, the poor people of these resettlement sites have to starve to death for want of food. They have to walk several kilometers to the nearest town to offer themselves as wage labour. What a great irony! In the forest they gathered everything they needed—food, fuel, fodder and what not. In their old houses, they had no money, but they were insured. If the rains failed, they had the forests, where they could get all the things of their day-to-day life. Moreover, in the villages, they felt a sense of affinity, congeniality and above all, stability. But here in the town, they are suffering from a sense of claustrophobia and nostalgia. It is not for nothing that Andrew Marvell, a great metaphysical poet, praises the solitude of the village and feels that plants may grow only among plants:

> Your sacred plants, if here below
> Only among the plants will grow:
> Society is all but rude
> To this delicious solitude.[6]

As a matter of fact, a man who leads a pastoral life is always simple, innocent and ignorant. But when he comes in contact with society, his innocence and simplicity begin to bleed. So far the tribal man lives in the lap of nature, he is nearest to goodness. The forest dweller has the opportunity to study Nature in a very intimate manner, and the intimacy thus established with even the inanimate things is of such a profound order that it becomes possible for him to replace human society with all that is implied by the companionship of these forms of Nature. Whatever wisdom these forest dwellers gather comes from such an intimate study and observation of Nature and her myriad forms. It, thus, comes to happen that what books and sermons do the people in the public life of the world of urban civilization, the trees and books and stones do to these forest dwellers.

Thus, here Arundhati Roy stands like a lawyer to plead the case of the rural folk that what they are losing must be restored to them justifiably. With a hammer in her hand, Roy wants to blow hard on the ill-treatrrent of the state and the government who turned a deaf ear to the requests of the forest dwellers or the sufferers of the dam projects. In this sense, the book may be termed as an elegy on the pathetic and miserable condition of the villagers of the big dam area. The author weeps on the absolute neglect of the poor and the deserted. She feels that there is human dignity in them which ought to be recognized. A nation ought to be thankful to them because they live on their produce and create no nuisance. They are happily engaged in their rural vocation of cultivating the land. Further, they have the pleasure of the limited domestic life where they are looked after by their housewife and children. It is affection they get from them, but in the resettlement site, they feel like fish out of water. Here joy's portrayal tantamounts to that of Thomas Gray's "Elegy Written in a Country Churchyard" in which the poet mourns:

> Let not ambition mock their useful toil
> Their homely joys, and destiny obscure
> Nor grandeur hear with a disdainful smile
> The short and simple annals of the poor.[7]

"The Greater Common Good" also shows the tyranny and injustice, insult and abuse of the wealthy caste people to the outcastes and the have-nots. The author mentions an event of the village Jalud, in the Nimad plains of Madhya Pradesh where the scourge of the shameful caste divisions can be felt. Here, in this village, a majority of the land-owning farmers is the Rajputs. Their houses are always filled with sacks of wheat and rice. The Dalits of this area were badly beaten when they objected to their land ceiling. They told the author how when they objected, cement was poured into their water pipes, their standing crops were bulldozed and the police occupied the land by force. Consequently all the 12 families became landless and they have to work as wage labour. It reminds us of the author's Booker prize winner book, *The God of Small Things* in which Velutha, a Dalit of the village, has to suffer a lot. He was so mercilessly tortured by the dishonest and cruel police that he breathed his last in the police custody. The author very beautifully presents a heart-rending picture of Velutha:

> Velutha appeared on the scummy, slippery floor. A mangled genie invoked by a modern lamp. He was naked, his soiled mundu had come undone. Blood spilled from his skull like a secret. His face was swollen and his head looked like a pumpkin, too large and heavy for the slender stem it grew from. A pumpkin with monstrous upside-down smile. Police boots stepped back from the rim of a pool of urine spreading from him, the bright, bare electric bulb reflected in it.[8]

Thus, we see that the outlook of Arundhati Roy conforms to that of the Father of the Nation who had a strong belief in the existence of the villages in which the soul of India resides. Mahatma Gandhi believed that unless the miserable condition of a large number of people, mostly the villagers, is improved, we cannot claim the progress of the nation in the true sense of the term.

The last portion of the book rings the note of Roy's anger and her harsh and direct satire on the big men of society which she termed the 'Laltain' in her book, *The God of Small Things*. She compares the Big Dams to nuclear bombs. She concludes:

> Big Dams are to a Nation's 'Development' what Nuclear Bombs are to its military Arsenal. They are both weapons of mass destruction. They are both weapons governments use to control their own people. Both twentieth century emblems that mark a point in time when human intelligence has outstripped its own instinct for survival. They are both malignant indications of civilization turning upon itself. They represent the severing of the link, not just the link—the understanding—between human beings and the planet

> they live on. They scramble the intelligence that connects eggs to hens, milk to cows, food to forests, water to rivers, air to life and the earth to human existence. (29)

The book is not simply the work of lines and statements but a fine piece of a good art. The thoughts and feelings of the author are not vague, dry and monotonous but are woven into the fabric of art and literature. Some of the words and phrases, images and symbols of this book are highly suggestive. Sometimes the author uses such a fine way of words and diction that the sound of the sentence suggests the sense. Like T.S. Eliot, her expression is not the 'turning loose of emotion,' but it is an 'escape from emotion.'

We get some sentences intermittently in the course of the book which very well express the author's great anger and emotion. The sentence is independent in nature and it separates two paragraphs. It reminds us of T.S. Eliot's "The Waste Land." Take for example:

> I stood on a hill and laughed out loud. (4)
> I feel like someone who's just stumbled on a mass grave. (7)
> Did I hear someone say something about the world's biggest democracy? (8)
> There is a hole in the flag that needs mending. (11)
> Old Nazis probably soothe themselves in similar ways. (17)

The book is also saturated with fine similes and metaphor. The similes used here take us back to the realm of Yeats and Eliot, Pound and Auden. One of the salient features of the similes used is a fine correspondence between the major and the minor terms. Let us see some of them:

> I could see little children with hitler goats scuttling the landscape like motorised pea nuts. (4)
> I went because writers are drawn to stories the way vultures are drawn to kills. (6)
> I feel like someone who's just stumbled on a mass grave. (7)

> The relationship between us is exactly like the relationship between a landless labourer steeped in debt and the local Bania. (11)
>
> It's like the riddle of trying to ford a river with a fox, a chicken and a bag of grain. (13)
>
> The ancient teak beams dismantled from their previous homes, carefully stacked away like postponed dreams, now spongy, rotten and unusable. (20)

Thus, Arundhati Roy has amply lived up to the ideals of great art—the article is a blending of both 'poetic truth' and 'poetic beauty.' Though right from the beginning of the book up to the end, the author seems to be berserk with great anger and contempt against the prevailing drawbacks of the big dam projects of the government and unsympathetic attitude of the state and the administration against the people of the resettlement sites, yet her satire is not rugged and abusing in nature like that of Alexander Pope; but it is mild and congenial, refined and sublime like that of Dryden in the Neo-Classical period.

To sum up "The Greater Common Good" expresses the author's unremittingly hostile outlook to the adverse and entirely inhuman treatment inflicted upon the displaced sufferers of the government's big dam projects. It also shows how the tribal people habituated to live in the lap of nature are being forced to live in an entirely new and uncongenial atmosphere devoid of their natural instincts and nostalgic affection. It describes 'Big Dams' as 'Nuclear Bombs' in military arsenal. But what matters most is the new and original style—a style that lulls us away from the world of dream and fantasy to the world of grab reality; a style that turns and twists language to conform to the feeling; a style that has sometimes ungrammatical construction, bizarre phrases and idiosyncratic capitalization. The author's sympathetic attitude to the 'Dalit' and the deserted, the have-nots and the defenceless and her elegiac vision for ecological imbalances will last for generations so far as men will be a creature of flesh and blood, emotion and imagination.

NOTES

1. Wordsworth, "The World is Too Much with Us," *Golden Treasury*, ed. Palgrave (Calcutta: Oxford University Press, 1964), p. 299.
2. Arundhati Roy, "The Greater Common Good," *Frontline*, May 22-June 4, 1999, p. 4.
3. William Shakespeare, *As You Like It*, II.i.15-19.
4. W.B. Yeats, "The Second Coming," *Golden Treasury*, p. 224
5. J.B.S. Haldane, "The Scientific Point of View," *Prose-Poetry Selection* (Patna: Sunrise, 1994), p. 41
6. Andrew Marvell, "Thoughts in a Garden," *Golden Treasury*, p. 92.
7. Thomas Gray, "Elegy Written in a Country Churchyard," *Golden Treasury*, p. 146.
8. Arundhati Roy, *The God of Small Things* (New Delhi: IndiaInk, 1997), p. 320.

Contributors

SANGEETA DAS	D.G. College Kanpur
JAYDIPSINH K. DODIYA	Saurashtra University Rajkot
RANJANA HARISH	Gujarat University Ahmedabad
SURENDRA NARAYAN JHA	M.K. College Darbhanga
MADHU JOSHI	Kumaun University Nainital
JENNIFER KELLY	University of Calgary Alberta, Canada
PRAHLAD A. KULKARNI	S.M. Dr. Bapuji Salunkhe College Miraj
GAJENDRA KUMAR	Rajendra College Chapra
NEETA KHURANA	Gujarat College Ahmedabad
PRASENJIT MAITI	Burdwan University Burdwan
SEEMA MALIK	M.L. Sukhadia University Udaipur
ROSY MISRA	Govt. M.K.B. College Jabalpur

A.K. MUKHERJEE	Government College Bhawanipatna
UDAY SHANKAR OJHA	Jagdam College Chapra
K.M. PANDEY	M.G. Kashi Vidyapeeth Varanasi
AMAR NATH PRASAD	Jagdam College Chapra
M. RAJESHWAR	Kakatiya University Warangal
CHANDRA SHEKHAR RAJHANS	Government College Pakhanjore
C.R. VISWESWARA RAO	S.K. University Anantapur
PRADIPSINH RATHOD	G.D. Modi College of Arts Palanpur
ALKA SAXENA	D.A.V. College Kanpur
D.K. SINHA	Veer Kunwar Singh University Ara
K.K. SINHA	C.M. Science College Darbhanga
SHUBHA TIWARI	A.P.S. University Rewa
M.A. WAHEED	Govt. Arts and Science College Armoor